Deleuze and Geophilosophy

Deleuze and Geophilosophy

A Guide and Glossary

MARK BONTA AND JOHN PROTEVI

EDINBURGH UNIVERSITY PRESS

© Mark Bonta and John Protevi, 2004

Edinburgh University Press Ltd
22 George Square, Edinburgh

Reprinted with corrections 2006

Typeset in 11/13 pt. New Baskerville
by Servis Filmsetting Ltd, Manchester and
printed and bound in Spain by GraphyCems

A CIP record for this book is available from
the British Library

ISBN 0 7486 1838 4 (hardback)
ISBN 0 7486 1839 2 (paperback)

The right of Mark Bonta and John Protevi
to be identified as authors of this work
has been asserted in accordance with
the Copyright, Designs and Patents Act 1988.

Contents

Preface

If you open *A Thousand Plateaus* (*ATP*) at any page you'll find terms such as 'plateau', 'deterritorialization', 'rhizome', 'cartography', and so on. If you would then say to yourself that this is a 'geophilosophy', you'd be right, and in fact you'd be anticipating the term Deleuze and Guattari will apply to themselves ten years after they finished writing *ATP*. And if you were to further say to yourself that *ATP* provides an excellent opportunity for philosophers and geographers to collaborate, and in so doing to effect deep and deeply needed changes in both their disciplines, then you'd have anticipated our motivation in writing this book.

We wrote this book with (at least) two audiences in mind: geographers interested in a helpful guide to a new theoretical framework – or, more modestly, a new set of conceptual tools – and philosophers and others interested in the demonstration that Deleuze and Guattari have a rigorous, clear, precise, and useful engagement with scientific disciplines. Although the treatment of science in contemporary French philosophy and in the 'cultural studies' allegedly inspired by it was bitterly criticized in the 'Science Wars' of the mid- to late 1990s, there is good cause to take seriously the work of Deleuze and Guattari as providing a bona fide philosophical engagement with that loose collection of scientific endeavours known as 'complexity theory'.

Perhaps it's not too much, then, in our view, to say that Deleuze – once his work is fully understood – can be the Kant of our time. By this we mean not the author of mediocre and racist geographical works replete with the common prejudices of his age, but the great philosopher who provided the philosophical 'grounding' of classical modern science. Just as Kant's *Critiques* were in a sense the epistemology, metaphysics, ethics, and aesthetics for a world of

Euclidean space, Aristotelian time, and Newtonian physics, Deleuze provides the philosophical concepts that make sense of our world of fragmented space (the fractals of Mandelbrot, the 'patchworks' of Riemann), twisted time (the so-called anticipatory effects of systems that sense their approach to a threshold), and the non-linear effects of far-from-equilibrium thermodynamics. To provide such an ontology, Deleuze examines the self-ordering and emergent properties of material systems in widely differing registers – the physical, chemical, biological, neural, social, and anthropological – and sets forth the basic concepts that make sense of the world as it must be to provide the results elicited by complexity theory.

But Kant is not the only philosophical analogue expressing the importance of Deleuze and Guattari for the contemporary earth and environmental sciences. Descartes, the very inventor of that rigorously gridded or 'striated' space known as the Cartesian coordinate system, is a complementary choice. David Harvey points out that Kant and Descartes together (what he calls the 'Cartesian–Kantian' framework) have grounded almost all Western geographical endeavors of the last two centuries, whether or not their geophilosophical presuppositions are relevant to the questions under consideration. We see *ATP* as the key to a new materialist geophilosophical paradigm because it combines Kant's insistence on the importance of the earth sciences and Descartes' attempt to provide a new cartography and coordinate system.

The pluridimensional utility of *ATP* lies in its attempt to develop a new materialism in which a politically informed 'philosophy of difference' joins forces with complexity theory to rethink the earth. Now *ATP* is a book of strange and terrifying new questions: 'Who does the Earth think it is?', 'How do you make yourself a Body without Organs?', 'How does the war machine ward off the State?' and many others that are equally perplexing and even intimidating to the first-time reader. Despite its difficulty, we have found *ATP* to be not only comprehensible but also extremely useful and enlightening, and we have written the second part of this book in the form of a glossary to provide some guideposts that will help others work their way through it. Thus we do not present a unified interpretation of the meaning of *ATP*; rather, we try to render it useful to others.

We'd like to thank the following people for their support and helpful comments at many stages of our writing. Of course, as the saying goes, while they should get much of the credit for the parts that make sense, we'll take the blame for the obscurities that remain.

Phil Adams and James Madden graciously and patiently provided help with technical scientific aspects, despite what must have been a sometimes exasperating scientific naïveté. Manuel DeLanda and Rich Doyle helped blend philosophy and science for us in many detailed interchanges, while Evan Thompson and Dan Smith generously provided manuscripts of forthcoming publications, which proved invaluable. Jon Cogburn gave detailed philosophical critiques of the work from a rigorous analytic perspective; it was very generous of him to reach across the 'continental/analytic' divide. Miles Richardson, Kent Mathewson, and Bill Davidson were excellent mentors to Bonta and warm and generous colleagues to Protevi. J. P. Jones III and Ed Casey have been strong supporters of the project all along. We'd also like to thank all the organizers of sessions at the 2001 SEDAAG (Southeastern Association of American Geographers) and 2003 AAG (Association of American Geographers) meetings for inviting us to present materials from the work in progress, as well as the panelists and audience members for their contributions to the ensuing discussions. Finally, we'd like to thank Jackie Jones, Ian Buchanan and the anonymous reviewers at EUP for their support and encouragement.

Abbreviations

AO	*Anti-Oedipus* (Deleuze and Guattari 1984 [1972])
ATP	*A Thousand Plateaus* (Deleuze and Guattari 1987 [1980])
DG	Deleuze and Guattari
DR	*Difference and Repetition* (Deleuze 1994 [1968])
LS	*The Logic of Sense* (Deleuze 1991 [1969])
WP	*What Is Philosophy?* (Deleuze and Guattari 1994 [1991])

Part I: Guide

1

Introduction

GEOPHILOSOPHY

'Be true to the earth', Nietzsche wrote, and the geophilosophy of Deleuze and Guattari seeks to do just that. But as their notion of truth is always ethical and performative, this means constructing a 'new earth'. Although neither were professional geographers – Deleuze was a philosopher, Guattari a psychoanalyst and political activist – in *A Thousand Plateaus*[1] they link Spinozist, Marxian, Nietzschean, and Bergsonian notions with the scientific researches known popularly as 'complexity theory' to create their geophilosophy.[2] Researchers in complexity theory investigate the way certain material systems in the inorganic, organic, and social registers attain both higher levels of internal complexity and a 'focus' of systematic behaviour without having to rely on external organizing agents.[3] Because of their insistence on a politically informed use of complexity theory when considering social systems, Deleuze and Guattari's work enables us to re-conceptualize major problems in philosophy and geography, and, in particular, the seemingly unsolvable structure/agency dilemma.

Despite the brave efforts of Giddens 1984 to provide an alternative in structuration theory that would overcome the dilemma, the oscillation between structure and agency continues to haunt social science. In the structure/agency debate, 'structure' can mean: (1a) a functionalist/naturalist variant of General Systems Theory (Parsons); or (1b) its successor 'autopoietic theory' (Luhmann); or (2a) a structuralism of the Lévi-Strauss school; or (2b) one of its 'postmodernist' variants. In terms of the first two kinds of structure, then, we can say Deleuze and Guattari are both functionalists and

3

naturalists. However, for them functional structures are not limited to homeostatic self-regulation, as they are for many thinkers, but extend to the systematicity of 'free' and 'open' networks, which they will name variously 'consistencies', 'rhizomes', and 'war machines'. Consistencies have found their 'reterritorialization' precisely in their capacity for 'deterritorialization', or, in other words, they most feel at home when they are creatively changing. Thus for Deleuze and Guattari the limitation to homeostasis is characteristic only of a limiting case of a system, the freezing or congealing of consistencies they will call the 'strata'. Similarly, regarding their naturalism, while they do want to analyze social systems with the same basic concepts they use in order to analyze organic and inorganic systems, their biology is not solely oriented to investigating the homeostatic capacities of individuals, a focus they will name an orientation to the 'organism'. For them, the 'organism' is precisely a type of stratum, 'that which life sets against itself to limit itself' (ATP: 503).

In terms of the third and fourth types of structure, Deleuze and Guattari break not only with Lévi-Strauss, but also with all forms of 'postmodernism'. This sort of antihumanist linguistic structuralism, by dint of an exclusive analysis of signifying texts wherever signs are deployed, has trapped too many philosophers and geographers in debates over problems of reference and the surplus production of meaning in signifying chains. Deleuze and Guattari's historically and politically informed engagement with complexity theory helps us break free of the postmodernist trap by rethinking sense and reference, and in so doing shatter the postmodernist equations of signs with signifiers, of meaning with position in a signifying chain, and of reference with the relation of signifiers to each other.[4] Deleuze and Guattari accomplish this by reminding us of the findings of complexity theory, which show that at critical thresholds some physical and biological systems can be said to 'sense' the differences in their environment that trigger self-organizing processes. In this way, signs – thresholds sensed by systems – are not only conceptualized as occurring beyond the register of the human and even the organic, but also are understood as triggers of material processes.[5] The problematic of the external reference of the signifier, which so troubles post-Saussurean doctrines, is thus bypassed. Signs are no longer limited to linguistic entities that must somehow make contact with the natural world, and sense or meaning need no longer be seen as the reference of signifiers to each other. Rather, the 'meaning' of a sign is a measure of the probability of triggering a particular material process.

While seeing social systems as structures, in either of the two above senses, has always been attractive to social scientists, because the rules by which structures operate are amenable to formulation in terms of laws, 'agency', or the ability of human subjects to effect novel and creative changes in the world – and especially in those 'rules' determining 'social structure' – has always been a sticking point. The key to understanding the form that 'agency' thinking has taken is to understand its relation to positivism, which took classical mechanics and its search for universal laws as the model of 'scientific method' to which the social sciences must conform. Thus the classic defense of agency lies in an anti-positivist hermeneutic insistence on the irreducibility of understanding to explanation (and hence an insistence on anti-naturalism in dealing with human beings, since natural phenomena were assumed to be mechanical). Recently, 'agency' thinking seems mired in a quasi-existentialist affirmation of 'resistance'.

To allay the fears of agency thinkers, we can say straightforwardly that Deleuze and Guattari do not deny that human subjects can initiate novel and creative action in the world.[6] However, they refuse to mystify this creativity as something essentially human and therefore non-natural. For them, the creativity of consistencies is not only natural, but also extends far beyond the human realm. Thus not just the creative work of territorial animals on the 'alloplastic stratum' they share with humans (i.e. precisely, their 'deterritorialization') but also the creativity of 'nonorganic life' (DeLanda 1992) would always outflank any form of hermeneutic or existentialist humanism.

Now although not all methodological individualists are agency thinkers, many agency thinkers are methodological individualists, that is, they deny the desirability or even the possibility of using social structures to explain human behavior.[7] In other words, they deny emergence above the level of the subject: social phenomena are mere aggregates of individual actions. In these cases, we should note that just as complexity theory's insistence on the natural creativity of open systems enables Deleuze and Guattari to outflank hermeneutic humanism at the same time as its thematization of signs as triggers of material processes enables them to escape from the anti-humanist linguistic structuralism of postmodernism, their thematizing of the subject as an emergent functional structure embedded in a series of structures enables them to escape from methodological individualism. Complexity theory, or more precisely Deleuze and Guattari's politically-informed version of it, focuses our attention on the subject as a functional structure emerging from a multiplicity of lower-level components, which they call in *AO* 'desiring machines'. In *ATP* the physiological and social-psychological genesis of subjectivity (what we may call 'political physiology') is not as comprehensively treated as in *AO*, but is summarized as follows: 'schizoanalysis . . . treats the unconscious as an acentered system . . . as a machinic network of finite automata' (*ATP*: 18). This sort of emergent subjectivity arising from a multiplicity of components is what philosophy of mind calls a 'society of mind' composed of a population of 'autonomous agents'.[8] Unlike most cognitive scientists, however, who practice an implicit methodological individualism, Deleuze and Guattari allow emergence above the plane of the subject at the level of what they term 'social machines' (with various stops in-between, at the institutional, urban, and state levels).[9] This latter move is an all-important feature of *ATP* upon which we will continue to focus.

Thus, in its politically-informed complexity theory, where signs are triggers of material processes and emergence extends to subjectivity from 'desiring machines' below and from subjectivity to social machines above, *ATP* provides an escape route from the conceptual gridlock of 'structure' as either a merely homeostatic self-regulation or a postmodernist 'signifier imperialism' and 'agency' as a mysterious exception somehow granted to individual human subjects in defiance of natural laws and blithely free of social structure. Our book can thus be encapsulated by the following formula: via Deleuze and Guattari, geography and philosophy meet a politically informed complexity theory in a general field of geo-bio-sociality (a 'geology of morals' as it is called in *ATP*). And it is on this field, we claim, that two good things can happen: geographers (both physical and human) can talk to each other again without riding the functionalism/postmodernism/hermeneutics/existentialist (resistance) merry-go-round, and geographers and philosophers can collaborate in new and important research projects. If our endeavor is successful, then perhaps Deleuze and Guattari's thought can be said to have enabled emergence on the interdisciplinary scholarly level as well as thematizing it at work in the world.

Manuel DeLanda (1991, 1992, 1997, 2002) and Brian Massumi (1992) deserve the credit for first pointing out the connection of Deleuze and Guattari with complexity theory, beginning in the early 1990s.[10] As the potentials of extending nonlinear dynamics from natural to social systems came to be appreciated in the 1980s, there was a widespread interest in the general field of 'biosociality'[11] and consequent endeavors that come close to the range displayed by Deleuze and Guattari. Though more recently we have seen a specialization in disciplinary studies, one of the hallmarks of this research is its interdisciplinary nature: it is often conducted by teams of specialists from different disciplines, or workers in one discipline using techniques and findings from other disciplines. A brief and decidedly non-comprehensive survey of fields of interest to geographers reveals works that can be roughly grouped as anthropology,[12] cognitive science,[13] history,[14] organization theory,[15] philosophy,[16] political science,[17] as well as, of course, geography itself,[18] in subfields ranging from geomorphology[19] through urban studies,[20] to land use and ecology.[21] Therefore, though we claim to be neither the primordial champions of Deleuze and Guattari in geography,[22] nor the geographic pioneers of complexity theory, we are among the first to bring Deleuze and Guattari together with complexity theory explicitly for the questions facing geography.

IMPASSES IN GEOGRAPHY AND PHILOSOPHY

This book grew out of our concrete experiences with the conceptual gridlock that paralyzed geography and philosophy in the 1990s. Bonta's primary dissatisfaction stemmed from the status of language and meaning implicit in both postmodernist human geography and its critics.[23] In the late 1980s and early 1990s, 'new' cultural geographers developed the notion of landscape as text, drawing from literary criticism, the work of Roland Barthes, and a certain perspective on Derrida's work that highlighted what they saw as a 'play of signifiers'. Although the reduction of text to signification misses the interplay that Derrida insists upon between 'force and signification' (the title of one of his early essays), and hence the asignifying (or at least more than signifying) nature of the 'general text', it was unfortunately one of the most popular ways his work was received in geographical circles (and in 'spin-off' postmodern applications in general). Despite Derrida's insistent revelation of the effects within written texts of an unnamable 'outside' or 'force' that destroys pretensions to pure signification (in other words, the inscription of written texts in the 'general text'), we nonetheless feel that Deleuze and Guattari's framework is more productive because of their historical situating of the signifying regime as one among several semiotic systems ('regimes of signs'), and their insistence on the 'triggering' relation of signs to material production.[24]

Few geographers, however, have grasped Deleuze and Guattari's insistence that meaning be re-conceptualized as the triggering of material processes, or their demonstration that the signifying regime, a semiotic of signifiers, is only one among many and hence that its dominance in analyses of landscape, region, space, and place has been too confining. Furthermore, because the signifying regime of signs is uniquely developed by State societies, it is insufficient for conceptualizing non-State geographies and philosophies, or, more precisely and most crucially, the 'mixed' semiotics (what Bonta calls the *enredo* or entanglement) occurring in the complex spaces of the real world. Although Deleuze and Guattari's analyses and examples are mostly drawn from the West (with the obvious and controversial exceptions of their treatment of the Steppe nomads, and their references to anthropologies of 'territorial' tribal societies by figures such as Clastres, Lévi-Strauss, and Leach),[25] their situating of the signifying regime and thematization of 'mixed' semiotics helps at least prepare the way for a more nuanced approach to other cultures.

ATP, we repeat, escapes the textual trap both through the materialization of meaning as triggering and in the historical-political situating of the signifying regime among other regimes of human semiotics. Conversely, the emphasis on landscape as text in cultural geography explains why many geographers are anti-postmodern: they feel more or less explicitly that the postmodernist critique of the play of signifiers and the slippage of meaning is self-defeating, trapping us in words – in a version of what, for better or worse, Fredric Jameson has called the 'prison-house of language'. We can thus sympathize with the reaction of anti-postmodernist geographers (and field-oriented social scientists in general) faced with what they see as such a naïve idealism: 'away with such self-reflexive indulgences, let's get out and do some good old-fashioned fieldwork. The evidence is out in the landscape, isn't it?' Such a naïve realism is ultimately unsatisfactory, however, and, in attempting to break through these impasses, we offer our work on *ATP* as a contribution to a new, materialist paradigm for all human/physical geography that supersedes the quibbling of entrenched postmodernists and their detractors of atheoretical, functionalist, or positivist bent.

As far as the situation in 'Continental philosophy' went, Protevi found that the post-phenomenological starting point of Derrideans and Levinasians, along with a certain quasi-Heideggerian allergy to science, prevented this branch of philosophy from fruitful engagement with Marxist, leftist, or other types of materialist analyses of the economic, political, cultural, and environmental effects of phenomena such as globalization.[26] Also missing from the post-phenomenological orientation was the ability to connect with fields of research as important as the cognitive sciences, which were left to the tender mercies of analytic philosophy and its cramped and apolitical 'philosophy of mind'. The unabashed materialism of Deleuze and Guattari, however, encourages an engagement with materialist political, economic, and cultural analysis, while the historical and political dimensions of their thought provide needed leverage in exposing many of the individualistic and ahistorical assumptions of the human sciences, cognitive science included.

We will demonstrate in the course of this book that Deleuze and Guattari's geophilosophy entails a profound and sustained engagement with dominant trends in philosophy and geography, but at the same time is a challenge to their orthodoxy. Starting with the title (a 'plateau' is a self-ordering set of productive connections between forces without reference to an external governing source of order),[27] *ATP* is rife with geological and geographical terms – along with those of a host of other sciences, mathematics, physics, biology, ethology, and anthropology among them – that Deleuze and Guattari orchestrate to create new philosophical concepts such as 'deterritorialization' and 'stratification', terms that not only resonate with geographical concepts but can also be fed back to guide geographical research endeavors as divergent as postcolonial theory and global climate change. As we stress repeatedly below, the geographical terminology in *ATP* is no accident and is neither poetic metaphor nor frivolous wordplay. Their fundamental geophilosophical project entails thinking earth, ground, land, and territory, and even terms as seemingly arbitrary and playful as 'striated space' have precise utilizations and reasons. At the register of the social, striated space is that imparted by the signifying regime or by the State – gridded, hierarchical, suffocating, pre-determined, taxed, and containing subjects that are situated and controlled from some central place 'above'. The seemingly bizarre reference to striation evokes Louis Agassiz's discovery of glacial striations; hence *ATP* likens the spatial effect of the State to the all-powerful suffocation and almost irreversible landscape modification of the continental glacier. This is no convenient metaphor but rather a challenge to think through the glacial effects of the State and perhaps vice versa.

BODIES POLITIC

Deleuze and Guattari's political version of complexity theory is unique and badly needed in providing clues for experimentation with flows of energy and matter – and the attendant attempts at channeling them in ways that produce an excess off which leaders, capital, and subjects feed – that make up the contemporary world. As we have intimated, the materialism of Deleuze and Guattari has an explicit political dimension, insofar as it is a historical-libidinal materialism – an assemblage of Marxian, Nietzschean, and Freudian components.[28] A key dimension of Deleuze and Guattari's work is the investigation of ~~bodies politic~~, material systems or 'assemblages' whose constitution in widely differing registers – the physical, chemical, biological, neural, and social – can be analyzed in political terms. Such an analysis proceeds along an ethical axis (the life-affirming or life-destroying character of the assemblage) and a structural axis, the poles of which Deleuze and Guattari name 'strata' (the domination or putting to work of one body by another in a fixed hierarchy) and 'consistencies' (what Deleuze and Guattari also call 'war machines' or 'rhizomes', which entail the formation of a network or assemblage of bodies with multiple, shifting, and increasingly intense internal and external connections).

On the structural axis for the analysis of bodies politic, the geophilosophy of Deleuze and Guattari names 'stratification' as the process whereby the implantation of codes and territories form dominating bodies. This is opposed to the construction of a 'new earth' that entails new human relationships to the creative potentials of material systems to form consistencies, war machines, or rhizomes from a variety of means. In the construction of the new earth, care must be taken not to confuse the structural difference of strata and consistency with an a priori moral categorization, but rather to retain always the pragmatic and empirical nature of Deleuze and Guattari's work and perform the ethical evaluation of the life-affirming or life-denying character of assemblages. Strata, along with codes and territories, are always needed, if only in providing resting points for further experiments in forming war machines. Strata are in fact 'beneficial in many regards' (*ATP*: 40), though we must be careful not to laud the stability of strata as instantiating the moral virtue of unchanging self-identity espoused by Platonism. The mere fact that an assemblage or body politic is flexible and resilient, however, does not guarantee its ethical choice-worthiness, for what Deleuze and Guattari call 'micro-fascism' is not rigid at all but rather a supple and free-floating body politic, even if fascists are reterritorialized on the 'black hole' of their subjectivity: 'there is fascism when a *war machine* is installed in each hole, in every niche' (*ATP*: 214; italics in original). And not only those practices that 'intend' to produce a life-affirming assemblage will result in such.[29] Because of this intersection of political-ethical evaluation and scientific disciplines, a knowledge of the scientific context for Deleuze and Guattari's thought can be very helpful in grappling with its philosophical difficulties, while their philosophical concepts can inform concrete geographical investigations of their irreducibly political dimensions.

Let us now turn to a more detailed examination of Deleuze and complexity theory.

2

Philosophy and science

DELEUZE'S ONTOLOGY

In discussing Deleuze and Guattari's articulation with science, a distinction must be made between their project and the one Deleuze undertakes in his single-authored works. Deleuze and Guattari's conceptual toolkit enables the humanities' and social sciences' practical engagement with contemporary physical and biological sciences, and vice versa. In his solo works, Deleuze strives to present a basic ontology or metaphysics adequate to contemporary physics and mathematics.[30] We stress the need to engage Deleuze's ontological project first, because it feeds forward into the wider applications presented in his collaborations with Guattari. Indeed, it is a truism of contemporary life that there is a relay between theory and practice: not that one first gets one's theory straight and then applies it, but that conceptual clarification must be linked with practical feedback just as practice is informed by ongoing conceptual work.[31]

Deleuze's quest for a metaphysics or an ontology (for our purposes, we need not distinguish these terms) may shock those who identify contemporary French philosophy with the early thought of Jacques Derrida, who, following Martin Heidegger, thematized the 'closure' or 'overcoming' of 'metaphysics' and indeed of 'philosophy' *tout court*.[32] Deleuze always avoided this approach, insisting that 'I've never been worried about going beyond metaphysics or any death of philosophy'.[33] Instead of denying the possibility of a new metaphysics, Deleuze tried to construct one, stating 'I feel myself to be a pure metaphysician . . . Bergson says that modern science hasn't found its metaphysics, the metaphysics it would need. It is this metaphysics that interests me'.[34] The solution to this

12

[handwritten annotations at top: "Metaphysics of presence ≠ Metaphysics (ontotheology) (ontology)"]

seeming antagonism between great philosophers is the following. The difference between what Deleuze calls metaphysics or ontology and that 'metaphysics of presence' thematized as passé by Heidegger and Derrida is precisely the 'differential' nature of Deleuzean metaphysics or ontology. In the 'metaphysics of presence' the structure of Being is grounded in, or exemplified by, a transcendent or 'highest' being or entity. Hence the 'metaphysics of presence' is also called an 'onto-theo-logy'. By contrast, the Deleuzean ontology developed in *Difference and Repetition,* and sketched out below as Manuel DeLanda interprets it, rigorously avoids any presence or identity in its 'virtual multiplicities'.

To claim a straightforward ontological project would be equally surprising to positivists, for whom 'metaphysics' was an insult that denoted speculation unhinged from empirical observation. Positivism was the dominant philosophy of science in most of the twentieth century. Whether in its Vienna School verificationist or Popperian falsificationist modes, positivism posits a 'deductive-nomological' theory of scientific explanation (called the 'covering-law' model in social science and history). Here we make inductions from observations to form universal and exceptionless laws, which are treated as axioms. Hypotheses are then deduced (as 'theorems') from these laws for specific subfields of experience. Further experimental observations are then compared to the predictions garnered by hypothetical deduction from laws, and, if the observations match the predictions, then we have achieved scientific explanation. Note that the general laws are linguistically formulated so that explanation has the form of logical proof. Thus explanation, prediction, and proof are equivalent.

An excellent guide to this positivist version of the 'scientific method' is David Harvey's *Explanation in Geography* (1969).[35] Positivism based its 'scientific method' on classical physics as a model of scientific rigor, and proposed a reductionist program so that the soft sciences should strive to attain the rigor of the hard sciences. Through following a strict positivist program, it was thought that the laws of psychology, biology, chemistry, and finally physics could account for the phenomena of society as each step along the way had been 'reduced'. In such a reduction, one strives to analyze complex systems into components; the claim is then made that adding together the solutions to the equations that account for the behavior of components will account for the behavior of the system without remainder. Reductionist and positivist approaches thus deny emergence, insisting that all 'wholes' are mere aggregates.

Once again, we see an echo of this reductionism today in methodological individualism in the social sciences, for example, in rational choice theory.

As Harvey points out in *Explanation,* vast problems are created for social sciences when they adopt a positivist model. Chief among these problems is the irrelevance of time in classical physics (the 'reversibility of time's arrow' thesis). In physics, there are in principle no unrepeatable events (replication of results is an essential requirement), but the irreversibility of time and the uniqueness of events is essential to historical events and therefore to human experience.[36] Furthermore, making the prediction of human behavior the goal of social science raises the specter of a search for methods of intervention and control. The sort of disciplinary practices investigated by Foucault can in fact be said to be a tool to try to bring about the social conditions which would yield behavior fitting a rational choice model's prediction.[37] As we will see, Deleuze and Guattari's notion of 'minor science' or 'problematics' is irreducible to positivism (which is called 'axiomatics' in *ATP*), with which it nonetheless maintains a complex relation.

Having cleared the ground by this brief discussion of the very idea of Deleuzean ontology, we are now in a position to sketch the most important concepts in Deleuze's ontology. All commentators agree that the major distinction made in Deleuze's ontology is that of actual and virtual (e.g. Boundas 1996; Smith 1997). Manuel DeLanda, however, usefully adds a third concept, the 'intensive', in his reconstruction of Deleuze's ontology in *Intensive Science and Virtual Philosophy* (2002). We will present the outlines of DeLanda's reconstruction here, beginning with the actual and moving to the intensive and the virtual.

The first aspect of Deleuze's ontology and the one most recognizable in everyday life is the actual, which is named the 'system of the strata' in *ATP*. Actual or 'stratified' substances are equilibrium, steady state, or stable systems, and hence display most prominently extensive properties (such as length or volume), which are by definition divisible without a change in the kind of system (a ruler cut in two would be two rulers), and definite qualities (for instance, the pieces of the ruler would display the same weight-bearing capacity per unit measure as the original ruler). Actual or stratified systems lend themselves to linear models that, for certain practical purposes (that in turn depend upon a certain fit of temporal and spatial scales between system and 'observer' [or better, 'manipulator']), strive to isolate a law-like relation of independent and dependent variables.

14

For Deleuze and Guattari, a science that uses linear models to deal with stratified systems does so by means of a 'striated space'. Now, as the 'Geology of Morals' chapter of *ATP* makes clear, the 'strata' are certainly not limited to the geological register, but also occur in the biological and social registers. Thus it is crucial to remember that 'stratification' for Deleuze and Guattari is not a metaphor when used to discuss the biological and social registers. Although 'stratification' was first discovered in geology, such precedence in the 'order of discovery' is relegated to the arena of historical accident by the demonstration that the same (virtual) 'abstract machine' lies behind the geological, biological, and social strata. In this way, Deleuze and Guattari remove the use of the term 'stratification' in *ATP* from the realm of linguistic effects to that of ontological demonstration.

The next aspect of Deleuze's ontology highlights the intensive morphogenetic processes that operate far-from-equilibrium and produce equilibrium/steady state/stable systems. Processes exhibiting intensive properties are those that (1) cannot be changed beyond critical thresholds (the 'line of flight') in control parameters without a change of kind (a 'becoming'), and that (2) show the capacity for meshing into 'consistencies', that is, networks of bodies that preserve the heterogeneity of the members even while enabling systematic emergent behavior. Deleuze and Guattari employ various names for consistencies, such as 'assemblages', 'war machines', and 'rhizomes'. In the inorganic register, we see consistencies in phenomena of chemical autocatalysis (DeLanda 1997: 62); in the organic register, we see them in ecosystems and in certain evolutionary phenomena ('transverse communications' or 'involutions' where genetic materials cross species borders [*ATP*: 238]); and in the 'alloplastic' register, we see them in animal or human bands, gangs, packs, movements, and even certain social institutions. Intensive morphogenetic processes are characterized by linked rates of change such that any change in those internal relations past a threshold will trigger qualitative change in the assemblage. An ecosystem example of an intensive process forming a simple two-species assemblage would be a predator–prey relation. Now of course such an assemblage is only an abstraction from a far more complex assemblage or 'problem' involving processes and products not only among many other biological species but also in the multiple interacting dimensions of the geomorphological, climatological, economic, political, social, and cultural registers. All these dimensions are involved in the 'mapping' or 'cartography' Deleuze and Guattari prompt us to enact, and, because of the tremendous complexity

15

involved, the choice of which dimensions to study – the interplay of complex reality and simplifying models – is brought to the forefront.

As we detail below, one of the key theses of Deleuze's philosophy is that the extensive properties of actual substances hide the intensive nature of the morphogenetic processes that give rise to them. Actual or 'stratified' substances are the result of the 'congealing' of intensive far-from-equilibrium processes as they reach equilibrium, a steady state, or stability. This congealment is a temporary fixing of an underlying flow that enables the emergence of functional structures; such structures are nonetheless always subject to the flight of particles from the grasp of the structure, even though the time scale of the structure is very long and the rate of flight is very low.

Last, we come upon the third aspect of Deleuzean ontology, the virtual structures of those intensive processes.[38] Deleuze conceives of such structures as 'multiplicities' defined by 'singularities', which are laid out by a 'quasi-causal operator' (in *ATP*, the 'abstract machine') and collectively form a realm (in *ATP*, 'the plane of consistency', the 'Body without Organs', the 'Earth'). The structure of the virtual realm can be explicated as a meshed continuum of heterogeneous multiplicities defined by zones of indiscernability or 'lines of flight'. The virtual realm contains the patterns and thresholds of behavior of the material systems in their intensive (far-from-equilibrium and near thresholds of self-order) and actual (equilibrium, steady state, or stability) conditions. These processes and their resultant actual substances are said to be 'divergent actualizations', which means that the same virtual multiplicity can provide the structure for intensive processes that yield products with vastly different extensive properties. To illustrate divergent actualization, DeLanda uses the example of minimal free energy as a pattern for some steady state physical systems yielding a sphere in soap bubbles, but a cube in salt crystals (2002: 15–16). Finally, let us remember that the 'aspects' of Deleuzean ontology should not be thought of as 'levels', as if the virtual were more (or less) 'real' than the actual. Rather, DeLanda proposes that they are moments in a process of unfolding marked by symmetry-breaking cascades (2002: 26; 74; 86; 105).[39]

COMPLEXITY THEORY

In this section, we present a brief primer on complexity theory, the scientific endeavors whose results prompted Deleuze to distinguish the actual/extensive, intensive, and virtual in his ontology. A basic definition of complexity theory is the study of the self-organizing capacities of 'open' systems (those through which matter and energy flow). Some elementary terminology is necessary to help us understand the basics of this approach.[40]

First, let us distinguish models and the real systems they simulate and remind ourselves that all modeling (in fact, all understanding) is a simplification of the complexity of real systems. The simpler the model, the more 'knowledge' in the sense of predictability you can potentially achieve. But if in building a model too many simplifying assumptions are made (that is, too many relative to the real complexity of the situation you're trying to understand), the result is an illusory 'knowledge'. The trick is to match model and system by balancing simplification and complexity. Constructing a 'state space' is the procedure for modeling complex systems. The great French mathematician Henri Poincaré developed the idea of 'state space' to provide a visual representation of the behavior of dynamical systems. There are five steps in constructing a state space portrait of a system:

1. Identify important aspects of a system's behavior, which are called its 'degrees of freedom' (what constitutes 'importance', of course, must be defined relative to the interests of the model builder).
2. Construct a space with as many dimensions as the degrees of freedom of the system under consideration.
3. Represent each state of the system by a single point, with as many coordinates as there are dimensions.[41]
4. Follow the movement of the point, which represents the changing states of the system as it produces a trajectory through state space, with time as a running parameter.
5. Attempt to solve the equations governing the trajectory and thereby predict the system's behavior.

Before we proceed with our expositions, let us reinforce the difference between 'state space' as a representation or model, and space itself as the locus of interaction of dynamic forces of material systems. Because Deleuze, for various reasons related to his project of developing a 'philosophy of difference', wants to restrict the term 'representation' to the conscious recognition of the properties of constituted bodies,[42] his notion of the 'virtual' should not be seen as state space qua representation, that is, as an actual visual image. (Such images nonetheless let us have a 'window on the virtual', as DeLanda puts it.) Rather, the virtual is the modal status of the set of possible states of the system, along with the probabilities of attaining a particular sub-set of those states. In other words, the concept of the virtual is a way to understand the relation of any system to the patterns and thresholds of its intensive processes and actual behaviors.

After this clarification, we must next distinguish linear and non-linear models. Linear models assume an internal homogeneity of components, an environment in which friction can be disregarded, and that the system is at or near thermodynamic equilibrium (for large quantity, statistical or 'molar' systems) or is in a 'steady state' or 'stability' condition (for other systems). With such models we can achieve a level of accuracy in correlating independent and dependent variables such that we can arrive at a clearly defined equation for a trajectory of the system (when there is only one trajectory to be calculated). Although pure internal homogeneity and completely frictionless environments are simplifications of reality, in some cases (for example, a solid projectile big enough to discount air resistance) modeling the system as if it were homogeneous and frictionless is acceptable because the approximate knowledge is useful for our purposes.[43] Where it is assumed that linear models are representative of all reality, however, LaPlace's demon is at work. Knowledge of the initial conditions and basic laws of a system would yield knowledge of all possible states of the system, both 'past' and 'future' – but here the terms lose their meaning in the face of such omniscient retrodiction and prediction. (To be precise, LaPlace concocted his demon to demonstrate that, because of the limits of human knowledge, we must settle for probabilities.)

In equilibrium thermodynamics, where there are too many trajectories to be individually calculated, we can arrive at statistical laws for large numbers of particle trajectories by treating the average behavior of particles (that is, assuming the homogeneity and normal behavior of particles by discounting greater-than-average fluctuations as quickly damped out). In far-from-equilibrium thermodynamics, complex mechanics, and most organic and social systems, in contrast, nonlinear models are called for (thus they fit the 'intensive' aspect, where 'assemblages' are composed). In systems where a flow of matter and energy has pushed them far-from-equilibrium and into a 'crisis' situation, the emergence of functional structures that focus system behavior lead us to say that the system has 'self-organized' without an external source for that order, solely by achieving threshold states set by its own internal relations. (Though a system can certainly be nudged toward one of those thresholds by external stimuli, these are to be seen not as the source of the order the system assumes, but only as occasions or 'triggers' for internally generated order.) Such open, self-organizing systems are the provenance of complexity theorists.

At this point, we must review an important distinction in elementary calculus. On the one hand, differentiation is the means for determining the instantaneous rate of change of a position function and thereby producing a field of velocity vectors. Such a field is populated by 'singularities', points where the derivative of the function changes direction, and hence points that determine a range of solutions to a problem.[44] The distribution of singularities thus establishes the dynamical landscape of a complex system, including the patterns of behavior (the attractors), and their basins of attraction, the limits of which determine critical points in the history of a system where radical changes of behavior occur. Integration, on the other hand, is the means of establishing a function to vectors, and is used to construct a field of possible trajectories for a system. Although the exact nature of any one system is not established until the construction of the trajectory field using integration, the 'existence and distribution' of singularities can be established in the vector field produced by differentiation (Lautman 1946: 42; cited at DeLanda 2002: 31). Using differentiation and integration together in linear equations is sufficient for calculating simple systems such as the trajectory of projectiles, since here we find well-defined constants such as the acceleration provided to bodies by gravity, and unidirectional and punctual causality (the action provided by the source of movement to the projectile does not continue and does not change once the trajectory has commenced). In these cases, a two-dimensional state space is sufficient, as time and distance are the only dimensions of interest. In such systems, only one singularity is at work, the one that indicates the end state of the system, the landing point of the projectile.

Sometimes, however, we can't solve the equations of systems due to their internal complexity, which demands nonlinear equations to account for the feedback loops that produce a multidirectional causality (the action of one component on another is subsequently modified by the behavior of the acted-upon component, which then must be seen as acting upon the first). This tends to be the case for 'open' systems, those in which a matter-energy flow has pushed them far-from-equilibrium and into 'crisis'. Such open systems tend to be of two kinds. Open random systems are those in which no patterns emerge in our state space representation; by contrast, open self-organizing systems are those in which patterns do emerge. In this case we have a qualitative knowledge of the emergent properties of the system, the patterns of the macro-behavior of the system, but no quantitative knowledge of the micro-behavior of the system arrived at by analysis of the actions of the elementary particles of the system followed by aggregation of the results.

The three basic constituents of the state space of self-organizing systems, revealed by the study of the dynamical landscape established by the singularities of the models used in representing them, are:

1. 'attractors', which determine regions of state space ('basins of attraction') toward which systems tend once their states enter a range of parameters (attractors thus represent patterns of behavior of the system);
2. 'bifurcators' (singularities themselves), which are points where systems flip between one region of state space and another (bifurcators thus represent thresholds where a system changes patterns); and
3. 'symmetry-breaking events', which occur in 'zones of sensitivity' where bifurcators cluster and amplify each other's effects so that a new set of attractors and bifurcators is produced (such events are opportunities for 'creativity' in response to 'crises' in the history of a system).

We must remember many 'actual' or 'stratified' systems settle into such deep 'steady state' basins of attraction that any potential for qualitative change in behavior (associated with the accessing of another attractor) is not only hidden from view (an epistemological point) but is also hard to access (a practical matter). As we have seen, Deleuze calls this property of strata the 'burying' of the intensive beneath the extensive and/or the burying of the virtual beneath the actual.

Attractors are patterns of behavior, then, and bifurcators are thresholds where behavior patterns change. Many typologies isolate three types of attractors: point, loop, and chaotic, corresponding to three patterns of behavior: steady state, oscillation, and turbulence. 'Triggers' are events (either endogenously generated fluctuations or exogenous 'shocks') that move a system to a threshold where its behavior changes. We can note two types of bifurcator, one in which the system moves to a pre-established pattern and another in which a new set of patterns and thresholds is released. The former type of bifurcation is called by Deleuze and Guattari 'relative deterritorialization', while the latter is named 'absolute deterritorialization'. Both types of deterritorialization are accompanied by 'reterritorialization', but in the case of relative deterritorialization the reterritorialization is on specific patterns, while in absolute deterritorialization the reterritorialization is on the system's very capacity for self-transformation.[45]

Although we have used 'complexity theory' as a generic term, one leading researcher in the field, Peter Allen, distinguishes the models used in studying nonlinear dynamical systems, complex adaptive systems, and complex evolutionary systems.[46] Let us conclude this section by a brief recounting of Allen's typology. According to Allen, nonlinear dynamical models produce the most probable trajectory of an ensemble of systems. Nonlinear dynamical systems can have several equilibria (represented by point attractors), or several cycles (loop attractors), or exhibit chaotic behavior, that is, occupy the basin of attraction of a 'strange attractor'. Allen emphasizes that non-linear dynamic systems of themselves cannot cross the borders of such basins (what he calls 'separatrices') – in Deleuze and Guattari's terms, they are bound to their territories. These are still 'mechanical' systems because they exhibit no learning, no local detail, and no individual diversity. Thus the use of such models will gravely distort many complex systems. The presuppositions of these models are 'simply not going to be true for almost any human system. It is probably equally untrue for biological and ecological systems'.[47]

By contrast, Allen's next type, self-organizing models, do not assume that component behaviors are normalized. Here one models systems that have non-average fluctuations; one thereby accounts for all possible trajectories, not just the most probable (as in nonlinear dynamics). Self-organizing systems can thus move across borders separating basins of attraction in response to minor fluctuations (if they happen to be near a border). According to Allen, such collective adaptive response to external change takes the form of new spatial or hierarchical organization. This is still a 'stereotype' model, however, that excludes learning on the part of participants. Thus environment changes are only triggers. Here we see Deleuze and Guattari's 'relative deterritorialization'.

Allen's third category is evolutionary complex models, which do not assume that components have identical structure or behavior. Evolutionary complex systems perform an exploration of behavior space (due to a diversity of inherited traits and a transmission of learned behavior) subject to a selection process. We also see, and this is the critical point, the evolution of the behavior space itself (what Allen calls the 'possibility space' of the system). This change in the very nature of what constitutes change is 'creativity', the 'life' of the 'plane of consistency' of Deleuze and Guattari, or the 'expanding biosphere' of Kauffman (2000).

CARTOGRAPHY AND CRITIQUE

At this point we can enunciate a Deleuzean principle of critique: the extensive properties of actual substances cannot be used to predict the virtual structures of intensive processes, because the extensive properties of actual or 'stratified' systems hide the intensive nature

21

of morphogenetic processes. An actual product, as product, has reached an equilibrium, steady state, or stable condition that hides the far-from-equilibrium, 'intensive crisis' nature of the process that gave rise to it. (As DeLanda notes, the virtual is impossible to access directly from the actual. This is because complex systems, when studied in equilibrium, steady state, or stable conditions, are so locked into the basins of attraction governing habitual behavior that the influence of other attractors is silenced. Indeed, the external stimuli needed to nudge these systems into their intensive crisis state and from there map the virtual realm of the potential behavior patterns might be so extreme that such experimentation is either too expensive or too dangerous to be worthwhile for most practical purposes.) The example Deleuze often uses to illustrate these ideas is that of the egg. Laden with gradients and singularities, the egg is the stage for the intensive processes of embryogenesis, but the adult product of those processes contains structures whose intensive nature has been for the most part 'cooled off' as cell types have been stably differentiated.

Deleuze and Guattari's 'cartography' respects the principle of critique by abjuring all requirements of resemblance in moving through all three ontological aspects: we begin mapping a region by using measurements of extensive and intensive properties of a system to establish the degrees of freedom of the system (the components of the assemblage, the elements of the multiplicity) to be modeled as dimensions of a manifold. But we do not then seek to establish law-like relations between those variables by correlating independent and dependent variables (this is done by a regression analysis when there are many combinations of variables: a regression analysis seeks to isolate law-like relations among multiple factors). Rather than stay on the register of the extensive properties of actual substances in this manner (the striated space typical of 'Royal science'), we move to the study of the virtual structure of the intensive morphogenetic processes that give rise to such substances by 'placing the variables themselves in a state of continuous variation' (*ATP*: 369), that is, by the techniques of 'minor' or 'nomad' science. Minor science operates either experimentally by pushing the system inputs to trigger intensive processes (or simply studying those processes as they occur in high-intensity nonlinear 'crisis' situations), or by using computer modeling to study 'what if' scenarios in changes in variables among populations of 'agents' set free in an informational environment. Minor science is equivalent to establishing the vector field of a system by differentiation ('differential equations irreducible to the algebraic form' [*ATP*: 369]), which serves to 'determine singularities in the matter instead of constituting a general form' (*ATP*: 369). Minor science is also called 'itinerant' science, because Deleuze and Guattari find the procedures of smiths, masons, and the like to be qualitatively different from those of Royal science: 'There are itinerant, ambulant sciences that consist in following a flow in a vectorial field across which singularities are scattered like so many "accidents"' (*ATP*: 372).

In minor science, one maps the virtual realm, establishing the existence and distribution of the singularities (attractors and bifurcators; patterns and thresholds) of that field by differentiation prior to integration, which establishes actual trajectories and the precise nature of such singularities. Once you have a working cartography, you can experiment with real intervention, but you must be cautious: there's no guarantee that destratifying or deterritorializing (that is, moving from extensive to intensive and within the intensive to critical thresholds that trigger either the move to a previously established attractor ['relative deterritorialization'] or that prompt the unleashing of a new set of attractors and bifurcators ['absolute deterritorialization']) will yield a beneficial effect. Here we encounter one of the most important hints we can provide in using Deleuze and Guattari's work: always be careful of the contrast between the gleeful destruction of *Anti-Oedipus* and the cautious experimentalism of *A Thousand Plateaus*.

PROBLEMS AND SOLUTIONS

Earlier, we flagged the political uses of positivist social-scientific projects. Specifically, we warned of ways such projects can be employed to mold social structures so that system behavior conforms to the predictions of models. Why would a Deleuzoguattarian cartography be exempt from the temptations of political control? The answer lies in the status of prediction within complexity theory. We can cautiously and experimentally intervene at points our map predicts are the system's zones of sensitivity. However, confident interventions that aim to control the system cannot be made on the basis of complexity theory models, for there is no strict prediction with such models. Two reasons – one practical, the other in principle – explain this lack of exact predictive power. First, their sensitivity to initial conditions builds practical unpredictability into complex systems thanks to the cascading effects of minuscule measurement errors. Second, some highly complex systems create new possibilities of behavior as they go along; this is the creativity of 'life', the 'Earth' or 'absolute deterritorialization'. Radical systemic changes in such systems can be examined only after the fact, and no improvement in measuring accuracy can affect such radical unpredictability, because of the creation of new basic laws at 'emergent' levels. Such emergent effects are characteristics of a 'multiverse' (*ATP*: 'Cosmos' or 'Mechanosphere') possessing layers of level-specific laws. Reductionism is impossible within this creative, 'multiversal' cosmos, for analysis and then aggregation of unit behaviors is in principle unable to account for emergent effects. Although some writers have attempted to attribute to quantum effects the radical unpredictability of complex systems, in keeping with the general anti-reductionist ethos of complexity theory we prefer to restrict quantum indeterminacy to its own level and claim only a relevant unpredictability at other levels.[49]

Deleuze and Guattari discuss such unpredictability under the rubric of 'problematics', which they oppose to 'axiomatics'. Problematics, as the concern of minor science, treats figures according to their affects, while axiomatics or Royal science is a type of essentialism, which defines figures by their necessary characteristics.[50] In discussing the relation of Royal and minor science it is important first of all to stress that they inhabit 'ontologically, a single field of interaction', even though they are 'two formally different conceptions of science' (*ATP*: 367). Their interaction is one of capture and flight: 'Royal science continually appropriates the contents of vague or nomad science while nomad science continually cuts the contents of Royal science loose' (*ATP*: 367). Among the examples Deleuze and Guattari offer of such interaction is Archimedean and Euclidean geometry, as instantiated in the building of Gothic cathedrals by the interactions of journeyman artisans and Church-employed architects (*ATP*: 364–5).

What do the 'minor sciences' do? As Deleuze and Guattari put it, the minor sciences 'subordinate all their operations to the sensible conditions of intuition and construction – *following* the flow of matter, *drawing and linking up* smooth space' (*ATP*: 373; italics in original). Such problematics overflow the ability to solve the problems posed: 'however refined or rigorous, "approximate knowledge" is still dependent upon sensitive and sensible evaluations [of embodied artisans] that pose more problems than they solve; problematics is still its only mode' (*ATP*: 373). As irreducibly problematic, there are no exact quantitative solutions to the problems of minor science. Instead, they are 'resolved' by 'real life operations' (*ATP*: 374). Let's take the problem of irrigation that Lansing examines in Bali in *Priests and Programmers* (1991). Here, a complex geographic problem involving multiple dimensions in geomorphology (the slope of the hills and the cutting of terraces into them), climate (wet and dry seasons), agriculture (crops vs weeds), irrigation (canals and locks), ownership patterns, population-carrying capacity, and labor availability is modeled. While Lansing's computer simulations can indicate the complexity of the problem, and show how central planning is inferior to the distributed decision-making the Balinese have developed, there is no exact quantitative solution to this problem. Nor can there be any qualitative, 'thick' narrative (for example, a Clifford Geertz-inspired ethnographic account) or even a qualitative-quantitative hybrid approach (for example, a cultural-ecological treatise) that provides a full set of instructions for reproducing this system within the complex spaces of Bali. Rather, it is 'resolved' only by the irreplaceable, un-reproduceable, adaptive 'real-life operation' of the canal and lock system itself. Our conclusion is that in the highly complex problems explored by a Deleuzoguattarian cartography, complexity theory is a complement to minor science, and indicates the irreducibility of distributed spatiotemporal networks of embodied artisans in 'resolving' complex problems by real-life operations rather than by the solution of exact equations or descriptions. As the partisans of the embodied mind school of cognitive science put it in *Naturalizing Phenomenology*:

what Husserl called 'inexact morphological essences' [the objects of 'minor science'], essences foreign to fundamental classical physics [the paradigm 'Royal science'], are indeed amenable to a physical account, provided that we rely upon the qualitative macrophysics of complex systems (and no longer upon the microphysics of elementary systems). (Petitot, Varela, Pachoud, and Roy 1999: 55)

To sum up our account so far, the realm of the actual or the 'system of the strata' is the realm of bodies produced by intensive morphogenetic processes (proceeding via the construction of 'assemblages') while the virtual (the 'plane of consistency') is the differential field of potential transformations that structures such intensive morphogenetic processes. In other words, the virtual is the ontological equivalent of the state space of a system, the set of patterns of processes and the thresholds at which it either adopts or changes those processes. With this sketch in mind, let us examine first Deleuze's work of the late 1960s (*Difference and Repetition [DR]* and *The Logic of Sense [LS]*) and then Deleuze and Guattari's 1991 *What Is Philosophy? (WP)*, thereby contextualizing the 1980 *ATP*.

THE VIRTUAL AS DIFFERENTIATING 'IDEA'

In his late 1960s works, *DR* and *LS*, Deleuze shows that the main characteristic of the virtual is that it is self-differentiating, or 'difference in itself'. A simplified and composite account of Deleuze's thought in this period, developing only those features relevant to our attempt to articulate that thought with complexity theory, follows.[51] The virtual realm is not an undifferentiated chaos, but is articulated by 'Ideas'[52] that serve as 'regional ontologies', laying out the many ways in which 'a' society, 'a' language, 'an' animal, and so forth can exist. Ideas are sets of 'singularities', which are the virtual counterpart of attractors of systems, and are thus determinate 'solutions' to the 'problem' (the Idea, the regional ontology) that lays out the manifold options for incarnating bodies of that nature. We might even say, shifting for the moment from mathematical to everyday language, that a singularity is an opportunity to 'solve the problem' of being a body of a certain nature. (As we have noted above, Deleuzean 'problematics' or 'minor science' establishes the existence and distribution of singularities in a manifold, thus laying out the complex structure of a multiplicity. Now it is precisely those *unsolvable* problems, those with many interacting singularities, which are the important ones, the ones that can only be practically 'resolved'.)

Deleuze shows in great detail how Ideas have a complex internal structure, being composed of series of singularities that:

1. make up regions of intensity (they are thus 'multiplicities' that cannot be divided without a change in nature);
2. are in continuous variation (they are not arranged around a center that provides a standard); and
3. have borders linking them to other Ideas, which are themselves regions of intensity linked in turn to still others.

Deleuze calls the triggering of a bifurcator an 'Event', which unleashes an 'emission of singularities', providing for a new set of attractors and bifurcators, or patterns and thresholds of the intensive processes that are 'buried' under forms of actual behavior. This internal structure of Ideas, or, better, the self-differentiating process by which Ideas spread throughout the virtual as the possible ways of being of different formations become more complex (the 'divine game' of *DR*, the 'unfolding of the plane of consistency' in *ATP*), is named differentiation by Deleuze, in contrast to differenciation, which names the process of actualization, for example, the 'incarnation' of the Idea of 'a' society in one particular actually existing *actualization or differenciation* [handwritten annotation]

society. The series of singularities in an Idea are arranged in 'inclusive' disjunctions, so that they are 'compossible', even those that when actualized would be 'incompossible', that would preclude each other. Thus actualization or differenciation is the construction of 'exclusive' disjunctions, the selection of a series of singularities whose actualization precludes the simultaneous actualization of others, which would then have the modal status of the (virtual) 'road not taken'.

At the risk of some repetition, which we hope will be forgiven as pedagogically justified, let us now see how DeLanda's reconstruction of the 1960s Deleuzean terminology can provide the basic concepts that illuminate the phenomena with which complexity theory deals. We can see that an actual system might, say, oscillate at one frequency within a certain range of parameters, and at another frequency within another range. The actual behavior of the system, its oscillation at frequency #1 or #2, would be a trait, while oscillation frequencies #1 and #2 would occur as the result of the (near-)actualization of virtual attractors, a selection of a divergent series that actualizes a certain set of virtual singularities. The transition between #1 and #2 would be an Event, an actualization of a virtual bifurcator, the selection of a different series of singularities. As we have stated above, 'attractors' are so named because they capture the behavior of systems within a range of parameter values – their 'basin of attraction' – while 'bifurcators' are so named because they are the thresholds at which a system moves from one attractor to another, or, indeed, sets forth a new set of attractors and bifurcators.

This last point lets us reinforce the extremely important distinction between static and changing state spaces, or, in our terms, between a static and creative virtual. While some simple systems can be modeled by a fixed state space with a stable set of singularities representing attractors and bifurcators that are merely 'explored' by the system, in more complex systems the activities of the inhabitants of the system change the very nature of the space itself. Stuart Kauffman of the Santa Fe Institute, for instance, considers the 'mutual bootstrap' effect between the 'landscape' of a particular state space and the specific trajectories that reside within it.[53] In this way the interactions of actual agents serve to change the virtual field, creating new attractors and bifurcators, new 'fitness peaks', as in co-evolution phenomena such as that of an 'arms race' between predator and prey species. Even more challenging to the notion of a fixed virtual is the case in which two systems interact, so that there is a dynamic of dynamics as it were, a veritable explosion of singularities caused by the interaction of ever changing landscapes.[54] The

[handwritten margin notes: "In complex systems activities of inhabitants change nature of space ✳"; "actual changes / virtual → virtual is not dynamic."; "the process of differentiation"]

atractors: structures of self-organization of organizing matter-energy flows → even chaos.

virtual is thus not static, but a constantly self-creating process of differentiation. (As we have noted above, Kauffman 2000 makes this point in terms of the constant expansion of biosphere into the 'adjacent possible'.)

The basic Deleuzean distinction set forth in *DR* between virtual and actual enables us to account for unpredictability in physical systems while still maintaining a consistent materialism. Attractors are structures for the self-organization of processes in which physical systems of matter–energy flow can become organized, even if currently random or laminar.[55] Even turbulent fluids, for instance, which were classic symbols of 'chaotic' matter, are embodiments or actualizations of virtual attractors, albeit 'fractal' or 'strange' ones. There's no real chaos in turbulence, rather fiendishly complex interactions of matter. However, laminar flows (paradoxically, 'calm' fluids) or gases come close to the original sense of chaos. In some self-organizing systems, we find creativity, novelty, unpredictability, but this creativity is inherent in material systems themselves, in two main ways:

zones of sensitivity are potential lines of flight.

1. The 'zones of sensitivity' of material systems provide a source of creativity. What Deleuze in the 1960s calls 'Events' (and later with Guattari will call 'lines of flight') are changes brought about unpredictably when sensitive systems pick up slight cues that trigger a bifurcation, allowing them to move themselves onto another basin of attraction, or keep themselves moving about within a zone of unpredictability, trying out one 'solution' after another in novel combinations.
2. When two or more material systems, with their attendant virtuals, come together in a 'becoming' that provides an unpredictably new 'Idea', a new state space erupts with a new geography of singularities. (It is precisely the use of 'space', 'landscape', and 'geography' in these commonly used explications of complexity theory that sets up Deleuze and Guattari's use in *ATP* of 'cartography', 'mapping', and so forth to denote the exploration of the virtual realm of material systems.)

becoming as coming together of 2 material systems.

CONCEPTS AND FUNCTIONS

To provide a context for their work in *ATP*, let us briefly discuss Deleuze and Guattari's last work, *What Is Philosophy?*. Here they also provide an extended thematization of the relation of philosophy and science, but it is important to remember at the outset, as DeLanda points out (2002: 178–80), that the nomad or minor science evoked in *ATP* – the sort of 'cartography' we promote here – is not the Royal or major science that makes up the entirety of what *DG* call 'science' in *WP*. In *WP* Deleuze and Guattari vigorously deny that philosophy is needed to help science think about its own pre-suppositions ('no one needs philosophy to reflect on anything' [*WP*: 6]). Instead, they emphasize the complementary nature of the two. First, they point out a number of similarities between philosophy and science: both are approaches to 'chaos' that attempt to bring order to it, both are creative modes of thought, and both are complementary to each other, as well as to a third mode of creative thought, art. Beyond these similarities, Deleuze and Guattari distinguish between philosophy as the creation of concepts on a plane of immanence and science as the creation of functions on a plane of reference. Both relate to the virtual, the differential field of potential transformations of material systems (once again, the 'state space' of systems), but in different ways. Philosophy gives consistency to the virtual, mapping the forces composing a system as pure potentials, what the system is capable of. Meanwhile, science gives it reference, determining the conditions by which systems behave the way they actually do. Philosophy is the 'counter-effectuation of the event', abstracting an event or change of pattern from bodies and states of affairs and thereby laying out the transformative potentials inherent in things, the 'roads not taken' that coexist as compossibles or as inclusive disjunctions (differen*t*iation, in the terms of *DR*), while science tracks the actualization of the virtual, explaining why this one road was 'chosen' in a divergent series or exclusive disjunction (differen*c*iation according to *DR*). Functions predict the behavior of constituted systems, laying out their patterns and predicting change based on causal chains, while concepts 'speak the event' (*WP*: 21), mapping out the multiplicity structuring the possible patterns of behavior of a system – and the points at which the system can change its 'habits' and develop new ones.

Let us concretize the discussion. First, let's take as a simple example of the contrast of philosophy and science, the becoming-orange of a tree's leaves. Science would construct a causal explanation of this change by means of a function describing the properties of the chemical composition of the tree and its relations to other elements in the ecosystem. In contrast, philosophy would create a concept that would 'map' the tree in terms of the 'affects' or capacities of change composing the tree, singularities expressed in the infinitive: to bloom, to take root, to change colors, and so on. The event of the change of colors is thus expressed as 'pure reserve', as the relation of one series (this particular change) to the other series of which the tree is capable (all the other changes it may or may not happen to ever actualize).

science tracks differenciation
philosophy tracks differentiation.

This deliberately over-simplified example, however, doesn't bring out the social import of Deleuze and Guattari's contrast of philosophy and science, which proposes ways of dealing with such extremely high-dimension phenomena as those encountered in social systems. Philosophy's highest calling is to create concepts of events that summon us to new opportunities, or that make us aware of events that promise a 'new earth' through constructing their concepts. For example, let us consider 'the events of May 68', with which Deleuze and Guattari are linked via *AO*, and the importance and reality of which they never stopped defending.[56] The story has often been told, but bears repeating. In France, a threshold of social unrest was passed, as turbulent post-war affluence and concomitant life-style experimentation was countered by government regulation in the form of education reform. May 1968 brought together students and workers in a completely unexpected heterogenous assemblage, to the befuddlement of the established guardians of the revolution, the French Communist Party. Days of general strikes and standoffs with the police led de Gaulle to call a general election. To very few people's surprise in the non-Communist French left, de Gaulle's call for a parliamentary solution to the crisis was backed by the Communists, who were evidently as scared of any revolution from below – which by definition would lack the party discipline they so craved – as were the official holders of State power, to whose position they aspired. The worker–student movement collapsed eventually, leaving memories of non-scripted social interactions and revealing the investments of the Party, lampooned thereafter as 'bureaucrats of the revolution'.[57]

When it deals with May 68, philosophy needs to construct the concept that will allow us to see, to feel, to live a new life on the basis of the becomings – the transformative potentials – of that event. We could contrast this philosophical approach with a (positivist, 'Royal', or 'axiomatic') social-scientific attempt to construct causal chains that would explain May 68 on a plane of reference: such-and-such level of unemployment and such-and-such level of education combined with such-and-such concentration of mass media images would yield a function explaining the event as the consequence of the properties of that constituted entity called 'French society'. It's not that science is inferior to philosophy as a mode of creative thought: producing such a function would be an amazing achievement indeed! It's just that science travels a line 'downward' from the virtual multiplicity of all that *a* society can be to that which *French* society has become and on that basis predicts what it probably will change into, while philosophy moves 'upward' from the actual changes *French* society has undergone to the virtual multiplicity of all that *a* society can be in order to call for an experiment that will create a new society (one no longer recognizable as 'French' perhaps) along untold 'lines of flight', novel combinations of bifurcators, attractors, and zones of sensitivity, that would deviate from the probable pattern science predicts.

For Deleuze and Guattari in *WP*, then, science deals with properties of constituted things, while philosophy deals with the constitution of events. Roughly speaking, philosophy explores the plane of immanence composed of constellations of constitutive forces that can be abstracted from bodies and states of affairs. It thus 'maps' the range of connections a thing is capable of, its 'becomings' or 'affects'. In contrast, science explores the concretization of these forces into bodies and states of affairs, tracking the behavior of things in relation to already constituted things in a certain delimited region of space and time (the 'plane of reference').

How can we entangle these two ways of seeing the relation of philosophy and science (providing an ontology [*DR* and *LS*] and complementary creations [*WP*])? One way is to focus on how concepts can relate to functions. Just as there is a 'concept of concept' there are also 'concepts of functions', but these are purely philosophical creations without 'the least scientific value' (*WP*: 117). Thus concrete concepts like that of 'deterritorialization' are philosophical concepts, not scientific functions, even though they might resonate with, or echo, scientific functions. Nor are they metaphors, as Deleuze and Guattari repeatedly insist:

Of course, we realize the dangers of citing scientific propositions outside their own sphere. It is the danger of arbitrary metaphor or of forced application. But perhaps these dangers are averted if we restrict ourselves to taking from scientific operators a particular conceptualizable character which itself refers to non-scientific areas, and converges with science without applying it or making it a metaphor. (Deleuze 1989: 129)

Deleuze and Guattari's refusal to recognize that their work contains metaphors is owing to their struggle against the 'imperialism' of the signifying regime: not every relation between different intellectual fields can be grasped by the most common notions of 'metaphor', reliant as they are on the notion of a transfer of sense from primary to secondary signification.[58]

3

Toward a geography of complex spaces

EMERGENCE

To begin this section, let us briefly consider emergence, which to our point of view is the biggest question in social science, implicated as it is in all the controversies surrounding methodological individualism, the structure/agency debate, Luhmann's differentiation of social systems, and so on. Now it is important not to exaggerate the current state of scientific research dealing with emergence; we can more easily define emergence than demonstrate its existence, or even determine the criteria for demonstrating its existence.[59] First, the definition: an emergent structure is that which enables focused systematic behavior through constraining the action of component parts. This definition encapsulates what Thompson and Varela (2001) call 'reciprocal causality': the mutual constitution of local-to-global or 'upward' causality that produces focused systematic behavior and the global-to-local or 'downward' causality that constrains the local interactions of components. How though to demonstrate the existence of such an emergent functional structure rather than just asserting its presence? A negative demonstration would be pointing out any systematic behavior that cannot be accounted for by analysis of the system into its components and then aggregating the results of measuring the behavior of the parts. But as Silberstein and McGeever (1999) point out, this explanatory failure might simply be epistemic (due to sensitivity to initial conditions and so on) and so we have here merely 'epistemological emergence' and are not any closer to being able to claim 'ontological emergence' or emergence as a real feature of the world. A stronger approach would be to link ontological emergence to the ontology of complex systems we sketch above. If we can show the presence of attractors of the same type in many different physical actualizations, then we can plausibly claim these as evidence of ontological emergence, as they are produced by nonlinear feedback processes which are widely accepted in contemporary ontologies (Silberstein and McGeever 1999: 197–8). Such a demonstration of ontological emergence often takes the form of demonstrating the formation of singularities in agent-based computer modeling of systems, since such singularities are said to represent attractors in real systems (though here again the epistemic questions are difficult to assess). Such attractors would entail a reduction in the state space of the system, and hence the possibility of focused behavior achieved through the constraint of components. While such agent-based modeling has had some success in ecosystem studies, we are still far away from being able to model social systems successfully. The biggest problem here, as DeLanda (2003) puts it, is the modeling of bounded rationality (the facile assumptions of rational choice theory concerning information availability and rational performance not being very useful for those committed to a realist attempt to capture features of the world rather than merely modeling phenomena). For the time being, then, it seems we will have to be satisfied with the intuition that social systems at a variety of levels (group, family, institution, corporation, and so on) are complex systems with emergent functional structures, without being able to model them. This limitation does not mean, however, that we cannot use complexity theory as a 'folk ontology', that is, that we cannot look for patterns, thresholds, and radical evolution of structures in far-from-equilibrium 'crisis' situations in social systems.

We have stressed the political dimension of Deleuze and Guattari's encounter with complexity theory as bearing on the question of emergence above the subject to the level of social (institutional, urban, State) machines. They also show the importance of complementing the move 'below' the subject to a multiplicity of 'agents' by showing that the distribution of agents in a population of subjects is itself amenable to analysis on the level of social systems, thereby attacking the implicit methodological individualism of much cognitive science. To cite one example among many of the methodological individualism in philosophy of mind, especially pertinent here because it deals with complexity theory, Alicia Juarrero states in *Dynamics in Action*:

Since the global level of all complex adaptive systems contextually constrains the behavior of the components that make it up, I postulate that behavior constitutes action (a wink, as opposed to a blink) when the *brain's* self-organized dynamics, as characterized by consciousness and meaning, originate, regulate, and constrain skeleto-muscular processes such that the resulting behavior 'satisfies the meaningful content' embodied in the complex dynamics from which it issues. (Juarrero 1999: 7; emphasis added)

Deleuze and Guattari's political focus prompts us to ask: why stop at the brain as the 'global level'? Why not posit the brain as an intermediate global level, caught up in turn by higher-level institutional and social 'machinic assemblages', so that we add other levels of constraints and enablings? Undoubtedly, we need to account for the novelty and unpredictability of individual, 'molecular' human subjects, but we also need to account for social predictability in 'molar' populations. Human beings are rule-followers as well as free agents; in fact, many free agents break rules but in so doing form new patterns that can become rules for others, a phenomenon Deleuze and Guattari term deterritorialization accompanied by compensatory reterritorialization.

Juarrero's emphasis on the irreducibility of possible rule-breaking (and hence the irreducible unpredictability of human behavior) is common in complexity theorists when they discuss humans, owing to the lingering effects of their struggle against positivism's insistence that any real science of human behavior must establish universal laws that allow prediction. The entire problematic of rule-following and rule-breaking shows why Deleuze and Guattari's emphasis on moving above and below the subject, their 'political physiology', is crucial for anyone interested in the structure-versus-agency problem. To take an example closer to the interests of economic geographers, Peter Allen, on the very first page of an interesting work on complexity theory and urban growth (Allen 1997), shows how most complexity theorists still conceive their work as a struggle against positivism and its insistence on classical mechanics as the model of all science:

Planets, billiard balls, and point particles are helpless slaves to the force fields in which they move, but people are not! People can switch sources of energy on and off and can respond, react, learn and change according to their individual experience and personality.[60]

Well, of course human beings *can* break rules, learn, adapt, and so on, but the question is under what conditions *do* certain sections of human populations develop new fundamental behavior patterns, rather than merely move between the already constituted patterns they predictably adopt due to their social position? Such questions of human freedom are only explicable when we address emergence above and below the level of the subject.[61] In moving us above and below the subject Deleuze and Guattari do not deny that there is a genuine subject (on the level of practical effectiveness, not as an ontological substance), but they do stress that it is only an intermediate global level of organization. There is thus a way to talk about degrees of freedom of human action or agency. We are more free: (1) the greater the constraints the subject level can exercise over 'autonomic' sub-systems (for example, yogic experimentation with physiological processes); (2) the more one's 'subject position' allows one to negotiate social constraints embedded in institutions and free-floating or 'peer pressure' systems (for example, gender and race constraints); and (3) the more money one has (in some places gender and race constraints are being replaced by economic constraints), because then, to complete the system, you can buy somatic training and/or move to places where economic power mitigates race and gender constraints, etc.[62]

As should be clear by now, the largest problem considered in our book is the extension of the notion of self-organizing material systems – systems with no need of transcendent organizing agents – to the social, political, and economic realms. In such a view, systems no longer need conceive of themselves as in need of leaders, capital, subjects, or codes (for example, DNA) as sources of transcendent order, although of course such leaders, codes, etc. may have catalytic effects on independently existing intensive processes. The question Deleuze and Guattari raise is how then do leaders, capital, subjects, and codes come to claim total credit for the order and novelty generated by the system which incorporates both them and the people, the workers, the body/brain/environment, and the cellular metabolism, respectively? The catalyst and the process together form an emergent structure, and confusing catalysis, which requires an independent process in which to intervene, and a hylomorphic scheme in which a transcendent source of order 'rescues' a chaotic matter, is equivalent to the sort of 'vampirism' in which a higher-level constraint claims credit for reciprocally generated emergent order. (This is, of course, only the mirror image of a methodological individualist denial of emergence in which wholes are nothing but aggregates of components.) Emergent structures do have real effects via a systemic enabling, achieved through a top-down constraint of the probabilities of a system; in other words, the emergent structure forms a new virtual field for the population of components. But such structures are nothing without the components. A

35

No

no?

Emergent structures
form new virtual fields.

constraint without lower-level activities to constrain would be empty, just as, to complete our paraphrase of Kant, lower-level activities without the constraint of emergent structures would be blind. (In contrast, while a catalyst without a process is completely useless, a process can get along just fine without a catalyst, although it might be too fast or too slow to reach a specific threshold.) The difference from a hylomorphic schema is that although emergent structures are real and have real effects, they are not already formed, self-present and transcendent agents swooping down to rescue a chaotic system from itself (using 'chaos' here in the ancient, cosmogonist sense). Rather, they themselves are produced when intensive flows – often aided by catalytic agents (themselves the product of other processes) – reach certain thresholds that activate self-ordering patterns inherent in the material interactions of the components. However, by the same token, even though Deleuze and Guattari argue indefatigably against the 'transcendental illusion' of hylomorphism, there is no a priori morality here in favor of flow, as the naïve postmodernist reading of Deleuze and Guattari would have it. As we mentioned above, stratification, one of the types of emergence, is 'a very important, inevitable phenomenon that is beneficial in many respects', as Deleuze and Guattari say on the very first page of *ATP*'s 'Geology of Morals'.[63]

Time scale is all important for understanding emergence. In one of his last works, Francisco Varela shows that neuronal resonant cell assemblies cohere and then fall apart on a time scale measured in milliseconds (Varela 1999). But during their period of resonance they can trigger simple motor responses, which can trigger further real effects when picked up by the appropriate assemblage. They can also stay around longer and guide more complex behaviors by forming constraints via attractor formation in a quick-forming basin of attraction ('dynamical landscape').[64] This notion of temporary emergence must be set against both structuralism, which puts structures into a universal unconscious, and methodological individualism, which denies the efficacy of structures.[65] As we remarked above, DeLanda (1997) is very good at thematizing the difference between 'strata' and 'consistencies', the two types of emergent substances Deleuze and Guattari detail. As always with Deleuze and Guattari, these are only ideal distinctions, for in reality there are only de facto mixes: bodies, and the networks of bodies called 'assemblages' that contain processes moving in both directions at once. Strata are homeostatic (that is, they are characterized by negative feedback loops, as theorized in the cybernetics movement) and have a fixed virtual realm. Strata are stable, returning quickly from perturbation to a set point. This is the Deleuzoguattarian sense of 'organism', which can be related to the received notions of the autopoietic school of Maturana and Varela. (In social theory, Niklas Luhmann is the leading figure in extending notions of autopoiesis to the realm of social systems, conceived as self-regulating systems.)[66]

In terms of political physiology, stratified 'organisms' force their organs to serve the system of which they are parts, and here we find the received notion of functionalism. In contrast to strata, consistencies have changing virtual realms: they amplify diversity by virtue of positive feedback loops (but successful consistencies are always dampened by negative feedback loops to avoid a suicidal explosion – the fascist war machine lacks precisely this 'instinct for self-preservation'). Beside stability, consistencies also exhibit resilience: creative adaptation to environmental change (actually, here with assemblages, 'environment' is coupled to bodies in networks of 'affects', so that there is no servitude, but symbiosis, the assemblage of heterogeneity as such). Once emerged into their temporary stability, strata and consistencies exert top-down constraint (turning components into content) as well as enabling emergent effects, the teamwork in which the whole is greater than the sum of its parts and is able to exert focused systematic behaviour (expression). Once again, we must insist that Deleuze and Guattari are not simple 'flow enthusiasts': there is no enabling without constraint. (In Foucault's terms, power is not negative, but productive.) Constraint here is a reduction in the dimensionality of the connection space of components while emergent effects mean the substance has increased the dimensions of its connection space (it can do more things, relate to more bodies – or at least more powerful bodies – than a heap of lower-level substances can).

Let us take one last example of emergence to illustrate our points. A properly legitimated judge utters a certain 'order word', let's say, 'guilty'. This utterance triggers the 'incorporeal transformation'[67] of the prisoner from accused to convict, which means real changes in the probability distribution for the location of the prisoner's body as a whole, and perhaps in the organization of his sub-systems by application of electricity or gas. All these real effects are conducted by temporary structures, but note the time scales involved. While the resonant cell assembly in the judge's brain that triggers his or her pronunciation lasts only a few milliseconds, the body of the prison to which the prisoner is sent will *probably* retain its (actual) structure (concrete and steel forming walls and cells) long after the (actual) organic materials of the body of the prisoner lose their (virtual) organization (= 'death'). Of course, the body politic of the prison system can change (riots can breach prison walls; governors can commute death sentences; legislatures can change laws), but maybe not fast enough for this prisoner. So simply recognizing that structures are temporary products of morphogenetic processes is abstract until you specify time scales: for the dead prisoner, the prison is just as present a 'judgment of God' (*ATP*: 40) as if it 'really' had been made by a world-transcendent force. Alternatively, the first truism of any political action is that you need to recognize the historically constructed nature of a body politic before you bother to try to change it: no one mounts a political struggle against gravity. So just because the prison system is long standing and exhibits great resilience doesn't mean it can't be struggled against, even though it has outlasted many individuals. The point is to organize patterned movements, consistencies, that can effectively struggle against the strata and consistencies that harm us. Yes, some consistencies, some emergent 'war machines', are poisonous assemblages. But not all of them! So Deleuze and Guattari's twin injunctions should always be kept in mind: (1) don't be satisfied with the 'organism' or 'subject' you've been given, so go ahead, be creative, experiment with the strata, but (2) always evaluate carefully, because you can never tell ahead of time what is going to work: 'never believe that a smooth space will suffice to save us' (*ATP*: 500).

DOING GEOGRAPHY AFTER DELEUZE AND GUATTARI

Once we have accepted Deleuzean geophilosophy as a viable ontological and epistemological framework for geography, how do we go about putting it to work in the discipline? What positive projects can we undertake that engage the complex systems approach employed in *A Thousand Plateaus* to break free of conceptual deadlocks, circumvent crises of representation and the textualist trap, overcome imposed dichotomies (for example, 'human' vs 'physical'), and challenge subdisciplinary boundary-drawing? How can Deleuze help us cure the plagues of a science David Harvey (1984) once challenged to construct an 'applied "peoples" geography', what we would call a 'new Earth'? If we accept *ATP*'s post-post-structuralist union with complexity theory as a way forward, we agree implicitly that we are engaged in a struggle against hegemonic and oppressive spaces such as those of Empire (Hardt and Negri 2000) and those imposed or favored by the State, by globalizing corporations, by development organizations, and so forth. Deleuzean action means neither nihilism nor escapism, but rather reorganization of spaces along other lines, and particularly – if we are engaged in geo-thinking that threatens the emerging post-9/11/2001 world order – a retreat to 'holey space' to launch sallies against the ever-more-'striated' spatial regimes colonizing our minds as well as our bodies.

ATP is designed not as an anarchists' cookbook (it doesn't give you any recipes to copy) but as an *n*-dimensional 'rhizome' of entangled lines of inquiry whose 'plateaus' can be plugged into productively for nonlinear geophilosophical inspiration. The geophilosophy behind *ATP* can be put to work once the terms and concepts are explicated, as we do in the Glossary. We do not want to situate *ATP* alongside works of Foucault, Derrida, et al. as the latest contribution to a gene-alogy of post-structuralist critical texts. Though we do recognize the need to engage *ATP* critically and comparatively, in the present work we attempt to move it out of its post-structuralist neighborhood and into a place of its own as a unique geophilosophical blueprint poten-tially as important as Descartes or Kant. We repeat, however, that *ATP* is NOT a geophilosophy of flows and nomads per se, and Deleuze and Guattari did not intend the 'smoothing' of every space. Rather, they give us the tools to analyze and intervene in the mixture of smooth-ing and striating forces at work in the complex spaces we inhabit.

Because we do not seek to alienate non-materialist post-structuralists, we offer a few final comments on the break *ATP* makes with that tradition. *ATP* demands of critical post-structuralist geog-raphers that they figure out how things work in a real material sense. Deconstruction is necessary, but only as a first step to spatial expla-nations that articulate the interweaving of material and semiotic in the 'general text' in a way the post-phenomenological perspective of Derrida, which remains bound to merely marking the disruption of signification by 'force', cannot allow. But *ATP* demands we go out and describe complex systems – including complex spaces, at our scale of observation – as they exist in their own material-semiotic imbrications, beyond the mere effects they cause on signifying chains. There can be – there *must* be – a Deleuzean cultural ecology, a post-post-structuralist biogeography, a Deleuzean geomorphology, and these are not critiques of discourses that cling to the ideal of a purely rational and self-grounding signification – or that by contrast 'affirm' the disruption of such an ideal by a mute 'force' – but new ways of explaining complex systems as only geographically-minded individuals, teetering on the balance of human and non-human, can achieve.

Spaces are NOT constructed by discourse alone, and thus are not configured solely to be read. 'Haecceities' (places as events, for example) offer endless opportunities for the emergence of new materials that irrupt from multitudinous points and ripple outward across landscapes. These irrupting, smoothing forces need to be mapped and described, and even exploited (by the activists among us), for the State is never and should never be the last or only word in any landscape. Once post-structuralists – those who have already moved beyond structure – come to believe in the far-from-equilibrium crisis potentials of unstable matter-flows, materials, signs, products, and discourses, they can move on to encounter complexity even within the most seemingly 'closed' of systems. We think this is already happening in the discipline of geography (the post-textual emphasis on phenomenological corporeality and performance, as noted above, for example; also, the growing fascination with Latour's actor-networks), so we hope that for many post-structuralist geographers and allied social scientists this book will be more than anything else a nudge toward wider applications. Another thing: it is fully possible for humans to engage and include the nonhuman and the transhuman ('nature': biology and geology in particular) in a geophilosophy of immanence, particularly through careful observation and attunement to what is going on, and a humility in the face of the inhuman that reins in humanist pride. Physical geography, in other words, doesn't have to include people, because human 'regimes of signs' are not the be-all, end-all of the Earth – far from it. Humans and our semiotic systems can be between and among complex transhuman systems, or on the outside looking in. For example, when *ATP* discusses birds, it is concerned with them as birds, not as metaphors that allow us to understand ourselves better. *ATP*'s discussion of bird song allows us to understand bird song, and from there geophilosophical concepts such as the refrain, landscapes, territories, and so forth. Similar processes operate in human territorial phenomena, but *ATP* does not use the bird only to get to the human.

For structuralists antipathetic to post-structuralism, sympathy for or conversion to Deleuzean geophilosophy may be a hard sell indeed. The structure in *ATP* is more akin to a pattern, a 'flat' and emergent network 'machine' 'extending' the intensive and actualizing the virtual. Structures that appear deep and eternal – particularly those in the anthropogenic realm – nevertheless always have spatio-temporal limits, thus room for maneuvering, manipulation, and (trans)mutation. Structures, no matter how rock-solid they appear, never entirely predetermine actions, thoughts, or speech, and certainly not spaces.[68] Individuals are not wholly produced by structures, only co-produced (structures never conquer all one's degrees of freedom). The non-human is also this way: constantly mutating, forever shuttling off materials into other networks, endlessly forming new connections. To escape, to transmute, to disrupt structures, the human, intertwined with the non-human at myriad junctures, can draw off the forces of 'nature' but also can serve as an event, a haecceity whose single efforts and effects achieve wider societal and spatial transformations. If it is true that some structuralists need a prime mover to account for structures in the first place, then this points to a lack of understanding of the immanent, creative qualities of the cosmos. The prime mover is not an alpha–omega, transcendent, overcoding, force, but rather (in the 'multiverse') an ever accessible virtual realm presided over by 'abstract machines'. For a structuralist to engage Deleuze and Guattari fully, the need for origin and depth must be replaced by the intercourse of virtual, intensive, and extensive registers. The bond between Marxists and Deleuzeans, of course, is their insistence on material production and sidelining of signifiance; it is just a matter, then, of agreeing on the source and organization of what is produced.

Beside theory, what are the sources for a 'geography of complexity' or a geographical study that employs geophilosophy? One of the attractions of *ATP* is its eclectic collection of texts drawn from an astounding array of disciplines. Many of the sources are straightforward, non-philosophical accounts of material systems, and it is fair to say that one can find materialist accounts in even the most atheoretical sources. Also, because we have a certain fondness for ethnographic research based on the geographical knowledge of informants, we can say that whether or not a source is theoretically aligned has no bearing on its value in a geography of complexity. Indeed, clues to material processes can be gleaned from such a wide array of sources that it is not even necessary to agree with the theories that do underpin them. We grant, however, that it is necessary to separate the wheat from the chaff in terms of the validity of a source's factual assertions, and this never fails to be an extremely tricky endeavor. Particularly tricky when you claim, as Bonta has done in his study of Honduras (pp. 169–90), that facts and ideas of separate sources never match up because not only are they anchored in disparate discourses but also they are derived from separate (though intertwined) complex systems and spaces. The question for Bonta, after he was barraged with multiple 'interpretations' of land use, became not 'who is right?' but 'where do I situate them?' Nobody's interpretations of space were 'wrong' per se: they were just derived from disparate world-views and different experiences of reality, produced by immersion in separate cultural and spatial milieus often only loosely imbricated.

In searching for voices of authority within geography, when one is researching a certain region such as the province of Olancho in Honduras, Bonta found that the works of the Sauerians were exemplary for their no-nonsense, materialist approach to the land; so what if they didn't analyze the role of capital? The truth is that while Bonta disagreed strenuously with their epistemological and ontological stances (as much as those were evident at all), this did not take away from the fact that certain Sauerian sources were mines of information. Denevan's (1961) study of highland pines in Nicaragua and Johannessen's (1963) research on interior savannas in Honduras were invaluable for their nuanced human-environment details, and though they may fall short 40 years later, what studies do not become dated? That, in any case, is the point of 'science': no one produces an authoritative statement for all time. Geographers can and should draw off accounts no matter how 'outdated' (and this includes travelers' accounts and so forth, not just academic geographical treatises).

'Geohistory' (we would call it historical geography) appealed to Deleuze and Guattari (as manifested in *WP*, by way of Braudel) because it builds on and up from the microhistories of places and regions linked by flows of products, rather than down to the local by way of the 'universal'. In Bonta's study there was a lot of geohistory, something that we argue must necessarily feed into understanding the complexity of spaces. This is probably taken for granted by most geographers, but within reductive social scientific pursuits (not to mention within universalizing natural sciences), geohistories may not be a factor: one strives for uniformity and repeatability in the 'field', which becomes nothing more than a vast 'laboratory'. Place, in other words, does not matter for far too many researchers who have burdened us with the 'molar' rain forest, biome, life zone, frontier, town, city, *campesino*. There are indeed molarizing – normalizing – processes at work that ensure we will encounter similarity and linkages wherever we go (these forces of uniformity and standardization are certainly not restricted to the human 'stratum'), but through Deleuze we may see difference as also at work in the field, and identity produced through difference, rather than vice versa. In this thinking, 'I am in Juticalpa' supersedes 'I am in yet another typical Third World regional political capital and market center'. One starts in the middle – in a place – and researches outward, finding out things that may or may not be 'applicable' elsewhere, but that can't necessarily be understood in terms of elsewhere.

In sum, we would say that, after Deleuze, one's research focus and one's theoretical framework are not necessarily as important as one's disavowal of 'Royal science' (science in the service of the State and like-minded apparatuses). It is basically impossible to engage Deleuze and Guattari's geophilosophy fully without at least admitting that the State, the corporation, and their minions need to be challenged. Whether one is asking ethnographic questions, coring lake beds, taking *GPS* points, or critiquing the discourses of Victorian travelers (or all the above), what is important in the construction of 'a new earth' is the realization that hierarchization, centralization, signifiance, identity, 'overcoding', and so on are produced and can thus be the objects of transformative projects where they are construed as norms and become oppressive. Outside the laboratory and off the pages of the planning document, the only 'norms' are emergence and complexity. As these are not guaranteed to be in line with 'progressive' political ideals, *ATP* leaves us only with the tools for careful evaluation and cautious experimentation. Not much, perhaps, by the standards of the master discourses of the past, but more than enough for us, and we hope for you as well.

Part II: Glossary

Deleuzoguattarian geophilosophy

We provide the French term after the translation only when the translation is not a simple English cognate. For example, we give *agencement* after 'assemblage' but not *architecte* after 'architect'.

All page references are to *ATP* unless otherwise noted.

ABODE [*demeure*]. See Territory.

ABSTRACT MACHINE: the most general sense of 'machine' for DG is a linkage between heterogeneous elements, so an abstract machine links virtual singularities to form multiplicities on the plane of consistency. An abstract machine defines multiplicities by their lines of flight, that is, the thresholds beyond which a material system undergoes qualitative change. An abstract machine, in other words, defines the patterns and thresholds (the attractors and bifurcators, to use complexity theory terms) of a complex system. DeLanda glosses the abstract machine as the 'quasi-causal operator' that links virtual multiplicities together; as evidence justifying the postulation of the abstract machine he cites the emergent capacity, near-phase transitions in complex systems, for linked changes in the distribution of the singular and the ordinary events in a series (DeLanda 2002: 75–80).

　　DG discuss abstract machines in three main ways in their conclusion (510–14): (1) as 'singular and immanent' abstract machines directing concrete assemblages; (2) as THE abstract machine or measure of creativity; (3) as responsible for creativity, stratification, and capture, the three major productive and anti-productive practices of the world.

47

1. Defined by the cutting edges of deterritorialization (the invitations to novel connections) of an assemblage, a singular and immanent abstract machine links 'unformed matters' and 'nonformal functions' operating on a plane of consistency (141). In other words, an abstract machine lays out what an assemblage can be made out of and what it can do, not just in its current state, but in future states as it enters into becomings or transformative relations with any of the other assemblages it can reach by virtue of inhabiting a 'plane' allowing for mutual interaction. An unformed matter is defined by its virtual capabilities; such matter is spread across a 'phylum' which links materials according to their possession of traits that indicate such capabilities and thus indicate the various materials out of which an assemblage can be made (406–10). Similarly, a nonformal or virtual function is expressed in a diagram, which lays out the transformations, the affects or becomings of that assemblage (141–2). Beside being outside the form–substance grid, singular and immanent abstract machines are also beyond content–expression, although by virtue of bringing together traits of matter (intensities) and function (tensors) they do have a semiotic, which consists of indefinite articles, proper names, infinitives, and dates (263–5).

   Let us consider two examples of singular and immanent abstract machines: a heat motor and discipline. As a virtual operator, the abstract machine links material phyla and functional diagrams that are then subject to 'divergent actualization', that is, they are 'incarnated' in widely differing registers. The abstract machine of a heat motor links unformed matter (any medium for storing and transmitting heat) and nonformal functions (separate, channel, exploit heat differences). Such a diagram can be found in hurricanes, steam engines, and refrigerators (DeLanda 1991: 141–3; 1999: 58). The abstract machine of discipline takes as its unformed matter 'any human multiplicity' linked to the nonformal function: 'impose any conduct'. Such a diagram can be found in schools, prisons, factories, and so on (Deleuze 1988a: 34; 72; translation modified).

2. DG also point to THE abstract machine 'serving as a transcendent model, under very particular conditions' (512) to which concrete assemblages are related and assigned a coefficient of creativity. In other words, there is a veritable quantity of creativity that can be determined for any one assemblage, according to its ability to create new connections on its plane of consistency. In this way, DG can establish the relative closeness of the war machine and the relative distance of the State to the abstract machine of life.

3. DG isolate three main types of abstract machine: (1) those creative ones on the plane of consistency that create new connections by decoding and deterritorializing; (2) those that stratify the plane of consistency by means of coding and territorialization, creating new

planes organized along the axes of substance–form and content–
expression; (3) those that, on the alloplastic stratum, overcode and
reterritorialize, producing order-words in language, significations
and subjectivities linked in faces, and axiomatics or striations of the
earth (223; 513). This typological classification of abstract machines
enables DG to underscore the complexity of the 'Mechanosphere',
because all these machines 'are as intertwined as their operations
are convergent' (514). Thus the three main activities of the world
are creation, stratification, and capture, or, in other words, life (creation) and 'that which life sets against itself to limit itself' (stratification and capture).

ACTUAL: an ontological term for Deleuze, 'actual' is replaced in
ATP by its correlate, 'stratified'. The actual is the aspect complex
systems display when, in a steady state, they are locked into a
basin of attraction. Actual, stratified, systems hide the intensive
nature of the morphogenetic processes that gave rise to them –
and therefore, a fortiori, the virtual multiplicities structuring
those processes – beneath extensive properties and definite qualities. It is as if the actual were the congealing of the intensive and
the burying of the virtual. This congealment is a temporary fixing
of an underlying flow to enable the emergence of functional
structures or substances, which are nonetheless always subject to
the flight of particles from the grasp of the structure, even
though the time scale of the structure is very long and the rate of
flight is very low.

ACTUALIZATION: the process of 'incarnation' of a virtual multiplicity. See Stratification.

AFFECT: the ('active') capacities of a body to act and the ('passive')
capacities of a body to be affected or to be acted upon; in other
words, what a body can do and what it can undergo. As Massumi
indirectly notes (xvi), the use of this term derives from Deleuze's
reading of Spinoza, in which Deleuze carefully distinguishes
'affect' as the experience of an increase or decrease in the body's
power to act from 'affection' as the composition or mixture of
bodies, or, more precisely, the change produced in the affected
body by the action of the affecting body in an encounter
(Deleuze 1988b: 49). In the main discussion of affect in *ATP*
(256–7), DG curiously do not use the word 'affection', although
the concept is there. DG distinguish the relations of extensive

parts of a body (including the 'modification' of those relations in an affection resulting from an encounter), which they call 'longitude', from the intensities or bodily states that augment or diminish the body's 'power to act [*puissance d'agir*]', which they call 'latitude'. In other words, the 'latitude' of a body comprises the affects or the capacities to act and to be acted upon of which a body is capable at any one time in an assemblage. What are these 'acts' of which a body is capable? Affects are 'becomings' or capacities to produce emergent effects in entering assemblages. These emergent effects will either mesh productively with the affects of the body, or clash with them. Meshing emergent effects will augment the power of that body to form other connections within or across assemblages, resulting in joyous affects, while clashing emergent effects will diminish the power to act of the body, producing sad affects. Affects as the capacities of an intensive body to act in forming assemblages are equivalent to the intensities passing on a Body without Organs (BwO), and are thus the object of ethical evaluation (165).

For DG, knowledge of the affects of a body is all important: 'We know nothing about a body until we know what it can do [*ce qu'il peut*], in other words, what its affects are' (257). (Note that the 'passive' and 'active' senses of affect are combined in the French verb *pouvoir*. One can say 'je n'en peux plus' for 'I can't take anymore of this' as well as 'je peux le faire' for 'I can do it'.) Now defining bodies in terms of affects or power to act and to undergo is different from reading them in terms of properties by which they are arranged in species and genera (257). According to affect as the capacity to become, to undergo the stresses inherent in forming a particular assemblage, a racehorse (carries a rider in a race; that is, enters the racing assemblage) has more in common with a motorcycle than with a plow horse (pulls a tool that gouges the earth; that is, enters the agricultural assemblage), which has more in common with a tractor. This is not to say that what is usually named in one regime of signs a 'plow horse' or 'tractor' cannot be made to race, just as 'race horses' and 'motorcycles' can be made to pull plows. These affects as changes in the triggers and patterns of their behavior would, however, constitute another becoming or line of flight counter their usual, statistically normal, or molar usages; it would constitute their enlistment in assemblages that tap different machinic phyla and diagrams than the ones into which they are usually recruited. Whether or not the bodies involved could withstand the stresses they undergo is a matter of (one would hope careful) experimentation.

AIR: a type of smooth space (387). In the sense of the atmosphere enveloping the earth, air was 'conquered' only in the twentieth century, by aircraft. The air is partially striated as 'air space' (the columnar territory of air 'owned' by a nation-state) but as in the historical striation of the sea, air has been smoothed again by a world-wide space effected by 'fleets in being' (DG borrow the term from Virilio), that is, military forces utilizing the atmosphere to survey and conquer any and all points in the striated space of the land (spy satellites, remote-controlled spy drone aircraft, 'Stealth' bombers and fighters). The United States' repeated attempts since the 1970s to install a missile shield ('Star Wars') may result in the most powerful smooth space yet devised. DG warn against such smooth spaces that are re-imposed to striate the land more intimately and exactly (480). See also Desert, Polar Ice, Sea.

ALLOPLASTIC STRATUM: that register where the creative production of signs constructs territories. It is not limited to the human or social, but extends to territorial animals (60; 314–37).

ANARCHISM: DG have little to say about it, despite the parallels to *ATP* in the disruptive, rhizomatic, and mutualist philosophy found in such anarchist-geographical writings as Reclus 1897 and Kropotkin 1989. However, at *ATP* 558n61, they do note that nineteenth-century European anarchists drew inspiration from 'nomadic themes originating in the East'.

ANTI-PRODUCTION: in *AO*, the full BwO as catatonia or interruption of desiring-production as well as the moment of waste or 'glorious expenditure', such as the potlatch, the feast, the monument, the sacrifice (see also Bataille 1988; E. Holland 1999). In other words, anti-production is an expenditure of energy derived from a consumption of products with no reference to a utilitarian goal; anti-production is thus, literally, 'good for nothing'. Anti-production does serve, however, the reproduction of the form of the productive network by wasting products (*ATP*: 440), which creates lack among the producers, which in turn focuses desire on mere survival (*AO*: 28). DG thus renounce any political economy based on natural scarcity and a separation in production between necessity and excess, or, in Marxist terms, use value and exchange value; anti-production, waste of excess, structures economies from the start. Uniquely, capitalism makes anti-production part of the economy as a spur to more production. 'Advertising, civil government, militarism, and imperialism' all realize surplus value outside consumption and investment in order, once again, to produce lack among the producers and send them back to work the next day to try, in Sisyphean style, to work off an infinite debt incurred in the midst of plenty (*AO*: 235).

APPARATUS OF CAPTURE [*appareil de capture*]: an assemblage that captures localized territories by overcoding them and channeling their flows into a centralized organism or system. DG devote a plateau of *ATP* to the apparatus of capture that molds States (via the State apparatus or 'megamachine' [444]) out of villages, towns and countryside, cities, and so forth. Through the process of overcoding, preexistent regimes of signs (in mixture) are decoded and subjected to the ends of an organizing, centralizing, hierarchizing machine that turns activity into work (labor), territories into 'the land', and surplus value into capital. Land ownership is the apparatus of capture of the earth; labor and particularly surplus labor (for example, of the type used to build imperial monuments and public works of all kinds) is the apparatus of capture of activity. See also Signifying Regime.

ARBORESCENCE: the virtual model of the tree used directly or indirectly to trace a hierarchy (15–18). DG derive their uses for this term from Pacotte 1936 (cited at 519n13). The terms 'root-tree' and 'tree' refer to different types of hierarchies. The tree model conceptualizes such diverse hierarchical systems as bureaucracy, democracy, and genealogy. The 'unit dipole' type of arborescence is the model of the wheel with spokes, partially applicable to certain State-forms, while the root-tree model is of the 'link dipole' type, whereby the trunk is the segment that connects the roots with the branches (16). For the sake of contrast, DG oppose trees to rhizomes, but also point out that any actual system is always subject to intensive forces moving it in the opposite direction. In other words, the roots of trees (hierarchies) are always beset by rhizomatic growths, while rhizomes (consistencies) are always prone to take root and develop centralizing hierarchies. (Technically speaking, however, there is no exact contrast, as the root-tree is a model for tracing development on a plane of organization or transcendence, while a rhizome is 'an immanent process' constantly constructing a plane of consistency [20].) The Western model of the rooted tree, with a strong central trunk (erect, phallic), an ever finer system of branches, the bearing of fruit, and the thinker who sits underneath, is to them a violence done to real trees. They point out that arborescence, and the power of trees as organs of power and as central nodes, are (like so many symbols) traceable to presignifying semiotics in the figure of the tree-climbing shaman, related to the 'world-tree' or *axis mundi* (211). Nevertheless, trees in the presignifying regime are only local black holes, and without the apparatus of capture of the State, they could not resonate together to become engraved as transcendent models. See also Thought.

ARCHITECT: the figure of hylomorphic production, that is, someone who thinks production occurs through the imposition of form on the chaotic matter of a body. DG derive the figure of the architect from their reading of Simondon (1995). DG analyze historical instances of architecture primarily in terms of the conflict of Royal and minor science (364–6), relying on Anne Querrien (cited at *ATP* 554n26), who studies Gothic cathedral building in the context of the growth of the French state. See also Artisan.

ARTISAN: an agent of production who coaxes bodies to thresholds of self-organization, and hence operates by the principles of minor science (409). The modern artist, because he or she taps the self-organizing and emergent capacities of molecularized material, is called a 'cosmic artisan' (345). Artisans are opposed to the architect, who operates under the illusion of hylomorphism and by the principles of Royal science (368). In artisanal production, the artisan must 'surrender' to matter, that is, transform it into material by pushing it into far-from-equilibrium crisis (408). In this way the artisan can follow the singularities of the material by attending to its traits and then devise operations that bring forth those potentials to actualize the desired affects; in other words, he or she must attend to hints that this material can withstand the intensities of heating and cooling, stretching and twisting, necessary to allow the product to do the things it is capable of, to perform its affects. It is this link of singularities and traits via operations that distinguish products as belonging to different machinic phyla 'deducted' from the singular machinic phylum (406).

ASSEMBLAGE [*agencement*]: an intensive network or rhizome displaying 'consistency' or emergent effects by tapping into the ability of the self-ordering forces of heterogeneous material to mesh together ('entrainment' in complexity theory terms), as in the 'man-horse-bow assemblage' of the nomads (404). Territorial assemblages cross the alleged nature/culture divide by instituting an 'imbrication of the semiotic and the material' (337), while technological innovations that enable emergent effects are also assemblages that work 'artificially and naturally' (406). In the latter case, these selections of singularities break up the 'machinic phylum' into 'technological lineages' (406–7). A territorial assemblage is a consistent 'material-semiotic' system that preserves the heterogeneity of its components even while enabling emergent systemic affects. Such assemblages are far-from-equilibrium systems operating in 'crisis' or near a threshold of self-ordering, and are thus poised between the strata (equilibrium, steady state, or stable systems) and the plane of consistency (the virtual field whose multiplicities outline the potential for linkages among assemblages [337]). A territorial assemblage links bodies (material systems that are themselves assemblages of organs at a lower level of analysis) and signs (triggers of change in those systems) to form 'territories' or systems of habit. The territorial assemblage is composed along two axes, content–expression and deterritorialization–reterritorialization (88–9; 140–1).

In the alloplastic stratum, territorial assemblages bring together bodies and regimes of signs as content and expression. The content, or that which is put to work, is comprised of 'machinic assemblages of bodies' (MAB), that is, arrangements of bodies that provoke and regulate a matter–energy flow and hence provide the concrete circumstances of an event or haecceity. The expression, or that which triggers productive change in bodies, is a 'collective assemblage of enunciation' (CAE), that is, a social framework of habits and institutions within which order-words effectuate their incorporeal transformations, the shifting of bodies from one region of their state space to another (from one pattern of behavior to another). The other axis indicates the types of relation into which content and expression enter. These are: (1) 'territories', which are in the broadest analysis the result of processes of (re)territorialization, that is, the creation of fields of material production in which the MAB and CAE work together more or less smoothly, producing repeatable patterns of behavior; and (2) 'deterritorialization', the invitations or feelers that search out opportunities for the positive creation of fields of bodily action where the previous fit of MAB and CAE breaks down and both mutate in ways that establish the conditions of new territories, that is, new patterns of behavior. Territories, or the conditions for repeatable patterns of behavior, thus result from reterritorializations that accompany deterritorializations. DG insist that deterritorializations, directed by abstract machines, be seen as the primary determinants of assemblages, the first things one looks for in classifying and interacting with them; in other words, one should look to the openness to novelty of each assemblage, the way it invites new connections with other assemblages. This is as much an ethico-political injunction as an ontological statement, indicating DG's profound pragmatism. In other words, the injunction to treat deterritorializations as primary should be taken as a directive for how one should deal with things (send out your own invitations to match those of others) in order to increase one's power (*puissance*: the ability to create new becomings and joyous affects). See Figure 1.

AXIOMATIC [*axiomatique*]: the key to DG's understanding of both capitalism and Royal science. In modern mathematics, an 'axiom' is an unprovable statement defining the relations between undefinable primitive elements in a formal system or 'axiomatic'. (NB: although 'axiomatic' is primarily an adjective in most English usage, 'axiomatique' is a noun in French and so Massumi uses 'axiomatic' as a noun in his translation of *ATP*.) In this manner such axioms are taken to fix, or implicitly define, the meanings of the primitive elements. In addition to axioms and primitive elements, an axiomatic includes a set of inference rules by which to derive further statements ('theorems') from axioms or other, previously derived, theorems. An ideal axiomatic system should demonstrate independence (no element can be defined by another element and no axiom can be derived from another axiom), consistency (axioms cannot contradict each other), completeness (any truths of the axiomatized theory must be either axioms or derivable as theorems), and effectiveness (the inference rules must allow a procedure by which the theorems can be enumerated). In the 1930s, Gödel proved that any consistent, effective axiomatic system powerful enough to be realized as arithmetic must be incomplete, that is, must contain at least one 'undecidable' statement, a truth of the intended theory that can

Figure 1   *The refrain*

CHAOS Un-organized milieus (actual)	EARTH Territorial assemblages (intensive)	COSMOS Plane of consistency (virtual)
Milieu = place of access to material	**Assemblage** = 'rhizome', 'war machine' = consistent heterogenous 'team' of components	**Abstract Machine** = operator that links unformed matters and nonformal functions to draw a phylum/diagram actualized in assemblages
Material = 'molecularized' matter = 'laden with singularities' = potential for self-ordering	**Consistency** = characteristic of an emergent process that preserves heterogeneity of components, operating far-from-equilibrium, in a sensitive condition, and thus forming an 'imbrication' of the material and the semiotic	**Diagram** = set of nonformal functions; what an assemblage can do
Matter = homogenized, stable state of elements		**Phylum** = set of unformed matters; what an assemblage can be made out of
Strata = systems locked into deep basins of attraction; strong habitual patterns for matter		

Code = periodic repetition of elements in a milieu.

Transcoding = resonance between codes.

Stratification = process by which milieus are captured by an 'apparatus of capture' so that material elements are layered in homogeneous layers (coding) and then functional relations are produced among those elements (overcoding).

Decoding = freeing of milieu elements so they avoid stratification and can be recruited into an assemblage or reach plane of consistency.

Destratification = intensification that produces a 'molecularization' of 'matter'.
Relative destratification = movement of material into an assemblage.
Absolute destratification = reaching the plane of consistency
= reaching condition of 'unformed matter'
= release of singularities or potentials of self-ordering that can be fit into a new assemblage.

Deterritorialization = intensification that produces a 'crisis' that reshuffles the 'material–semiotic' fit of an assemblage, so that 'signs' no longer have the 'meaning' they once did, that is, they no longer reliably trigger habitual material processes.
Relative deterritorialization = movement to a previously formed assemblage.
Absolute deterritorialization = reaching the plane of consistency
= providing unformed matters and nonformal functions for forming a new assemblage.

neither be proved nor disproved in the system. In other words, no rich axiomatic can be both consistent and complete.

We discuss three contexts of DG's use of axiomatics: their political economy, their epistemology, and their ontology.

1. In their political economy DG insist they are not using 'axiomatic' metaphorically when they discuss capitalism. Although the treatment of 'Axiomatics and the current situation' (460–73) is considerably more complex, we will present only three aspects of DG's notion of axiomatic capitalism: its operationality; its flexibility (its ability to add new axioms or subtract them); and its multiple realizability.

    First, the capitalist axiomatic is operational. When formalized, an axiomatic system has no truth value; its truth value must await its 'realization' in a 'model'. Thus an axiomatic is purely operational; the 'meaning' of axioms comes only in the realized model. For example, Euclidean geometry, on the modern understanding, is only a model realizing an axiomatic. (It was previously thought that the Euclidean axioms were self-evident truths, but the modern formalization of axiomatics eliminates this understanding of axioms.) In this way, an axiomatic is different from a code, in which meaning is inherent in the relation of bodily signs (tattoos, scars) to the territory, or an overcoding, in which meaning is inherent in the relation of signifiers to other signifiers in a chain (a mythic or legal system). This distinction between meaningful codes and overcodings and meaningless, purely operational, axiomatics forms the basis for DG's political economy in which they distinguish capitalist societies and 'savage' (coding) tribes and 'barbarian' (overcoding) empires. Capitalist axiomatics is meaningless, a purely operational mode of regulation of flows that 'deals directly with purely functional elements and relations whose nature is not specified, and which are immediately realized in highly varied domains simultaneously' (454). In other words, capitalism, by means of credit markets, labor regulations, and other 'modes of realization' overseen by the State, brings together decoded flows of wealth (now known as 'capital') and human energy (now known as 'labor power') as 'purely functional elements' (that is, elements with no predetermined use, no marked qualities, but open to any use, as opposed to societies in which productive elements are coded or overcoded and hence limited in their range of potential uses).

    Second, the capitalist axiomatic is flexible. It adds axioms continually as means of displacing its limits and accommodating new subject formations. 'Let's create the New Deal; let's cultivate and support strong unions . . . But within the enlarged reality that conditions these islands, exploitation grows constantly harsher' (*AO*: 373). At the same time, capitalism can also take away axioms, as in totalitarian 'anarcho-capitalism' such as Chile in the Pinochet era (*ATP*: 462).

Third, because of its operationality and its flexibility, the capitalist axiomatic is multiply realizable, so that the pure functions of capital and labor are 'realized in highly varied domains simultaneously'. To give historical examples from the period of the capitalist takeoff, English capitalism operated in slave plantations in the Jamaican colony and in Manchester factories in the home land which outlawed slavery. Capitalist models can be neo-liberal (USA and UK), social democratic (France and West Germany), socialist (Yugoslavia), totalitarian (Stalinist USSR), 'anarcho-capitalist' (Pinochet's Chile), and so on. (DG insist there is only one world capitalist market that subsumes the difference between 'East and West' and 'North and South'.) The current hegemony of the post-Thatcher and Reagan neo-liberal 'American model' which attacks the axioms of the social democracy of the New Deal type in favour of privatisation of public assets, minimal social welfare, and so on (and imposed through the 'structural adjustment' policies of the IMF or indeed by invasion, as in Iraq under the US/'Coalition' military occupation of 2003) can be seen as an attempt to restrict the multiple realizability of capitalism to a single model.

2. In their epistemology DG link axiomatics to problematics. The 'axiomatization' of a science means the formulation of basic principles so that theorems can be deduced from them. Problematics, by contrast, is the opening of a scientific field prior to its formalization in an axiomatic. For DG, an entire 'politics of science' (144) is involved in the interaction of axiomatics and problematics: 'Hilbert and de Broglie were as much politicians as scientists: they reestablished order' (143). However, despite the blocking effects of axiomatics, we must not see the construction of an axiomatic system as purely mechanical:

In science an axiomatic is not at all a transcendent, autonomous, and decision-making power opposed to experimentation and intuition. On the one hand, it has its own gropings in the dark, experimentations, modes of intuition. Axioms being independent of each other, can they be added, and up to what point (a saturated system)? Can they be withdrawn (a 'weakened system')? On the other hand, it is of the nature of axiomatics to come up against so-called undecidable propositions, to confront necessarily higher powers that it cannot master. (461)

3. Finally, in their ontology DG oppose axiomatics to diagrammatics. An axiomatic is the program of a stratum (143) rather than the diagram of an abstract machine for an assemblage (141). DG further connect axiomatics with the construction of striated space out of

smooth space. As part of the foundationalist program in twentieth-century mathematics, axiomatic set-theory sought to ground the nineteenth-century 'discretization program' of Dedekind and Weierstrass, which had previously sought to replace the geometrical notions of the continuum and motion with purely arithmetical ones. This might be what DG have in mind when they say 'axiomatics blocks all lines, subordinates them to a punctual system' (143).

BARBARIAN: term used in AO to designate the machine of the archaic empires ruled over by 'Despots'. In *ATP*, the term gives way to analyses of the 'signifying regime' and the State apparatus.

BECOMING [*devenir*]: the production of a new assemblage (257–8); a 'non-symmetrical double deterritorialization' (307); the entry into a 'symbiosis' in which what is real is 'the becoming itself, the block of becoming, not the supposedly fixed terms through which that which becomes passes' (238). A prime example of a becoming is the wasp-orchid (10). The orchid becomes necessary to the life of the wasp and vice versa: what is primary is the new assemblage, the wasp-orchid machine. The becoming of wasp-orchid does not have a subject separate from itself: it's not that the wasp, say, stays the same and merely adds a new property to the set of properties that defines it. Nor is there a goal or finish (or 'term' = terminus) distinct from the block of becoming, for the other in the pair is also changed by its entry into the new assemblage. In complexity theory terms, the new assemblage, the symbiosis, is marked by emergent properties above and beyond the sum of the parts. It is also important to remember that a becoming is a combination of heterogeneous parts; it is an alliance rather than a filiation, an 'unnatural participation', a 'marriage against nature', a 'transversal communication' (53; 239–40). Keith Ansell Pearson (1997: 132) cites Lynn Margulis's revolutionary work in contemporary biology on mitochondrial capture as the origin of the eukaryotic (nucleated) cells as a heterogenous becoming, a 'symbiogenesis' that produces a new assemblage. DG also use the Little Hans case study from Freud as a paradigmatic becoming, to buttress their argument that certain schools of psychoanalysis serve to block becomings by reterritorializing them on the Oedipalized family. The becoming-horse of Little Hans is not a matter of imitation or analogy in which the horse represents a family figure, but a symbiosis of speeds and affects on a plane of consistency. Can Hans change his assemblage, his body and regime of signs, so that the speed and slowness of its material elements, and hence its affects, what it is capable of, work together with those of a horse to form a new, third, assemblage, the 'becoming-horse of Hans'? In this third assemblage, the affects of the horse would trigger affects in Hans: 'An assemblage, for example, in which the horse would bare its teeth and Hans might show something else' (258).

BECOMING-WOMAN [*devenir-femme*]: one of the most heavily commented-upon of DG's concepts (for recent treatments, see Braidotti 2002; Buchanan and Colebrook 2000; Lorraine 1999; and Olkowski 1999), 'becoming-woman' is supposedly the 'key to all other becomings' (277), since 'White Man' forms the standard or major condition in contemporary Western social systems. Since a becoming is a change in the intensive 'speeds and slowness' of the material components of a body enabling a new set of affects ('what the body can do'), becoming-woman is not the imitation of the molar entity 'woman', that organism caught in a binary opposition to 'man'. Rather, becoming-woman is the ability of a 'molecularized' body to tap into the Body without Organs as the virtual realm for alternate orderings of organs, those that do not meet the 'Judgment of God'. See also Girl.

BERGSON, Henri. French philosopher (1859–1941). One of the primary influences on Deleuze, Bergson is mentioned by name only a few times in *ATP*, although his influence can be felt in many more places. The most prominent mention is in the title of the 'Memories of a Bergsonian' section of the 'Becoming-Intense' plateau (237–9), which picks up Bergson's notion of 'creative evolution' to develop DG's notion of 'creative involution', that is, genetic transfers across species barriers, a process DG call 'transverse communication' or 'surplus value of code' (53; 239–40; see also Ansell Pearson 1999). Bergson's distinction between intelligence and intuition is cited as analogous to DG's distinction between problematics and Royal science (374). Finally, Bergson is credited with having made important contributions to the theory of multiplicities by his notion of duration (484), which allows DG to distinguish intensive and extensive properties.

BLACK HOLE/WHITE WALL SYSTEM: a black hole is a point that captures everything coming into its reach or 'zone of proximity' (273). In complexity theory terms, a black hole is a basin of attraction from which a system cannot escape. DG apply the term to a wide range of phenomena. For instance, self-consciousness, when coupled to passionate love ('a cogito built for two' [131]), produces a black hole as absolute deterritorialization (133): 'I'll follow you anywhere!'; micro-fascism is defined by 'a micro-black hole that stands on its own . . . before resonating in a great, generalized, central black hole' of the fascist State (214); chaos can be a black hole (312), as can strata (40). That both chaos and strata are black holes makes perfect sense: either too much order or too little can be impossible conditions from which to escape. In fact, without careful experimentation, you'll move right from one black hole to the other. As we argue repeatedly, DG do not condone an a priori moralizing judgment in favor of change or flow: strata are 'beneficial in many respects' (40) and so 'staying stratified . . . is not the worst that can happen' (161). Constructing a black hole is among the worst things that can happen, and a black hole is the result of 'extremely sudden deterritorialization', a 'machine effect in assemblages . . . a closure of the assemblage, as if it were deterritorialized in the void' (334); all this sort of reckless experimentation does is 'throw the strata into demented or suicidal collapse, which brings them down on us heavier than ever' (161).

In the 'Faciality' plateau, DG focus on a dual system of the black hole of the subject and the white wall of the signifier, together creating the Western (Christ-)face in the mixed signifying/postsignifying regime (176). The black hole/white wall, working in tandem, comprises the abstract machine that produces faces (167–8; 180–2). Subjectification and signifiance, two strata, intersect to produce the face, whose white wall is the screen (the movie screen, essentially) on which the black holes (the film) are projected. Thus, the face is 'read' as a text for its passions and the emotions that flicker across it, particularly or perhaps uniquely (to an extreme) in Western culture, where the face is deterritorialized from the head–body system, to a degree so great that the face dominates not only the media and romantic love (for example), but even the landscape (which thus becomes a 'text' as well as a palimpsest [172]).

BODY [*corps*]: a system considered in terms of appropriation and regulation of matter–energy flows. At a lower level of analysis, a body is an assemblage of organs; at higher levels, a body may itself be an organ in a social body. A body is thus a node in a production network that is plugged into a network of other flows, slowing some down, speeding others up. A stratum is composed of homogenized bodies put to work by an overcoding agent, while a consistency is an assemblage that retains the heterogeneity of the bodies composing it. Machinic assemblages of bodies are linked with regimes of signs to constitute territorial assemblages. In both assemblages and strata, bodies are content, that is, they are linked up so that their output is used in functional structures or expressions. In other words, their behaviors are patterned in ways that are useful in realizing goals and are triggered by the operation of signs. See also Body without Organs, Organism.

BODY WITHOUT ORGANS or BwO [*corps sans organes* or *CsO*]: a misnomer, the BwO is responsible for much confusion; it would have been better to call it by the more accurate but less elegant term: 'a non-organismic body', as DG freely admit: 'the BwO is not at all the opposite of the organs. The organs are not its enemies. The enemy is the organism' (158). A BwO retains its organs, but they are released from the habitual patterns they assume in its organism form; in so far as the organism is a stratum (a centralized, hierarchical and strongly patterned body), a BwO is a destratified (decentralized, dehabituated) body. Adding to the potential confusion is a significant change in the term 'full BwO' from *AO* to *ATP*. In *AO*, the BwO is 'full' when it is catatonic, a moment of anti-production, a mere surface across which desiring-machines are splayed and upon which a nomadic subject moves (*AO*: 8). As such a surface, the full BwO allows for the recording of desiring-production; in the social register it is the socius (*AO*: 10). In *ATP*, however, the full BwO is positively valued; it is the 'empty' BwO that must be avoided. The full BwO allows for connection with other destratified bodies, while the empty BwO is a black hole for subjectivity, where nothing happens (citing William Burroughs, the junky is a prime example here [150]).

Although the organism is a stratum imposed on the BwO, it is equally true that a BwO is an object of construction, a practice; it is 'what remains after you take everything away' (151), after you take away all the patterns imposed on the BwO: 'The BwO howls: "They've made me an organism! They've wrongfully folded me! They've stolen my body!"' (159). A BwO has ceased to be content for an expression, that is, it has ceased working as part of a functional structure, and has entered a plane of consistency, a region in which it is now open to a field of new connections, creative and novel becomings that will give it new patterns and triggers of behavior. In other words, the BwO is the organism moved from 'equilibrium', that is, out of a stable state or 'comfort zone' (a certain functioning set of homeostatic mechanisms and regulated habits), to an intensive crisis realm (producing changeable, 'metastable' habits).

The relation of 'intensity' to the BwO is complex and the key to understanding the relation of a singular BwO as the limit of destratification of any one body and THE BwO as the plane of consistency, the virtual realm for all bodies or assemblages (72). On the one hand, a singular BwO is 'populated by intensities' (153) – in other words, in a molarized population of 'organisms' one can determine a standard measure or extensive property that will trigger production (producing such uniform reaction is the goal of disciplinary training), whereas, with a BwO, only experimentation with the cartography of a body, its immanent relations of intensities as matter–energy flows (longitude), will determine the triggers of production (affects or latitude) (260–1). But, on the other hand, in so far as any intensity of flow among the organs of a body will actualize a certain series of singularities indicating a pattern or increased probability of connection among organs, THE BwO is 'the earth' (40) at zero intensity of its flows (153). In this way a BwO is the state space of a body, its virtual realm, while THE BwO is the plane of consistency of all bodies, and hence the (virtual) arena in which all connections are possible, and hence where ethical selection must occur (153–4).

A BwO is not reached by regression, for a BwO is not the infantile body of our past, but the virtual realm of potentials for different body organization precluded by the organism form. Thus it is reached by a systematic practice of disturbing the organism's patterns, which are arranged in 'exclusive disjunctions' (specifying which organs can ever meet and outlawing other possible connections). Constructing a BwO is done by disturbing the organism, that is, by disrupting the homeostatic feedback loops that maintain organismic patterns by a shift in intensity that triggers a change of habitual practices – in complexity theory terms, by moving out of a basin of attraction and thereby leaving behind the singularity that unifies bodily patterns at an emergent level. In this way a body of purely distributed, rather than centralized and hierarchized, organs can be reached, sitting upon its underlying matter–energy flow. In other words, a BwO is purely immanently arranged production; matter–energy flowing without regard to a central point that drains off the extra work, the surplus value of the organs for an emergent organic subject in a 'supplementary dimension' (265) to those of the organs (159). A BwO has 'counter-actualized' the exclusive disjunctions of the organism to reach the virtual field where multiplicities are series of singularities ordered in 'inclusive disjunctions', that is, series in which any possible connection is equally probable. Since all actual bodies must make choices, the key ethical move is to construct a body in which patterning is flexible, that is, to stay in a sustainable intensive 'crisis' situation, where the BwO or the virtual can more easily be reached, so that any one exclusive disjunction can be undone and an alternate patterning accessed.

As an object of practice reached starting from the organism, the BwO needs to be cautiously constructed by experimentation with body practices: 'staying stratified – organized, signified, subjected – is not the worst that can happen' (159). Nor is the BwO an individualist achievement:

> For the BwO is necessarily . . . a Collectivity [*un Collectif*] (assembling [*agençant*] elements, things, plants, animals, tools, people, powers [*pusissances*], and fragments of all of these; for it is not 'my' body without organs, instead the 'me' [*moi*] is on it, or what remains of me, unalterable and changing in form, crossing thresholds). (161)

BOOK: DG constrast the root-book with the book as rhizome (3–7). The root-book may be a world unto itself (the final word, the decisive treatment); the development of themes from beginning to end; a mirror of the world, a mimetic or structural representation of 'reality' produced by an Author. The Book is the postsignifying regime of signs' answer to the Face of the signifying regime, and DG cite the flight of the Hebrews out of Egypt as the primordial example of the passionate subjective line of flight from the paranoid signifying regime; the Face of the Despot was replaced with the Word of God (127). They write of the root-book as a type of 'word of God', and contrast all this to the book as rhizome, which (without 'crazy talk' [138] or artifice) can be read starting anywhere, is a multiplicity, and is meant to be plugged into and engaged with at any point (not read beginning to end). They refuse the supremacy of the Book, or the Author (or even team of authors) as authoritarian figures that 'own' the 'work'. The book rhizome is good if it works for a certain purpose, not necessarily if it sounds pretty or argues effectively. It is astructural, amorphous, asignifying, and constrained only by its material limits (for example, length, publisher conventions, and the many limiting factors of language and script themselves). Needless to say, *A Thousand Plateaus* is written as a rhizome (22).

BORDER or BORDERLINE [*bordure*]: fuzzy, diaphanous edge of a multiplicity or molecular aggregate (245–6). DG contrast the borderline, and the process of bordering, to the hard edge of the boundary between states of beings. The borderline is the threshold, the edge beyond which a multiplicity changes in nature (437); in the dynamics of packs, flocks, or swarms (or flat rhizomes in general), bordering is effected by individuals that reach a zone characterized by a threshold of density beyond which they sense that it is 'unsafe' to venture, and they thus move back toward the inside (245). Beyond the borderline is the Anomalous, the exterior or Outside (DG cite H. P. Lovecraft at 240) which is populated by patrolling forces that keep the multiplicity dense and in motion. There are many Outsiders, ranging from sheepdogs to sorcerers (239–52). The sorcerer is the Outsider of the village, on the edge, slightly beyond the border, or at the halfway point between villages. The villages function largely by filiation (kinship networks); the sorcerer, friend of the Devil, ensnares by 'unholy' alliance, as in many European fairy tales. Multiplicities border multiplicities, with secret societies, outcasts, and outlaws prowling and populating the edges. The 'fiber' (249) is the string or continuous networks of lines connecting each borderline to its neighbors, threading multiplicities together, and effected (for example) by the voyage through space, such as that of the pilgrims going to Canterbury, or in any number of eventful tales wherein the voyagers travel along the edges of village-multiplicities, are attacked by wolf-packs, deceived by sorcerers, and so forth. DG also point out that shifting borderlines between multiplicities are waves or vibrations (252).

BOULEZ, Pierre. French composer (1925–). Boulez is noted by DG for his conception of smooth and striated spaces in music (518n22), which DG expand to the coding of space in general. See Campbell 2000 for an extended treatment of the Boulez/DG connection.

BOUNDARY [*frontière*]: the line between an interior and exterior, or between two states of being, that is in some way fixed rather than fluctuating or in free play (thus opposed to 'border'; see 222 for the *limes* of the Roman Empire). Because the State apparatus effects segmenting control over all aspects of human life and death, even death (uniquely) is claimed to be a boundary, a wall between two states (107). DG in this example oppose boundary to zone, highlighting the Western standard scientific conception of death as stopping of life, and of 'enantiomorphosis' (107–8, a term borrowed from Canetti 1963 whereby the change after death is that of a mirror-world [Heaven, for example]). In the West, or at least in Royal science and religion, there can be no metamorphosis, no seeing life as a phase, and death as a gradual transition to another type of body with rather different affects (Hindu conceptions come to mind here as an obvious contrast).

BRAIN: the exterior milieu for the alloplastic stratum (64), that is, the source of material for functions and affects constituting 'the human'. These evolutionary heritages derived 'from the organic substratum' form a 'prehuman soup' immersing us, a 'population' (64) of simple modularities arranged in a 'network of finite automata' (18). These modules or automata are recruited by social machines and differentially implanted by training (disciplinary or otherwise) in members of social assemblages. The distributed functioning of the brain itself makes it a prime example of a rhizome, 'a multiplicity immersed in its plane of consistency . . . an uncertain, probabilistic system' (15); despite this rhizomatic neural structure, thought can assume a State form (375–6). See also Epistemology, Memory, Thought.

BRAUDEL, Fernand. French historian (1902–85). DG adopt several of the themes from his three-volume history of capitalism (Braudel 1985), especially the contingency of the capitalist breakthrough in Europe (*AO*: 224), and the relation of town and State (*ATP*: 432–4).

CAPITALISM: DG discuss capitalism in the context of the 'universal history' of desiring-production (*AO*: 222–40) or that of the 'apparatus of capture' (*ATP*: 424–73). Capitalism operates by an axiomatic of flows that are decoded and deterritorialized and then conjoined on the assumption that their conjunction will yield a 'surplus value of flux'. Capitalism functions by purely quantitative calculation, dispensing with meaning systems of codings or over-codings. (This dissolution of meaning systems echoes Marx's famous 'all that is solid melts into air'.) However, just as capitalism decodes and deterritorializes, it also reterritorializes in its realization by State 'models', thereby displacing its limit of 'absolute deterritorialization', which is reserved for revolutionary war machines (472–3). Wealth in Europe was deterritorialized (land was no longer the arena of highest profit) and decoded (local currencies give way to national ones) and concurrently reterritorialized as capital (as ownership of command of labor), there being only an abstract overcoding in terms of a 'work ethic'. Similarly, labor was deterritorialized and decoded (serfdom was no longer viable and so labor was no longer caught in a system of mutual obligations with the lord) and reterritorialized as private (the worker now owns his or her labor power). According to DG, the historical contingency that these two de-/reterritorialized flows meet in Europe at a sufficient intensity to trigger a takeoff or autocatalytic loop is the accident of capitalism (*AO*: 224; *WP*: 98). (DG might here underestimate the importance of slavery and the Atlantic triangle to the capitalist takeoff. See Blackburn 1997.)

DG's account is recognizably based on Marx's thought, but it differs from a standard Marxism in several ways. (1) Their emphasis on anti-production destroys the distinction between necessary and surplus production or use-value and exchange-value (see E. Holland 1999). (2) They replace the concept of 'modes of production' with that of 'machinic processes' (435). (3) They adopt a notion of 'machinic surplus value' (surplus value generated through the emergent effects of cybernetic assemblages), moving beyond a simple labor theory of value (458). (4) They consistently deny any historical determinism of stages of development by emphasizing the contingency of capitalist formations (*AO*: 224). (5) They conduct a sustained polemic against reductive base-superstructure models of society (*ATP*: 68). (6) They consistently maintain that the line of flight is a primary component of assemblages, thereby preventing totalizing accounts (336). (7) Their use of axiomatics to characterize capitalism allows, at least in principle, the attempt to see capitalism as an adaptive consistency of economic, state and quasi-state (IMF, WTO, and so forth) institutions, rather than as a homeostatic organismic whole, as in crude functionalist accounts.

CARTOGRAPHY: making maps [*cartes*] that establish the contours of intensive processes. Cartography is opposed to tracing [*calque, décalquer*], which simply represents the (actual) properties of equilibrium/steady state/stable systems (12). There are many

calls to make maps in *ATP*. The cartography of a body is established by determining its intensive characteristics, that is, its 'latitude' or set of affects and its 'longitude' or speed and slowness of
its material elements (261). Lines of segmentarity are also the
objects of cartography (203; 222). Furthermore, the BwO is the
object of an 'intensity map', one that is 'not just a map of geography' (163–4), while maps are also made of regimes of signs
(119; 146). (While it seems at 146 that maps [*cartes*] are distinguished from diagrams of virtual multiplicities or abstract
machines, we do not think it too violent in the 'Cartography and
Critique' section above to suggest 'cartography' as a general term
for procedures that also establish the contours of the virtual
realm.) Finally, there is also a sense of cartography for DG that
refers to 'geographic traits' indexed in the flow of narrative of
North American authors (they mention F. Scott Fitzgerald):
'Every great American author creates a cartography' (520n18).

CENTER: a focal point of power [*pouvoir*]. A center is either physically at the 'center of gravity' (the unit dipole mentioned under
arborescence, for example), or 'behind' all resonating points
(what causes them to resonate), and even dispersed in 'micro-
centers' (especially in presignifying regimes where centers do
not, by definition, resonate). Centers, whether relatively diaphanous or relatively consolidated, have three zones (217). The zone
of power, in this example defined by a State apparatus, is the
command center through which diffuse flows are channeled,
captured, converted, stored, and otherwise segmented. The zone
of indiscernability is the milieu, the zone over which the power
center has a modicum of control. The third is the zone of impotence, which on the alloplastic stratum refers to all the flows of
the Ecumenon that can be converted but never controlled from
the center. DG employ the example of banking power, where the
zone of power is occupied by the public banks (central banks,
development banks), the zone of indiscernibility is occupied by
the relations between banks and borrowers, and the zone of
impotence is the mass of economic transactions (217). DG
employ 'center' in several other contexts, as synonymous with
black holes, as points in grids, and as places or nuclei of home.

CHAOS: in *ATP*, used in the ancient cosmogonic sense of a lack of
order, thus equivalent to the modern sense of entropy. However,
perhaps echoing Plato's *Timaeus*, DG write that 'chaos is not

without its own directional components' (313). Thus there is no overlap in *ATP* with the contemporary sense of 'deterministic chaos', the study of which provides a rigorous account of the limits of predictability due to the 'sensitivity to initial conditions' found in complex systems. The matter seen in hylomorphic schemas is chaotic in the ancient sense and hence in need of rescue by a transcendent ordering form. In *WP*, 'chaos' is used to describe the virtual realm, but with images drawn from an odd mix of disciplines (as two harsh critics, Sokal and Bricmont, put it: 'a verbal mélange of a description of quantum field theory with a description of a supercooled liquid', neither of which have any direct relation to deterministic chaos [1998: 156n199]). In other entries herein, we are careful to distinguish *ATP*'s sense of cosmogonic chaos from deterministic chaos. See also Cosmos, Earth, Milieu, Rhythm.

CHAOSMOS. See Rhythm.

CLASTRES, Pierre. French ethnologist (1934–77). Clastres studied New World 'primitive' societies and particularly such phenomena as violence and cannibalism. Clastres 1987 was a major influence on DG's conception of presignifying societies' relationships to black holes, striation, and the signifying regime.

CODING: the process of ordering matter as it is drawn into a body; by contrast, territorialization is the ordering of those bodies in assemblages. In milieus, codes are the 'periodic repetition' of elements, the characteristic vibration or block of space-time specific to an area serving as a source of materials; milieus are hence subject to transcoding (313). In the strata, both codes and territories are needed for double articulation (41). In organic strata, forms relate to the genetic code or DNA, which regulates parastrata, the production of sets of affects via various processes of decoding (53). In a social body or assemblage, codes regulate flows by a mark that indicates a certain quality of the flow (454).

The analysis of social codes is highly developed in *AO*, where coding is the semiotic of the so-called primitive or territorial social machine. Tribal codes mark bodies to indicate that the flows or products of their organs are owed to one segment of the earth or other via genealogies that trace clans to parts of the earth. Thus tribal initiation rites are 'cruel' in that they mark a body to indicate its place in a system of mobile debts: the works of this arm are owed to this group, while the children of this womb are owed to that group. Social codes thus give rise to 'surplus value of code', or the gain of prestige involved in circulating debt among members of the tribe. This analysis of social coding is the key to DG's polemic in *AO* against 'exchangist' anthropologists who miss the way coding incurs circulating debt in a system that never reaches economic 'equilibrium'. The movement of goods provoked by social codes reminds us that signs are triggers of material production, not signifiers representing a signified. Tribal codes are overcoded by a State apparatus, which marks flows according to their place on the body of the despot or God (Augustine's *Confessions*: 'even the milk of mother's breasts comes from you, O Lord') and thereby forms social strata. The capitalist axiomatic, which is quantitative rather than qualitative, overtakes codings and overcodings. See also Index, Presignifying Regime.

COLLECTIVE ASSEMBLAGE OF ENUNCIATION [*agencement collectif d'énonciation*]: the social character of language, of which free indirect discourse (hearsay) is the primary linguistic characteristic, and which from a pragmatic point of view is composed of social institutions or behavior patterns effectuating the incorporeal transformations brought about by order-words (80–5). The collective assemblage of enunciation is meshed with a machinic assemblage of bodies in a territorial assemblage (88). See also Expression.

CONCEPT: the central term in *WP*, DG's final collaborative work. Concepts are equivalent to 'Ideas' in *DR* and to multiplicities in *ATP*. In *WP*, philosophy is that endeavor that creates concepts, as opposed to science, which deals with discursive functions, and art, which deals with affects and percepts.

CONSISTENCY [*consistance*]: the linking together of heterogeneous elements (507) in a variety of registers. On the one hand, consistency is that characteristic of intensive territorial assemblages that denotes their ability to preserve the heterogeneity of their components and to form new assemblages and thereby expand their affects (327). Consistency is not achieved by imposing a form on matter, but by 'elaborating an increasingly rich and consistent material, the better to tap increasingly intense forces' (329); such assemblages are creative in their self-ordering, that is, their makeup lends itself to novel becomings. On the other hand, consistency is not 'restricted to complex life forms, [but] pertains fully even to the most elementary atoms and particles' (335). Thus not only territorial assemblages but also 'aggregates' [*ensembles*] can achieve consistency when 'very heterogeneous elements' mesh together to achieve emergent effects, thus forming a 'machinic phylum' (335). Because of this extension of consistency and its creative emergence beyond complex life forms (cf. 'non-organic life' [411]), technological assemblages, crossing the organic and the inorganic, are consistent as well (406; for example, the 'man-horse-bow assemblage' at 391). The means of achieving creatively self-ordering consistency are the three factors of consolidation: 'intercalated elements, intervals, and articulations of superpositions' (329). DeLanda glosses this difficult passage as the diagram of the abstract machine of self-orderings like autocatalysis: 'articulations of superpositions' are the bringing together of heterogenous but complementary elements or functions; 'intercalated elements' are catalysts that intensify the internal economy; and 'intervals' are 'endogenously generated stable patterns of behavior' (DeLanda 1997: 64). Finally, in the social register, DG distinguish the 'transconsistency' of networked towns in a trading circuit from the 'intra-consistency' of the State that makes points resonate together (432–3), while in the phrase 'plane of consistency' the term also denotes the manner of coherence of virtual multiplicities.

CONTENT [*contenu*]: that which is put to work in a stratum or assemblage. As the first articulation of stratification, content is composed of bodies whose recruitment from a substratum retrospectively qualifies them as matter for that stratum. (Since bodies as formed matters are substances, and substances are territorialized, such recruitment is a deterritorialization [53].) Stratified content has both form and substance. The 'substance of content' is homogenized matter selected out from a heterogeneous source or exterior milieu. The 'form of content' is the ordering of those selected elements by a code which is in turn overcoded by the 'form of expression' to produce an emergent functional structure or 'substance of expression' (41). In the double articulation characteristic of stratification, content is relative to its expression, so that what is content for one expression can itself be the expression of another content. Content and expression enter into different relations on the different strata

(57–64), one of the consequences of which on the alloplastic stratum is that, because content has its own code or 'form', content is never merely a 'thing' named by a 'word'; this complexity vitiates the signifier/signified model (66). The machinic assemblage of bodies in a territorial assemblage is also considered content, with the collective assemblage of enunciation as expression (88).

CONTROL SOCIETY: the subject of a late essay by Deleuze (1995: 177–82; see E. Holland 1999), the term denotes methods of imposing social order after the decline of disciplinary institutions and the consequent 'molecularization' or intensification of social relations (the monitored relaxation of molar normality), which is accompanied by the 'becoming-cosmic' of the forces released by that intensification. As always, the move from equilibrium/ steady state/stable zones to far-from-equilibrium, intensive crisis states is the key to exploring virtual (here 'cosmic') effects. DG show a prudent caution with regard to such triggering of self-organizing forces, which need not always be progressive ('never believe a smooth space will suffice to save us': 500), as the huge interest in self-organization theory among business and government agencies should make us aware (see Thrift 1999). In the shift from disciplinary to control society, 'the question then became [after the molecularization of society] whether molecular or atomic "populations" of all natures (mass media, monitoring procedures [*moyens de contrôle*], computers, space weapons) would continue to bombard the existing people in order to train it or control it [*le contrôler*] or annihilate it' (345).

COSMOS: another name for the set of self-ordering and emergence-producing capacities of the universe, the plane of consistency. At the end of the 'Refrain' plateau, DG use 'cosmic' to describe the 'modern' move from intensive to virtual (using the behavior of systems in far-from-equilibrium intensive crisis states to map the virtual) as opposed to the 'earth' as taken up by the 'Romantic' rendering-intensive of actual or stratified systems (342). These 'ages' are not to be taken as evolutionary steps but only as different assemblages instantiating different relations to the abstract machine (346), so the contrast of modern Cosmos and romantic earth cannot be pushed too far. (Indeed, 'earth' is used as a name for 'plane of consistency' at 40). DG mention the Cosmos in connection with the 'grandiose cases' of vast migrations of spiny lobsters and birds which seem to 'leave all [territorial] assemblages behind' in attaining 'another plane'; here deterritorialization seems to have left the earth itself and the sun directing the migrations is no longer the 'terrestrial sun reigning over a territory' (326; 549n26).

COUNTERSIGNIFYING REGIME [*régime contre-signifiant*]: the regime of signs of nomads, proceeding by numeration (118; 389–93), and operating by subtraction from the codes of territorial assemblages as well as by the constitution of a war machine directed against the overcoding of the State (390). The numeration of nomads is by way of the 'numbering number', that is, a number that does not represent an actual substance fixed in striated space ('a numbered number'), but a number that pertains to intensive assemblages occupying a smooth space. The numbering number 'marks a mobile and plural distribution' (118); it 'appears as soon as one distributes something in space' (389). In other words, instead of saying 'take control of area 15' (an order-word of the signifying regime utilizing the numbered number of striated space), the countersignifying regime of signs might offer the following order-word which would utilize the numbering number of smooth space: 'the first ten should disperse and hold the field'.

DG list three characteristics of countersignifying numeration: the arithmetization of the starting aggregates (people immersed in coded territorial 'lineages') in order to extract groups of complex numbers (the 'unit' of the nomad is always complex, as in the 'man-horse-bow' assemblage) (391); the numerical formation of the extracted groups into groups of 10, 100, and so on (118; 392); and the formation of a 'special body', a subset of the extracted sets, forming 'secret services', 'personal guards', and so on (392). The internal tension of these groups exists 'independent of quantity' and in constantly giving rise to power struggles [*luttes de pouvoir*] prevents the formation of a State and thereby informs the creativity of the war machine (392).

COUNTRYSIDE [*campagne*]: that which lies outside cities. In one of their few uses of non-Western sources, DG cite Ibn Khaldun's masterful ethnology of the dwellers in the countryside, which for him includes both cultivators and nomads (481). All in all, we must say that DG do not provide too much elaboration in *ATP* as to the historic realities of the smooth spaces of countrysides inhabited by transhumant peasants as well as by nomads, by itinerants, by landless migrants. Actually, using DG's principles if not their performance, it's best to say that the countryside was and is inhabited by mixtures of complex, heterogeneous multiplicities who did not possess a common identity until it was foisted upon them by the urbane literati. DG stress that the town [*la ville*] and in particular the city [*la cité*] (regional power center) created and continue to create the countryside (429; 481). The concept of 'the country' or 'rural areas' cannot exist except as what lies outside of towns, and by the State's definitions villages (sub-towns) are 'part of' the countryside: 'The State makes the town resonate with the countryside' (433). The countryside in Hispanic America, for example, is *el campo*, a supposedly striated space occupied by a homogeneous mass of people known as *campesinos* living in dispersed villages and farmsteads. This, anyway, has been the interpretation of the urban(e) elite. In reality, *campesinos* comprise heterogeneous populations existing in complex mixtures of filiation and alliance, half-inside anti-State territories, half-beholden to the lands of the State (the degrees vary by region). The *campesino*, like any classified and racialized human, does not exist per se; rather, 'he' is a statistical abstraction produced by molarizing a population of molecular particles.

CREATIVITY: the ability of a body or assemblage to create novel connections or becomings on a plane of consistency. In complexity theory terms, it is the ability of a system to generate new and emergent attractors and bifurcators. DG dispense with the need to posit a spiritual source of creativity, since their critique of hylomorphism has done away with the notion of a dead matter (material or 'molecularized matter' [345] must be homogenized and molarized to become 'matter'). Thus creativity is a property of material systems in certain circumstances. Insofar as the war machine is the paradigm of a social system aiming at creativity, it is thus the social machine that best actualizes life (422).

CRITIQUE: the principle that the properties of a product hold no clues to the production process that gave rise to it, because of the transcendental illusion whereby the actual hides the intensive and hence the virtual. Such hiding occurs because some complex systems, if studied at equilibrium/steady state/stability, are so locked into their habitual basins of attraction that the influence of other attractors (virtual ones not currently actualized) is silenced.

CROWD. See Mass.

DECALCOMANIA [*décalcomanie*]: the mimetic process of lifting a code, image, or text from one medium, then transferring it to another without transforming it; the practice of tracing or representation DG oppose to cartography (12). As *décalquer* means 'to transfer', *décalcomanie* is the mania of transference; DG's reason for using this odd term appears to be an effort to poke fun at the 'manic' nature of tracing what amounts to nothing more than a decal. The belief that decalcomania is possible arises from a rigid structuralism where one thinks that one can swap codes across media without changing their nature. A clear example of decalcomania is the transfer of genes through cloning, the process of making a perfect genetic copy.

DECODING: the process of dissolving a code. As codes pattern material elements in milieus, decoding liberates material for recruitment into a new body or assemblage (322). In the formation of parastrata or new sets of affects for bodies on the organic stratum, decoding takes two forms: (1) genetic drift or mutation allowing for differential production of traits in a population; and (2) 'transversal communication' (movement of DNA or transfer of code across species), which DG call 'surplus value of code' (53). Organic decoding entertains complex relations with deterritorialization (54–5). Decoding, transversal movements of code, is becoming or symbiosis, which DG call 'involution' (238). In imperial or capitalist social systems, overcoding or axiomatics attempt to catch up to decoding, but they themselves provoke further decoding by their very operation.

DESERT: a space (of 'sand') traversed primarily by smoothing vectors, productive of the nomadic countersignifying regime but produced in part by the excesses and overextensions of agricultural, hydraulic civilization (for example, in ancient Mesopotamia) (380–4). The desert smooth space was shelter and home to the war machines that attacked and overran sedentarist societies. DG's discussion of the 'sand desert' relies on Thesiger 1959 (557n55–6). In DG's materialist historical geographical account, the great deserts of Asia and Africa, along with the steppes, served as the staging grounds for nomadic war machines' attacks on civilization. DG recognize an environmental co-determinism of the desert and its tribe, showing how the smooth space of nature created the nomad and also welcomed the scapegoat of the Despot, the passionate, crazed prophet who led the People to safety through wandering.

DG point out that the desert itself wanders, as it is constituted by shifting elements – not only sands but also tumbling plants and rhizomatic vegetation that pops up following localized rains (382). The 'haptic' nature of the desert is made evident by its lack of perspective; the navigator of the desert relies on the 'song of the sands' and other shifting sets of relationships (haecceities) – as the mariner relies on the differential tastes of the sea – in the absence of fixed points. The oases – water points, dwelling points, assembly points – are prime examples of the places-as-points that DG cite as unobscured proof that places are the nodes of inter-laced networks (380).

DESIRE: as part of the complex term 'desiring-production', desire is the key term in *AO*, but is relatively absent in *ATP*. In *AO*, desire is not subjective hankering after what you don't have (that is, desire is not oriented to lack: see Anti-production), but is the material process of connection, registration and enjoyment of flows of matter and energy coursing through bodies in networks of production in all registers, be they geologic, organic, or social. Desire has two forms in *AO*, paranoid or fascist and schizophrenic or revolutionary. The paranoid-fascist pole of desire forms whole subjects who cling to their identities in a social production network that must not change and that reinforces the rigid (tribal or imperial) coding and channeling of flows. Faced with the release of uncoded flows in capitalism, paranoid desire turns fascist, that is, desires a State overcoding of the flows and an escape from the world economy into an autonomous ersatz economy. Schizophrenic-revolutionary desire, in contrast, rides the energies released by capitalism and takes them far beyond the pathetic reterritorializations on family and private property maintained by psychoanalysis and the capitalist State.

There are three main discussions of desire in *ATP*. The first (154–5) shows the way 'priestly psychology' focuses desire on lack, pleasure, and *jouissance*, that is, on three transcendent goals. (The 'priest' is one of DG's favorite whipping boys, inherited by them from Nietzsche. See the inspired rant, which would have done Nietzsche himself proud, at *AO* 268–9: 'depression and guilt used as a means of contagion, the kiss of the Vampire: aren't you ashamed to be happy? follow my example, I won't let you go before you say, "It's my fault"'.) In *ATP*, the 'triple curse' on desire cast by the priest is lack (you only want what you don't have), pleasure (once you get it, you needn't desire any longer, at least for a while), and *jouissance*, the 'transcendent ideal' (you can't ever really have overwhelming, pure pleasure, but that's the only thing you really want). The role of the priest in rendering desire transcendent is then taken over by the psychoanalyst, with the three principles of 'pleasure, death, and reality'. Instead of the transcendence of lack, pleasure, and *jouissance* to desire (pleasure as the arrival of the previously missing object whose momentary presence will temporarily stop desire), DG propose immanence, the 'joy [*joie*] that is immanent to desire' (155). The second main thematization of desire in *ATP* stresses the universal nature of desiring-production. Here the question is the constitution of the fascist desire for annihilation:

> Desire stretches that far: desiring one's own annihilation, or desiring the power to annihilate. Money, army, police and State desire, fascist desire, even fascism is desire . . . It is a problem not of ideology but of pure matter, a phenomenon of physical, biological, psychic, social, or cosmic matter. (165)

Finally, (social) assemblages are seen as 'compositions of desire', a formulation that reinforces DG's constant claim that 'desire has nothing to do with a natural or spontaneous determination; there is no desire but assembling, assembled, machined [*agençant, agencé, machiné*] desire' (399; translation modified). The main distinction here is between sedentary 'feeling' [*sentiment*] and nomadic 'affects' (400).

DESIRING-PRODUCTION: In *AO*, 'desiring-production' is a triple process in the somatic, social and natural registers. Desiring-production is universal production, operating beyond the nature/human distinction (*AO*: 4). The three aspects of this universal production are: (1) connecting and breaking flows of matter and energy (the 'desiring machines' are organs which regulate flows of food, water, sweat, saliva, air, urine, and so on, not only in somatic bodies but also in social networks: goods from the earth flowing in the tribe, village goods flowing to the imperial palace, commodities circulating in a capitalist economy); (2) 'registering' them (forming 'hot spots' or points of intensity that can later be recognized as the same when activated again; socially, 'ownership' patterns: those flows are mine!) on a Body without Organs (called a 'socius' in the social register); and (3) diverting a portion of them for the enjoyment of a 'nomadic subject' in anti-production (the momentary feeling of enjoyment from an organic function, or, socially, the tribe's feast or potlatch, the orgies in the emperor's 'stately pleasure domes', or, uniquely under capitalism, reinvestment in more production via the capitalist's bank account).

DESTRATIFICATION: decentralizing an organism or other hierarchical structure by pushing it past a 'crisis' threshold of its intensive properties to allow the components to find their own arrangements rather than submit to the overcoding of the stratifying agent. In complexity theory terms, destratification entails moving away from equilibrium/steady state/stability to destroy emergent unification by moving out of the comfort zone or basin of attraction of the emergent effect. By contrast, decoding pertains to changing what controls the characteristic rhythm of materials as they enter a body or assemblage, while deterritorializing moves bodies to another assemblage, that is, changes their thresholds and patterns of behavior.

DETERRITORIALIZATION: the always complex process by which bodies leave a territorial assemblage following the lines of flight that are constitutive of that assemblage and 'reterritorialize', that is, form new assemblages (there is never a simple escape or simple return to the old territory). Deterritorialization changes the 'imbrication of the semiotic and the material' (337), the fit of the collective assemblage of enunciation and the machinic assemblage of bodies (87–9). In complexity theory terms, deterritorialization works by increasing or decreasing the intensity of certain system states past a critical threshold, which either moves the system to a previously established but non-actualized virtual attractor ('relative deterritorialization'), or indeed prompts the release of a new set of attractors and bifurcators, new patterns and thresholds ('absolute deterritorialization'). In plain language, deterritorialization is the process of leaving home, of altering your habits, of learning new tricks.

There are several ways of relating deterritorialization and reterritorialization, as set forth in the 'theorems of deterritorialization' (174–5; 306–7) and in the concluding remarks (508–10). Negative deterritorialization occurs when the line of flight is immediately blocked by a 'compensatory reterritorialization': a new set of transcendent laws is immediately imposed (508). For example, European peasants fleeing manors went to cities where they became workers in the employ of the local bourgeoisie: 'it is because the bourgeoisie was a cutting edge of deterritorialization, a veritable particle accelerator, that it also performed an overall reterritorialization' (221). A positive deterritorialization can nonetheless remain 'relative' when its line of flight is segmented, as in the postsignifying regime of signs: you're set free to go for a certain distance, but then you run up against a wall, you run out of steam, you sink into a depression or 'black hole' (133; 508). DG reserve the term 'absolute deterritorialization' for the creative production of new attractors and bifurcators via a 'shared acceleration' (142), a 'connection of flows' (220), which enables the tapping of 'cosmic forces' (509) and the drawing of a 'plane of consistency' (510); the success of an absolute deterritorialization can never be guaranteed, as it always proceeds by way of relative deterritorialization (510). It can indeed 'create a new earth', but it can also overcode the earth in the worst of all dangers, the fascist State, which turns the lines of flight into lines of death and destruction (229; 510).

DIAGRAM: the outline of the traits of expression of an abstract machine, the 'nonformal functions' linked to the 'phyla' of 'unformed matters' or 'traits of content' (141–2; 511–12). As the outline of the absolute deterritorialized nature of abstract machines, diagrams themselves must be distinguished from indexes, icons, and symbols, which entertain various relations to territories and reterritorialization (142). 'Diagrammatics', as the third step in 'pragmatics' or the study of regimes of signs (145), is opposed to axiomatics, which establishes the program of a stratum (143). The diagram is not to be confused with a 'map' [*carte*], which deals with intensive assemblages, or with 'tracings' [*calques*], which reproduce properties of stratified bodies.

DIFFUSION: the machinic process of ecumenical organizations (DG mention long-distance trade [a specialty of Braudel], religions, and art movements), those that encompass heterogeneous social formations in a rhizomatic, consistent growth: 'diffusion occurs only through the placing in communication of potentials of very different orders' (435–6).

DISCIPLINE: used by DG in the technical Foucaultian sense of a system of corporeal practices aimed at increasing the productivity

of human multiplicities, enabling rigorous repetition of pro-
grammed action and teamwork among groups in response to
standardized triggers, all the while decreasing the chance of
immanent, horizontal, revolutionary political action (Foucault
1979). In *ATP* bodies are disciplined in the move from territorial
society to faciality as the intersection of signifiance and subjectivity (181), while discipline is said to be a characteristic of State
armies, rather than nomad war machines (358).

DOMAIN. See Territory.

DOUBLE ARTICULATION. See Stratification.

EARTH/LAND [*terre*]: Massumi uses two English words to translate
the French *terre*, which can mean both 'earth' in the astronomi-
cal sense of our planet and 'land' in the geographical sense of a
cultivated area. There is no consistency in DG's use of the majus-
cule in the French text; both *Terre* and *terre* are used in the sense
of 'earth' and 'land'. The Anglophone reader should keep in
mind the close proximity of *terre* ['earth' and 'land'] with *territoire*
['territory'].

1. Earth: (1) equivalent to THE Body without Organs, the virtual plane
   of consistency upon which strata are imposed (40); (2) part of the
   earth–territory [*terre-territoire*] system of Romanticism, the becoming-
   intensive of the strata, hence the gathering point, outside all territories, of all self-ordering forces ['forces of the earth'] for intensive
   territorial assemblages [the virtual seen from the point of view of territorializing machinic assemblages] (338–9); (3) the 'new earth'
   [*une nouvelle terre*], the becoming-virtual of intensive material, that is,
   the correlate of absolute deterritorialization [the leaving of all intensive territorial assemblages to attain the plane of consistency],
   tapping 'cosmic forces' [the virtual seen from the point of view of
   the abstract machines composing it, not the machinic assemblages
   that actualize a selection of singularities]; hence, new potentials for
   creation (423; 509–10; at 509 Massumi unfortunately translates *une
   nouvelle terre* as 'a new land').
2. Land: *terre* that is constituted by the overcoding of territories under
   the signifying regime and the State apparatus (440–1). Land refers
   exclusively to striated space, and is that terrain that can be owned,
   held as stock, distributed, rented, made to produce, and taxed. Land
   can be gridded, distributed, classified, and categorized without even
   being physically experienced, and a striking example of this is the
   township-and-range system of the US that imparted striated space to

a vast part of the North American continent ahead of actual settler occupation. The system of stockpiling territories and overcoding them as land for the State does not stop at the farm or even the ranch, but extends to the forest lands (as 'national' forests) and to the unusable spaces that become national parks, biosphere reserves, and so forth. These spaces are held as refuges for the State subjects who seek to escape from private property to find some sort of becoming-earth commons.

ECUMENON: the abstract machine as it composes a stratum, as opposed to the Planomenon of the plane of consistency (49–50; 56; 73). Although the Ecumenon composes the 'unity of composition' of a stratum by establishing 'the identity of [exterior] molecular materials, [interior] substantial elements, and formal relations [limits or membranes]', it is never unitary, but is broken by the diversity of epistrata and parastrata (52; 73). The ecumenon or universal reach of a religious body, for example, has an interior that contains the converted, an exterior consisting of the unconverted, and a border or membrane whereby the religion both protects its own integrity and projects its messages; missionaries are border patrols in search of converts by force of word or deed. But this unity is broken by the diversity of epistrata (different internal steady states or organizational nuances: ecclesiastical heresy) and parastrata (different affects, or capacities for becomings when encountering other assemblages: 'syncretism', doctrinal heresy). See also Diffusion (the discussion of 'ecumenical' organizations [which need not be religious]).

EPISTEMOLOGY: the philosophical study of knowledge (its conditions of production and the criteria by which one can be said to know something). The main distinction in DG's epistemology is between minor ('nomad', 'ambulatory', 'itinerant') science and major or 'Royal' science' (100–10; 361–74). Minor science is problematic, while major science is axiomatic. By means of the operations of artisans, minor science nudges systems from actual to intensive in order thereby to limn virtual multiplicities on a plane of consistency, while Royal science looks to extract constants from variables and determine laws of the relation of variables by means of functions linking dependent and independent variables. (In *WP*, DG conflate Royal science and 'science' *tout court*, and say science constructs functions on a 'plane of reference'.)

EPISTRATA: in the strata, stable states of bodies produced through territorialization and deterritorialization, 'variations that are tolerated below a certain threshold of identity' (50). In crystals, epistrata are 'discontinuous states of metastability', while, on the organic stratum, epistrata are 'interior milieus' that provide materials to internal organs, thus regulating 'the degree of complexity or differentiation of the parts of an organism' (50); in disciplinary organizations, epistrata are tolerated deviances. Epistrata fragment a stratum, as each crystalline solution, organic life form, or social institution will have different thresholds of tolerance for deviation from a norm. See also Ecumenon, Parastrata.

ESSENCE: in many standard philosophical accounts, the set of necessary and sufficient conditions for a thing to be a member of the set of things to which it truly belongs. Essence thus helps one to establish identity and difference among the things of the world by capturing the capacities of a body in a 'form of interiority' of thought prized by the State (375). For DG, essentialist thought stays at the level of extensive or actual properties which can be arranged in a grid or table with other essences by means of identity, analogy, opposition and similarity to produce a representation or picture of the world. In DeLanda's fine formulation, DG seek to replace essentialist thought with a thought attuned to virtual multiplicities and the intensive morphogenetic processes (all of which are impacted by contingent, non-average variations) that give rise to the diversity of given differences among the actual entities we encounter (2002: 3).

A 'nomadic essence' differs from a classically conceived essence, however. DG take the term from Husserl to be a 'vague and material' essence, such as 'roundness' as opposed to 'circularity', a fixed, exact, and geometrical concept (407). A nomadic essence is tied to corporeality, as determined by passages to the limit as events of spatial-temporal transformation that the body can undergo and by the affects the body can withstand; the nomadic essence is thus tracked by artisans who link singularities as implicit material forms to affects as the capacities of the body to form assemblages with other bodies (407–8). The 'essence' of the war machine described at 422 is presumably a nomadic essence; indeed, 'the war machine's form of exteriority is such that it exists only in its own metamorphoses' (360).

ETHICS: the immanent evaluation of interactions among bodies ('becomings') on a plane of consistency (165). The sole ethical criterion countenanced by DG is the ever increasing power [*puissance*] to form mutually enhancing or life-affirming assemblages: 'what is retained and preserved, therefore created, what consists, is only *that which increases the number of connections* at each level of division or composition' (508; italics in original). Ethics is opposed to morality, the judgment of a body or assemblage or event with regard to a pre-established standard. Morality is hence transcendent, as opposed to the immanence of ethics.

EXPERIMENTATION: the most radically anti-Platonic aspect of DG's thought. It is not simply the Platonic commitment to stability that they critique, but also the a priori character of that commitment. Thus, if your brand of 'anti-Platonism' amounts to nothing more than a simple denunciation of stability, as in the more naïve forms of a postmodernist affirmation of flow, you would have done nothing other than produce an equally a priori commitment. When a priori principles are abjured, you must experiment and evaluate to see 'what your body can do', to see if you can 'make a rhizome' (251). Sometimes a little more stability in a body or assemblage would be a good thing, would produce more positive affects: 'Staying stratified – organized, signified, subjected – is not the worst that can happen' (161). Sometimes, however, it's the opposite, a little more flow or escape, that is needed to shake up an overly rigid system. Caution is the key to successful experimentation:

> This is how it should be done: Lodge yourself on a stratum [your organism, your subjectivity, your regime of signs], experiment with the opportunities it offers [change your body patterns {sleep, exercise, diet}, your personality {your emotional patterns, thresholds, and triggers; what turns you on or off}, your writing or speaking habits {learn how to 'stutter in your own language', pick up some slang, or simply read new, 'minor' authors}], find an advantageous place on it [where you can be safe and still experiment], find potential movements of deterritorialization, possible lines of flight [listen to invitations to leave home, to change your habits]. (161)

This experimentation is not mere life-style management; it is an entire collective politics, for only by interacting with others can you experiment: 'you have constructed your own little machine, ready when needed to be plugged into other collective machines' (161). See also Body without Organs.

EXPRESSION: the takeover of content, putting it to work in a 'functional structure'. In stratification, expression takes part in a double articulation, and ultimately results in a new substance, with new emergent, albeit fixed, properties, while in assemblages, expression results in new affects, new capacities to form further assemblages (in the best case). Within the system of the strata, expression takes different forms. Following Simondon (1995), DG write that, in the inorganic strata, expression is the molarization of molecular content, that is, the carrying forth to the macroscopic scale of the 'implicit forms' of molecular interactions (57). On the organic stratum, both content and expression are each molecular and molar, with expression becoming autonomous in the linear genetic code, which results in the greater deterritorialization of organisms due to 'transductions' (59–60). On the alloplastic stratum, expression becomes 'linguistic rather than genetic', that is, achieves a 'superlinear' or temporal form allowing 'translation' (60).

EXTENSIVE. See Intensive.

EXTERIORITY: the condition of being outside a boundary: known and available, but not (yet) captured. On the organic stratum, the exterior milieu is the 'outside world' that can belong to one's world, but not as one's exclusive domain (49). A relative line of flight moves from an exterior milieu to an associated milieu, or, indeed, 'arises when the associated milieu is rocked by blows from the exterior, forcing the animal to abandon it and strike up an association with new portions of exteriority, this time leaning on its interior milieus like fragile crutches' (55). In epistemological terms, 'outside thought' [*une pensée du dehors*] makes thought into a war machine whose 'form of exteriority' attacks the form of interiority of State thought by 'situating thought in a smooth space' (376–7). Just as with the rhizome and the tree (20), there is no opposition of models here, for outside thought is not a model but 'a force that destroys' (377).

FACE [*visage*] – FACIALITY [*visagéité*]: faciality is at first the substance of expression of the signifying regime of signs (115; note that a 'regime of signs' is a form of expression [111]). This means that the face is the 'icon', the reterritorialization of the signifying system (115; a signifier is a deterritorialized sign lifted from territorial or 'primitive', 'pre-signifying' societies by an overcoding State apparatus: cf. *AO*: 206). Expressions flickering across the face ('the white wall for the signifier') guide the interpretation of the listener, according to the 'objective frequency' of signifiers: 'I've never heard that before!'; 'How many times do I have to tell you that!' (115; 167). By the constant display of his face, the Despot ensures his centrality to the signifying regime (115). (Recall the covering of the face on the statue of Saddam Hussein by the American flag during the 'Battle of Baghdad' in April 2003, or the pot shots taken at other Saddam faces, the tearing down of Saddam face posters as each town was taken, and so on.) Faciality is transformed in the postsignifying or passional regime: although the face is the 'body of the signifier', the book is the 'body of passion' in the postsignifying regime (127). In this regime of 'betrayal', the face of the god and the face of the subject turn away from each other, sending the prophet on his way (123–4). In passional subjectivity, the face is the 'point of departure for a deterritorialization that puts everything else to flight' (129); one look from the eyes of the beloved, lurking inside black holes (184), and you're ready to drop everything and move to the ends of the earth, making the look of the lover resonate in your own look (133).

The concept of faciality later shifts to become the abstract machine that produces faces at the intersection of significance (the despotic signifying regime of signs) and subjectivity (the passional postsignifying regime) (167–8; 180–2). As this intersection reaches its highest point of intensity in the crossing of the Roman Empire and prophetic, messianic religion (125), the face is 'Christ' (176; cf. 184: the duplicity inherent in the 'despotic Christ' and the 'passional Christ'). The face now is 'redundancy', repeating the frequency of significance and the resonance of subjectivity (168). The correlate of the face is the landscape [*paysage*] (172); and the face as 'White Man' is the standard implied in racism, which does not operate by 'othering', but by establishing degrees of deviation from the standard (178). Looking 'backward', the face is the absolute though negative deterritorialization of the head (172; 190), the head deterritorialized from the corporeal signs of the territorial or presignifying regime and overcoded (170); thus 'primitive' peoples as those without a face (176). Looking 'beyond the face', there is the 'probe-head', 'cutting edges of deterritorialization' which open humanity onto new becomings (190–1; cf. the function of metal as 'itinerant probe-head' of the machinic phylum, giving rise to the 'prodigious idea of *Nonorganic Life*': 411; italics in original).

FASCISM: in *AO*, the pole of paranoid desire opposed to schizophrenic or revolutionary desire. Historical fascism is explicitly addressed in *AO* relatively infrequently, but nevertheless DG's critique of the usual analysis of fascism in terms of ideology is important. Rather than being the result of the fooling of people by false consciousness, fascist desire has its own proper consistency, and spreads under certain social, economic and political conditions. Roughly speaking, fascist desire is the desire for codes to replace the decoding that frees flows under capitalist axiomatics; such codes would fix subjects to rigid boundaries of thought and action and fix bodies to pre-established patterns of flows, thus attenuating the fascist obsession with erotic perversion.

DG discuss both micro- and macro-fascism in *ATP*. Micro-fascism is the construction of a 'thousand monomanias' in 'little neighborhood policemen' resulting from 'molecular focuses in interaction . . . rural fascism and city or neighborhood fascism, youth fascism and war veteran's fascism, fascism of the Left and of the Right, fascism of the couple, family, school, and office' (214). Such micro-fascisms spread throughout a social fabric prior to the centralizing resonance that creates the molar apparatus of the State. In micro-fascism each body is a 'micro-black hole that stands on its own and communicates with the others' (228). Although DG do not do so, we can call micro-fascism 'molecular molarity': each subjective unit is self-contained, oriented to unity, an individual (molar), but they interact in solely local manner, independently (molecular). Macro-fascism (in its Nazi form rather than its Italian or Spanish forms) is characterized, following the analyses of Paul Virilio, as a 'suicide state' rather than a totalitarian one, which is 'quintessentially conservative' (230; Stalinist USSR is the target here). In *ATP*, then, fascism is too fast rather than too slow: it is cancer, a runaway war machine that, having taken over a State apparatus, forms a 'war machine that no longer had anything but war as its object and would rather annihilate its own servants than stop the destruction' (231).

FIBER. See Border.

FLOW: that which flees molar order; molecular deviation from a norm. DG are not simple enthusiasts of flow, despite the widespread but mistaken postmodernist reading of them in that regard. For DG, the key is pragmatic evaluation and cautious experimentation with the flows that traverse bodies. Stratification, the binding of flows into stable substances, is 'a very important, inevitable phenomenon that is beneficial in many respects and unfortunate in many others' (40). In the construction of social bodies (bodies politic), molecular flow is what escapes molar categories, returning to them to 'reshuffle their segments, their binary distribution of sexes, classes, and parties' (216). Following the French 'micro-sociologist' Gabriel Tarde, DG propose the study of molecular flows of 'belief and desire' that escape the codes that regulate molar representations (219). In other words, flow is that micro-deviation from the norm, that little nuance: 'sure, we're all Americans, but here we start our 4th of July celebration with a parade from our local Veterans Against War group, then we have the Dykes on Bikes group, then instead of hot dogs we have veggie burgers . . .' (Of course, on another level of analysis, there are always molecular flows escaping these representations: vegetarians who once in a while . . . and so on).

In evaluating flow, DG distinguish the 'segmented line' and the 'quantum flow' with a 'power center' at their intersection, regulating their interchange (217). The flow has poles, singularities and quanta: poles create and destroy the flow; the quanta of the flow are qualitatively different states; and the singularities are thresholds between quanta. In the example of monetary flow, the quanta are 'inflation, deflation, stagflation, etc.' (217); in this way quanta are 'signs or degrees of deterritorialization in the decoded flow' (219): they mark how far gone the flow is from its captured, stable, regulated state. DG further distinguish 'connection' and 'conjugation' of flows (220). A connection of flows indicates the autocatalysis of a set of decoded and deterritorialized flows, which 'boost one another, accelerate their shared escape, and augment or stoke their quanta' (220). A connection is a mutiny, a prison break, a bank panic: the more who join the flight, the faster it goes. 'Conjugation', in contrast, is the capture and overcoding of flows; it 'indicates their relative stoppage, like a point of accumulation that plugs or seals the lines of flight, performs a general reterritorialization, and brings the flows under the dominance of a single flow capable of overcoding them' (220). A conjugation is the rounding up and returning to prison of the escapees, or, better, the formation of a new State among them. Indeed, it is always, DG assert, the most deterritorialized flow that brings about conjunction and reterritorialization, as was the case, they claim, with the European bourgeoisie during the capitalist takeoff (220–1).

FORCE: when used without qualification, the self-ordering capacities of material or 'molecularized matter' (342), that is, material systems whose intensive properties are moved into far-from-equilibrium crisis and which thereby reveal the influence of virtual multiplicities (sets of singularities forming attractors and bifurcators). In Gothic cathedral building, the operations of artisans means 'the static relation, form-matter, tends to fade into the background in favor of a dynamic relation, material-forces' (364). In the 'Refrain' plateau, DG discuss 'forces of chaos' (entropic decay), 'forces of the earth' (machinic assemblages capable of selecting singularities underlying the construction of territories; they are themselves not territorial [339]), and 'cosmic forces' (the abstract machines laying out the plane of consistency [342; 509–10]).

FOREST: DG spend little time on this space, except to characterize it as striated by 'gravitational verticals' (that is, trees) (384) and as the annexed or associated milieu of many agricultural societies. They point out that the forest is the space of anti-state primitive societies that already contain the seeds of their striation by States. They stress the hostility of nomads toward forest dwellers, but also the relationships between forest dwellers (wood cutters, for example) and charcoal-using metallurgists.

We suggest an alternative map of forest space as holey space. The tree, far from being the standard for the forest, is rather deterritorialized by it, though perhaps not in the types of European wood-lot forests that DG imagined. DG failed to theorize the forest as anything other than a human space and precursor to civilization via short-fallow swidden agriculture. In seeing the forest as nothing more than a community of trees, they exclude the dynamics of tropical rain forests where the tree is but part of a vast rhizome with no center, no sense of perspective, no organizing principle, no ground [*sol*] (the soil itself is infertile, because nutrients are in constant cyclic motion throughout the system, and are not stored there), where plants can grow from top to bottom and then back (the strangler fig) or defy gravity altogether (epiphytes). The rain forest contains a high ratio of flow to order, and its complexity is engendered by this far-from-equilibrium crisis state. Its plateaus avoid climax.

Forest space, to remain a rhizome, can only be occupied and defended by anti-State forces, and many of its users – hunter-gatherer-swidden agriculturalists using long-fallow rotation (for example, in the Amazon) – are part of its rhizome. Forests are the Outside of the State (Latin *foris*, outside), the holey spaces that fend it off: the shelter for outlaws and misfits, the domain of guerrilla groups across the world today, powerful in their capacity to hide (thus, the necessity of the Agent Orange defoliant), they avoid the striations and overcoding of the State more than any other type of social formation. Harrison (1992) calls forests the 'shadow of civilization' and because they were not and are not to be trusted, they have been 'locked up' as the King's domain, and now as nature reserves. Tropical rain forests are often painted as multisexual or threatening bodies, as virgins, and so on: another threat to or possibility for the State. Forests, like deserts, also follow civilizations that overextend themselves, and grow along the borders between nation-states.

FORM: in ancient philosophy, the look or appearance [Greek: *eidos* or *morphē*] of something that indicates its essence, the set of necessary and sufficient conditions for a thing to belong to the set of things to which it truthfully belongs. In *ATP*'s analysis of stratification, form is a straightjacket for matter, restricting the affects of a body to a definite set by creating exclusive disjunctions among series of singularities. Form carves up the virtual realm by installing a fixed set of attractors and bifurcators, patterns and thresholds of behavior. By creating a restricted set of 'imprisoned' singularities a form-imposing power [*pouvoir*] seeks to determine once and for all 'what a body can do'. However, forms are always subject to processes of deformation. For example, the notion of organic form, the distribution of traits in a population, must take into account processes of decoding relating the organism to milieus. Decoding thus opens the organism to developing new sets of affects or parastrata (50–1; 322).

Form is tied closely to all three types of production. In hylomorphism, form is allegedly that which is imposed by a transcendent productive agent on chaotic or passive matter to allow bodies to possess the amount of order they do indeed possess (338). In artisanal production, the artisan coaxes forth the singularities or 'implicit forms' of the material (408–9). Finally, in machinic production, the abstract machine at work on the plane of consistency precisely operates by linking unformed matters (arrayed in 'phyla') exhibiting only 'degrees of intensity' and non-formal ('diagrammatic') functions exhibiting tensors (511).

FRACTAL: a mathematical object with a fractional number of dimensions; tentatively proposed as a 'very general mathematical model' of smooth space (486). Two examples of fractals that DG employ are 'Van Koch's curve' (487; correctly written 'Koch's Curve'), a line of potentially infinite length that (as 'Koch's Snowflake') can enclose a finite area; and 'Sierpensky's sponge' (487; correctly written 'Sierpinski Sponge'), a solid cube or other three-dimensional object that is hollowed out through a simple mathematical formula such that its volume approaches zero and its surface area approaches infinity. DG do not encourage us to go out into the landscape and look for fractals just as they do not call for the reinstatement of nomads. Fractals in the landscape are in our opinion necessarily restricted abstractions that, where 'found', might lead to conceptual simplification of complex, smoothing/striating processes better studied in combination with other models. For example, though shorelines and forests surely contain fractals, such smooth space qualities cannot by definition occur in pure form, or in isolation, because smooth spaces occur only in mixture with striated spaces as the product of a certain ratio of smoothing and striating forces. A fractalized shoreline, while intriguing, is but an abstraction of the real shoreline that is traversed by the striations contained in any system that is always-already striated by human forces.

FREQUENCY: the measure of the rate of repetition. Signs in a signifying regime repeat according to an 'objective frequency' (132), while towns impose a frequency on commercial flows (432). DG contrast frequency to resonance both in subjectivity and in the State. See also Face – Faciality.

GENDER. See Girl.

GEODESY. See Primitive Society.

GEOGRAPHY: DG make no statement about the academic discipline of geography per se, but presumably would characterize much of it as a Royal science serving States in colonialism and neo-colonialism by producing 'tracings' (*calques* instead of *cartes*). Their notion of geography as intensive cartography (261), however, means they oppose geography to history, calling the former 'untimely', equating it with forgetting, map, and rhizome. Thus nomads are said to have no history, only geography (393).

In *WP*, geography entails a focus on becoming: 'Geography wrests history from the cult of necessity in order to stress the irreducibility of contingency' (*WP*: 96).

DG also mention the geography of the human individual or group: 'we are traversed by lines, meridians, geodesics, tropics, and zones marching to different beats and differing in nature' (202). Although they do not treat academic geography explicitly, we can easily draw up a comparative list of Royal science geographers – geographers in the service of the State – and contrast them with minor science geographers: those who have actively resisted or downplayed the State as well as those who have tracked matter-flows not as petroleum geologists for the State but as students of mining societies and suchlike. Among the more recent Royal geographers are Ellen Semple, Ellsworth Huntington, and those in the 'spatial science' movement of the twentieth century, as well as legions of State-sponsored researchers tracing the boundaries of empires, revealing the best ways to colonize and educate, to establish transportation and communication networks, and to wage wars (the 'area studies' scholarship of the Cold War, for example; the Soviet Union had a parallel Royal geography).

Among the anti-State, 'minor geographers' were the anarchists Reclus and Kropotkin, both of whom worked actively for a new earth. Kropotkin (1989) and Reclus (1897) are both highly anticolonialist, rhizomatic, and sensitive to the struggles and potentialities of local bodies as well as translocal networks. Unfortunately for geography, the voices of Reclus and Kropotkin were drowned out by the environmental determinists in the service of empire. The anti-State or at least pro-traditional Sauerian current in North American geography also seems to be a minor science: from Fred Kniffen's mapping of house types (1936) to Robert West's tracking of the gold miners tapping into the machinic phylum in Colombia (1998), the Sauerians (including Sauer [Sauer and Leighly 1963] himself, who was the catalyst, not the originator, of the multiplicity that formed around him) focused on the 'anachronistic', what the State overlooks or does not care about, the anti-modern (as Mathewson [1985] argued). The 'traditional' Sauerian approach fed supplementary approaches that mapped commodity chains and complex adaptive systems but remained based typically on the idea that local spaces, traditional cropping systems, and mining societies contained numerous solutions to complex problems that the apparatus of capture of the State, or transnational development organizations, tended to interfere with or parasitize more

91

than improve upon. These ideas resonate strongly with the complexity theory work of Lansing 1991.

GEOLOGY: the 'Geology of Morals' plateau in *ATP*, in which DG map the energetic, physicochemical, geological, and organic strata, is a play on Nietzsche's *On the Genealogy of Morals*, and indicates DG's 'naturalism', that is, their desire to use the same concepts in thinking processes that traditionally had fallen on opposing sides of a distinction between 'nature' and 'culture'. (For them, of course, 'naturalism' entails just as much a politicizing of nature as a naturalizing of language and politics. Hence, their joke at 43: 'the Danish Spinozist geologist, Hjelmslev'.) The most noteworthy resonance of DG's terms with geological terms occurs with 'stratification'. DG present sedimentary rock formation as a brief geological example of the process of stratification (which also occurs in organic and social registers): first 'sedimentation', the differential deposition of material, then 'folding', the formation and deformation of entities with emergent properties (41; DeLanda 1999: 290n82 corrects this imprecise terminology and insists on 'cementation' as the second articulation, in place of 'folding', which occurs at larger scales).

GEOMETRY. See Riemannian Space.

GEOMORPHISM: the becoming-earth of the bird through song. The bird as musician can be happy or sad, or greet the sun, and this is not 'anthropomorphism . . . it is instead a kind of geomorphism' (318–19), in which the bird is in rhizomatic communication with the earth (the forces of territorialization and deterritorialization). This discussion is in the context of the territorial motif and counterparts that form rhythmic faces and melodic landscapes.

GEOMORPHOLOGY. See Holey Space.

GEOPHILOSOPHY: the title of an essay in *WP*, the term harks back to DG's attempt to refound philosophy as materialist, earthly, and spatial. They seek to reorient philosophy from a concentration on temporality and historicity to spatiality and geography, because 'thinking takes place in the relationship of territory and the earth' (*WP*: 85). All too briefly, geophilosophy in *WP* posits that philosophy needs the contingent connection (not 'conjunction': see

Flow) between the absolute deterritorialization of a thought of radical immanence and a relative social deterritorialization constituting a milieu of social immanence. The ancient Greek and modern capitalist moments that support philosophy are contingent events; there is no development of philosophy that passes by a Christian medieval moment. Rather, 'there is the contingent recommencement of a same contingent process, in different conditions' (*WP*: 98).

GIRL [*fille*]: in DG's recounting of the story of Oedipalization, it is the body of the girl that is 'stolen' first, in order then to shame the little boy (276). Femininity, the form of 'femaleness', is imposed on the girl as a stereotyped set of triggers and patterns; in other words, a feminine organism is produced by contraction of the affects of the girl's body to a small set, the feminine set (a restricted set of singularities is selected and arranged in exclusive disjunction). Masculinity is then produced in relation to an imposed essentialized femininity:

> The boy's [*garçon*] turn comes next, but it is by using the girl as an example, by pointing to the girl as the object of his desire, that an opposed organism, a dominant history is fabricated for him too. The girl is the first victim, but she must also serve as an example and a trap. (276)

Outside the Oedipal story, however, the 'girl' is the name for a treatment of the body in terms of material 'speeds and slowness' and affect because 'she' lives a body that avoids capture by the developmental line that leads from little girl to nice young lady (276). Because the 'girl' avoids this line, 'she' is not a tomboy [*garçon manqué*] either when acting against gender stereotype and experimenting with the capabilities of the body (how fast can I run? how tough can I be?). Accessing the 'girl' in all of us ('the girl is the becoming-woman of both sexes' [277]) is a question of constructing political and social frameworks: DG are never 'lifestyle' mavens, never 'individualists', as the collective sense of the French word *corps* (as in *corps sans organes*=Body without Organs) shows: Deleuze and Guattari urge us all to become a Corps of Engineers, cautious yet daring experimentalists who construct bodies politic, somatic and civic at once.

GROUND [*Fond*]: the experience of the earth in DG's account of romanticism (338–9). As opposed to the artist-God of classicism, who creates, the hero-artist of romanticism seeks to found; instead of confronting chaos, the romantic artist confronts the abyss [*sans-fond*] and has to deal with 'the pull of the Ground [*l'attirance du fond*]' (339).

GROUND [*sol*]: the condition of the earth in nomadic social formations. Insofar as the nomad reterritorializes on deterritorialization itself (the nomad most feels at home when on the move), 'the earth [*la terre*] deterritorializes itself to provide the nomad with a territory [*territoire*]. The land [*la terre*] ceases to be land [*terre*], tending to become simply ground [*sol*] or support' (381).

HAECCEITY [Latin for 'thisness']: a term taken from the medieval philosopher Duns Scotus to denote a 'nonpersonal individuation' of either a body or an environmental assemblage, a block of space-time (260–5). The concept of haecceity enables DG to write about the uniqueness of things or events without resorting to the traditional Aristotelian genus/species/individual scheme, which Deleuze rejects as subordinating difference to a horizon of identity (for example, *DR*: 30–5). In *ATP*, a body taken as a haecceity is defined in its cartography by its longitude (the 'speeds and slowness' of its material flows) and by its latitude (its set of affects) (260–1). An environmental assemblage, a 'set of relations' defined as a haecceity (382), treats spatio-temporal relations not as predicates of a thing (Aristotle's categories include 'where' and 'when') but as dimensions of multiplicities, components of the assemblage (262). The semiotic of haecceities links indefinite article + proper name + infinitive verb (263–5). The indefinite article indicates that elements find their individuation in the assemblage, not from their form or subjectivity. The proper name, as in military naming of an operation or meteorological naming of a storm, indicates the event-character of the assemblage. The infinitive verb, 'Aion', expresses the time proper to the virtual realm.

HETEROGENEITY: the natural order within multiplicities and rhizomes: jumbled-together, mixed-and-matched. Stratifying machines create homogeneity from heterogeneous elements by deterritorializing them from their disparate assemblages and overcoding them with a common semiotic, binding them together into a coherent and cohesive, but also segmented, body. Rhizomatic assemblages, in contrast, connect heterogeneous elements but leave them that way so that each retains relative independence and can be plugged simultaneously into other rhizomes.

HISTORY: the time-keeping and self-fulfilling prophecy of States; the constructed sequence of significant events that obliterates geography, the earth, and the non-historic presignifying and countersignifying regimes. DG's view of 'official' history is as hostile as their view of geography is sympathetic. They take for granted that history is a fabrication by sedentary societies to justify their importance and centrality. Even at its best, 'all history does is translate a coexistence of becomings into a succession' (430), that is, history establishes conditions for translation of co-existing diagrams (that is, for the actualization of virtual multi-plicities). In this way, 'the task of the historian is to designate the "period" of coexistence or simultaneity of these two movements' (deterritorialization and reterritorialization) (221). In the section on 'Geophilosophy' in *WP*, DG call for 'geohistory', following Braudel: materialist history, or in a wider sense, historical geography (*WP*: 95). See also Nomadology.

HOLEY SPACE [*espace troué*]: the 'third space' of the machinic phylum (of matter-flow), inhabited by itinerant metallurgists, and by extension the 'underground' space that can connect with smooth space and be conjugated by striated space (415). Holey space is the subsoil space of 'swiss cheese' (413) that bypasses both the ground [*sol*] of nomadic smooth space and the land [*terre*] of sedentary striated space (414). In this bypassing, holey space is suspect; for DG, the mark of Cain is not the biblical mark of the soil, but a mark of the subsoil [*sous-sol*] (414), since holey space is conceived of by surface dwellers as created by theft and betrayal.

Holey space has different relations to nomadic smooth and State striated space. Cave-dwelling, earth-boring tunnellers are only imperfectly controlled by the State, and often have allied with nomads and with peasants in revolts against centralized authority. Thus the machinic phylum explored in holey space connects with smooth space to form rhizomes, while it is conjugated (blocked) by State striation (415). The previously positive relation of holey and smooth space has turned around, however, now that States are able to create a smooth space of surveillance and global military intervention. Holey spaces have flourished, for the only way to escape the spying eyes of State intelligence is to go underground: 'Do not new smooth spaces, or holey spaces, arise as parries even in relation to the smooth space of a world-wide organization? Virilio invokes the beginnings of subterranean habitation in the "mineral layer," *which can take on very diverse values*' (480; emphasis added). Such a turnaround has not gone unnoticed; led by the Bush Administration, global States now trumpet the danger of 'rogue regimes' that have taken their weapons-making capabilities underground where they cannot be detected by satellites and spy planes. North Korea in 2003 remains the prime example, but much of the premise upon which the Bush Administration built its case for the 2003 'pre-emptive' assault on Iraq was the supposedly concealed nature of weapons laboratories and storage facilities. The post-9/11 Afghanistan war was also launched against the holey space of the so-called 'Al Qaeda' network, supposedly in possession of innumerable underground hideouts, indeed even elaborate bunkers (though these were discovered to be not nearly as luxurious as their reputations). The bunkers and tunnels of the American establishment are, of course, exempt from any suspicion.

Cyberspace and forest space may also be seen as holey spaces rather than as smooth spaces in that they provide protective cover for 'underground' operations. Guerrilla armies such as the FARC (Fuerzas Armadas Revolucionarias de Colombia) use forests to great advantage, and indeed a long line of guerrilla forces in Latin America has used rain forests in this way. The armies of the State cannot array on it as on a battlefield, and the trees must be defoliated before air war can be successful. Cyberspace is filled with gaps and voids, black matter from which hackers (these may of course be in the service of States) launch coordinated attacks on sites and servers. A study of the paranoid tunneling in Cold War suburban backyards to create 'fallout shelters' would yield yet another aspect of the interrelations of smooth, striated, and holey space, as would the innumerable urban legends concerning sewers, subway tunnels, and the like.

HOME [*chez soi*]. See Territory.

HOMOGENEITY: the condition of content in a stratum, the product of the first pincer of double articulation, which selects heterogeneous matter from a milieu and deposits it in homogeneous layers (40–1). It is also the extreme result of striation, at which point a smooth space is 'reimparted' (488). Homogeneity in strata is equivalent in thermodynamic systems to the fact that at equilibrium only the average behaviors of particles need be considered. Homogeneity is achieved in disciplinary systems by means of examination, evaluation, and intervention: what does not fit the norm is either isolated or reformed.

HYLOMORPHISM: the doctrine that the order displayed by material systems is due to the form projected in advance of production by an external productive agent, a form which organizes what would supposedly otherwise be chaotic or passive matter. DG follow Simondon in constructing an artisanal theory of production as part of the critique of hylomorphism (as well as constructing a full-blown machinic theory of production). The homogenization of matter by tools in a work setting enables the appearance of a hylomorphic production, but Simondon shows that, even in the paradigm case of baking clay for bricks, the pressure and heat applied by the brick maker coax forth implicit forms or self-organizing potentials so that colloidal microstructures of the clay interlock and are carried forth from molecular to molar scale (Simondon 1995: 39–40). DG also follow Simondon's lead in analyzing the political significance of hylomorphism. For Simondon, hylomorphism is 'a socialized representation of work', the viewpoint of a master commanding slave labor (1995: 49). For DG, hylomorphism also has an important political dimension, as a hylomorphic representation of a body politic resonates with fascist desire, in which the leader comes from on high to rescue his people from chaos by his imposition of order.

IBN KHALDUN: Arab historian and de facto geographer (1332–95). DG draw heavily from the 'magnificent' *The Muqaddimah: An Introduction to History* (555n31) for their discussion of the interrelationships of towns, cities, States, and Bedouins.

ICON: a sign that marks reterritorialization, that circumscribes meaning in a signifying regime; hence the face (112). Icons are often objects of veneration and adoration, for they stand for the whole but do not lose their substance and adorable materiality (unlike symbols, which are stand-ins for other materials). By this measure, icons populate the facialized landscape, and there is indeed an iconography of landscape – each signifying regime creates one. This phenomenon is explored particularly well in Cosgrove and Daniels (1988). See also Index, Symbol.

IDEOLOGY: the widespread Marxist notion that a false set of ideas hides objective political and economic conditions from potentially politically active subjects. DG name ideology a 'most execrable concept' (68) because it is insufficiently materialist, separating a realm of production from that of desire and positing a causal relation between content and expression in a social assemblage (89). Ideology thereby ignores the way order-words serve as triggers of material production (90), and this prevents an understanding of the way social machines construct desiring patterns of both corporeal and social 'bodies politic' in a sort of 'political physiology'. Accordingly, for DG the concept of ideology is particularly ill suited to the problem of fascism, which, like all problems of desire, is a 'problem of pure matter' (165). See also Theweleit 1988 and 1989.

IMMANENCE: in philosophical terminology, the act of being within a conceptual space. DG maintain a commitment to immanence in their refusal of transcendence as a philosophical option, that is, in their commitment to explain the order and creativity of the world as the result of the self-ordering capacities of complex systems rather than crediting such order and creativity to an extra-worldly source (spirit, God, prime mover). An immanentist position would account for the appearance of hylomorphic production by showing that hylomorphism is really artisanal production seen from the perspective of the architect or master. Similarly, the relative but real transcendence of overcoding agents in stratification processes must be accounted for by their status as products of previous morphogenetic processes. In his historical monographs, Deleuze constructs a genealogy of thinkers committed to immanence: Lucretius, Spinoza, Hume, Nietzsche, and Bergson (or at least gives immanentist readings of them).

IMPERCEPTIBILITY: the state of a destratified body able to enter into becomings with other bodies and form assemblages. Imperceptibility is one of the 'three virtues' along with indiscernability (to have traits that are nonsignifying signs of singularities and affects) and impersonality (to have left subjectivity or personality in order to assume one's haecceity or event-character) (279–80).

INCORPOREAL TRANSFORMATION: a change in the social status of a body within or across assemblages. DG take the notion from

Deleuze's analysis of the Stoics in *LS*; it maintains close affiliation to the theory of 'speech acts' developed by the English philosopher J. L. Austin. An incorporeal transformation is brought about by an order-word as uttered in the proper context as established by the collective assemblage of enunciation of a territorial assemblage (88). For instance, the pronouncement of the order-word 'guilty' by a judge moves the body of the addressee from the status of 'accused' to that of 'convicted'. If we conceive of a social state space, an incorporeal transformation moves a body into a different region of that space (in other words, it effectuates a bifurcation in the state space of the system). Another way of putting it would be to say an incorporeal transformation assigns a body to a different assemblage (in this case, from the court assemblage to the prison assemblage). Using their terminology of content (assemblages of bodies) and expression (assemblages of institutions supporting the work of order-words), DG note that this active element of incorporeal transformations means they do not represent bodies, but 'intervene' in them: 'expressions . . . are inserted into or intervene into contents, not to represent them but to anticipate them or move them back, slow them down or speed them up, separate or combine them, delimit them in a different way' (86). Incorporeal transformations are thus triggers of material production.

INDEX: a sign or group of signs that mark a territory. Indexes partition the worlds of animals into areas or 'zones': thus there is an audible, olfactory, visual, corporeal, movement-based index for zones of shelter, zones of hunting, zones of mating, neutral zones, and so forth. In the case of the New World bird family *Pipridae* (the manakins), the index of the mating ground contains signs such as the absence of leaf duff, the flashes of bright colors in the gloom, and the buzzing, whip-snapping sounds created by the males. The bowerbirds of Australia are an even more interesting case. Indexes of human territoriality have been explored extensively by geographers, anthropologists, sociologists, and other scholars, and range from body markings and possessive gestures to the strategic placement of items – even at a teen hangout – and the obvious locations of street signs, fences, and so forth. At a grander scale, whole cities and countries have indexes of this sort: flags of course, but also skylines, arches, statues, and so on. At some point, indexes become icons. See also Icon, Symbol.

INDIVIDUAL. See Haecceity.

INFORMATION: in the linguistic domain analyzed in the 'Postulates of Linguistics' plateau, information is the semantic or meaningful content of messages. For DG, language is not primarily for the transport of information from one consciousness to another, but is composed of order-words, that is, triggers of material production via incorporeal transformation (75–6). There must only be enough information contained in order-words to prevent their becoming confused, as in, for example, the difference between 'fire' and 'fore'. The technical (non-semantic) notions developed in the 'information theory' of Claude Shannon are used by DeLanda (2002) to explicate Deleuze's work in *DR* and *LS*, but they are largely absent in *ATP*, except for a brief mention at 179, and a few echoes in the notion of the 'acts of discernment' and the 'imbrication of the *semiotic* and the *material*' (337; italics in original) in an assemblage.

INTENSITY: in physics, the amount of energy transmitted per unit time per unit area. Deleuze derives his similar notion of intensity from his study of 'intensive magnitude' in Kant's 'Anticipations of Perception' in the *Critique of Pure Reason* (Deleuze 1978). An intensive magnitude [*grandeur intensive*] is 'that which fills space and time to such and such a degree'; for example, a volume filled with more or less dense matter, or a room heated to a certain temperature. Two characteristics of intensive magnitudes are noted. First, 'the apprehension of the unity of an intensive quantity happens in an instant'. In other words, while one must add together the parts of an extensive quantity to achieve a grasp of its unity ('one inch plus one inch plus . . . equals one foot'), one does not add, for example, three 'units' of ten degrees of heat to apprehend a temperature of thirty degrees. Second, 'the multiplicity contained in an intensive quantity . . . refers to a variable promixity to degree zero'. An intensive quantity is either growing away from zero or approaching zero or holding steady with regard to zero.

These characteristics of the intensive quantity are directly taken up in *ATP*'s notion of 'intensity', as in the discussion of the BwO: 'the BwO causes intensities to pass; . . . it is matter that occupies space to a given degree . . . it is nonstratified, unformed, intense matter, the matrix of intensity, intensity = 0; . . . Production of the real as an intensive magnitude starting at zero'

(153). In other words, the BwO is that body which has moved out of its comfort zone or steady state so that non-average fluctuations in matter–energy flows are not quickly compensated for by homeostatic mechanisms that return the system to normal, as in the 'organism' condition. In the BwO condition, intensities of experience (of love, of joy, of rage, of despair: all these 'emotions' are affects corresponding to affections or mixtures or compositions of bodies, that is, intensities of matter–energy flow) push the body toward crisis points so that new patterns and thresholds of behavior might be experimented with.

INTENSIVE: in basic scientific terms, the characteristic of properties of thermodynamic systems (for example, temperature, pressure) which when driven past a critical threshold trigger a change in the quality of the system (the system moves into another basin of attraction). As these thresholds are determined by immanent relations of the system (the boiling point for water is not that of oil), DG highlight the opposition of intensive properties to extensive properties such as length or volume, which are measured by an external 'metric' or standard (a cubic centimeter stays the same whether it is used to measure water or oil). Extensive properties are divisible without a qualitative change in the underlying system, and characterize actual or stratified systems (31). By extension, one can call 'intensive' any linked set of rates of change in assemblages or 'rhizomatic multiplicities' since changes in these ratios past an immanently determined critical threshold also trigger qualitative change (33). The key to Deleuze's ontology is the claim that intensive morphogenetic processes give rise to actual or stratified entities whose extensive properties and fixed qualities are the object of representational thought and occlude the intensities which gave rise to them. By further extension, and perhaps confusingly, the internal relations of virtual multiplicities are said to be intensive (70; 507), so in the final analysis strata hide not only intensive processes but also the virtual multiplicities that subtend them (in other words, equilibrium/steady state/stable systems are locked into a basin of attraction so that the possible effects of non-actualized attractors are not felt). Thus the triumph of minor science, when it attains insight into the plane of consistency or virtual realm by moving stratified systems into far-from-equilibrium crisis (moving them from actual to intensive registers), is to put variables into 'continuous variation' and thereby free an 'intense

101

matter' (109), or, more precisely, material which carries 'variable intensive affects' (408).

INTERIORITY: the condition of being captured by a stratum as part of its 'interior milieu', although even the 'exterior milieu' can be considered to be interior to a stratum in the sense of belonging to that stratum as its source of material (49). The two-fold structure of State thought (see Epistemology) results in a capture of the represented contents of the world and thus provides a 'form of interiority' to thought (375). Immanence is not to be confused with interiority; the immanent field of desire 'is not internal to the self [*intérieur au moi*]', but rather 'is like the absolute Outside [*le Dehors absolu*] that knows no Selves [*les Moi*] because interior and exterior are equally a part of the immanence in which they have fused' (156). See also Exteriority.

INTERPRETATION: in the signifying regime of signs, the process of establishing the meaning of signs by treating them as signifiers, that is, by positioning them in a signifying chain. Such chains form multiple circles and the priest locates himself at the point where he can direct the infinite interpretation of signifiers relating only to each other (116). Priests (and presumably hermeneuticians in general) suffer from 'interpretosis': 'In truth, significance and interpretosis are the two diseases of the earth or the skin, in other words, humankind's fundamental neurosis' (114). The nature of interpretation changes in the postsignifying regime, in which the book is the 'body of passion', the substance of expression, replacing the face (127). Here interpretation either disappears in favor of recitation, or becomes internal to the book itself, or becomes the translation of internal passion ('the book is written both in itself and in the heart': 127). Thus the center of significance has become the point of subjectification (127). DG oppose interpretation to pragmatic experimentation (162).

JUDGMENT: comparing the properties of a produced substance to a fixed and pre-established standard. Such judgment belongs to morality, and is opposed to (ethical) evaluation, which proceeds immanently to evaluate the production of affects in an assemblage: are they joyful and life affirming? Do they indicate an increase in the capacities of the assemblage to form mutually enhancing relations with other assemblages?

JUDGMENT OF GOD: the operation of stratification, producing actual substances according to an axiomatic as the program for the plan(e) of transcendence (40).

LABOR [*travail*]: work, occurring by definition only within striated space, is the segmentation, overcoding, and draining of surplus value of free human activity ('free action': 490), effected by the apparatus of capture of the State. Labor 'performs a . . . striation of space-time . . . a nullification of smooth spaces . . . [the State's] nullification of the war machine' (490–1). Labor, in other words, is the primary means by which the State achieves the transformation of 'earth' into 'land' (441) and the destruction of presignifying and countersignifying semiotics.

LAND [*terre*]. See Earth/Land.

LANDSCAPE [*paysage*]: the 'geographical' correlate of the face [*visage*] (172). Landscapes correlated to faces arise where the territories of presignifying or 'primitive' societies are deterritorialized by the State and reterritorialized by face-obsessed semiotic regimes. The landscape of the archaic State bears the reflection of the face of a semi-divine ruler, while in the postsignifying regime it may take on the characteristics of the Christ-face. Architects and engineers reproduce the face of the Despot on the land, molding it into a signifying face. In this context, it should be noted that DG believe the signifying regime has already melded corporeality to the face, such that viewing 'Mother Earth' as a body is the same as viewing it as a face, because the mother's body has been transformed semiotically into a face. Parallel to this, DG cite Maurice Ronai's (1976) discussion of the semiotics of landscape, and in particular Ronai's demonstration that the landscape is the 'face of the fatherland or nation' (533n13). DG also point out that the embeddedness of the face in landscape, and vice versa, is more obvious when one considers that schizophrenics may lose the ability to make sense out of landscapes and also lose or fail in their ability to read faces, as their ability to make sense out of language breaks down (188).

DG present a deterritorialized sense of landscape in discussions of painting in the 'Becoming-intense, becoming-animal' plateau. 'Put the landscape to flight. For example, what Mondrian correctly calls a "landscape": a pure, deterritorialized landscape'. And, 'the aim of painting has always been the deterritorialization

103

of faces and landscapes, either by a reactivation of corporeality, or by a liberation of lines or colors, or both' (301). Here, they expand 'landscape' to mean the heterogeneous array of features – a terrain – that in the painting is not and need not be represented as a face; the landscape in this context exists beyond and outside the face. Their treatment of *paysage* here appears to reflect a conception of a landscape populated by heterogeneous elements, what is jumbled together: milieus, territories, worlds, spaces.

They return to landscape in the 'Refrain' plateau in a discussion of the melodic landscapes created by bird song. 'Territorial motifs [of birds] form *rhythmic faces or characters* [personnages], and . . . territorial counterpoints form *melodic landscapes* [paysages]' (318; italics in original); furthermore, 'the melodic landscape is no longer a melody associated with a landscape; the melody itself is a sonorous landscape in counterpoint to a virtual landscape' (318). Here, the landscape in question is an array of melodic and rhythmic elements, not a physical terrain, though the discussion is a treatment of territorial refrains that is quite geographical in content. The idea that diverse birds (for example, in a dawn chorus) all sing their own territories but together form a landscape of song is further proof that DG conceive of landscape as heterogeneous terrain, as the interweaving of milieus and territories in specific places. What plays in this landscape is the 'machinic opera' (330).

LANDSCAPIFICATION: rendering of milieus into landscape (301).

LANDSCAPITY [*paysagéité*]: the correlate of faciality, it is the condition of creating and treating milieus as landscapes connected to the face (172). The face can also have 'landscapity' as it is treated as a landscape. DG describe a chiasma of face and landscape, where they are so correlated that they cannot escape each other: face = landscape = face = landscape = . . . This is the 'black hole' of subjectivity lodged in the face, projected onto the landscape: a trap of the signifying and postsignifying regimes. DG suggest that faces and landscapes have to be freed together from this catatonic visual embrace, that the face be freed from its faciality while the landscape be freed from its landscapity, from its reflection of and connection to the face.

LATITUDE: the set of intensive affects of a body, what the body can do and what it can undergo in joining assemblages. Along with longitude, it composes the coordinate system for the cartography of a body on the plane of consistency (261).

LIFE [*vie*]: (1) a certain set of beings ('organisms'), 'a particularly complex system of stratification' (336); (2) the creativity of complex systems, 'a surplus value of *destratification* . . . an aggregate of consistency that disrupts orders, forms, and substances' (336; italics in original). In the second sense, then, life is not limited to the organism form: 'the organism is that which life sets against itself in order to limit itself' (503). This notion of life as creativity, revealed by metallurgy and its sense of 'a life proper to matter', gives rise to 'the prodigious idea of *Nonorganic Life*' (411; italics in original). (Note that 'living thing' [*le vivant*] is used as a neutral term with regard to the distinction between organism and non-organic life [313].)

LIMIT: the membrane separating the interior and exterior of a stratified body (50). 'Limit' is synonymous with 'intermediary milieu' of an organism (51). The 'limit' as that within which a body or assemblage maintains its identity is thus opposed to 'threshold' as the point at which a system changes (440).

LIMIT-FACE: the ultimate result of certain operations of the faciality machine that produces and reflects subjectivity and significance through the 'white wall/black hole' system. White walls are the screen or the background of the face; black holes are the sinks of subjectivity (182–8). The first limit-face is that of the signifying regime, where faces and landscapes are populated by numerous black holes, centers of significance that are all reflections of the face of the Despot with eyes everywhere: the 'terrestrial signifying despotic face' (183). The second limit-face is that of the postsignifying regime, the 'maritime face or landscape: it follows the line separating the sky from the waters, or the land from the waters' (184). Here the 'landscape becomes a thread' (183); this is the 'maritime subjective passional authoritarian face' (184), the Christ-face that follows the wanderer in the desert and across the waters, that is always on the encircling horizon. DG wish for the overcoming of both these face-landscape pairs, and assert that it occurs as the regimes are overturned, as 'probe-heads' move to corporeality and rhizomatic spatialities (190–1).

LINE: DG distinguish three types of lines that transect and traverse us, that define our positionality within and in relationship to systems: the 'molar or rigid line of segmentarity' (195; 210–11); the 'line of molecular or supple segmentation' (196; 210–11); and the line of flight (222). The lines of segmentarity position and partition us within striated spaces, within the State, or within other hierarchized assemblages. The molar is rigid because it is what is laid down and imposed as the very defining line of the assemblage, and must be followed: the line from life to death but also the line from home to work, the line of logic and reason (linear thinking), the vertical line from pew to priest and up to heaven, and so forth. Supple lines (originating in the presignifying regime) are also segmented, but are molecular in that they are the lines that elude molar coding and/or are not effectively overcoded by the State. They can be variable, but only within the parameters of the system. In the final analysis, 'individual or group, we are traversed by lines, meridians, geodesics, tropics, and zones . . . we are composed of . . . bundles of lines, for each kind is multiple' (202). DG also peak of the 'entanglement' of lines: while flows and vectors define smooth space, lines of ever increasing imbrication achieve supple and rigid striation, twisted together (224). The cartography of any body or system consists in drawing lines.

LINE OF FLIGHT: the threshold between assemblages, the path of deterritorialization, the experiment; in complexity theory terms, a move that triggers a bifurcation. A relative line of flight is a vector of escape, a move between milieus – when, for example, the bull in the arena returns to its protective associated milieu (55); a move to a pre-established attractor. An absolute line of flight is an absolute deterritorialization to the plane of consistency, the creation of new attractors and bifurcators, new patterns and thresholds. Vanishing lines – what define perspective and depth in a Western landscape representation – are not active lines of flight at all, but rather fixed and frozen vectors, reterritorialized flows. Lines of flight or becomings are always segmented, never pure, because of the boundaries and borders that are crossed. They are the primary constituents of all assemblages, all bodies, all spaces, plugged by machines of enslavement and order but unplugged by forces of desire and smoothing. As vectors of (de-/re-)territorialization, they comprise the 'mappability' of one complex system to another, or any system to its state space. For example, the paths by which I convert myself from

106

membership in one religion to membership in another, or one profession to another, or one culture to another, are my relative lines of flight: the vectors by which I map (not trace) myself into a new assemblage. If I abandon one religion, or one culture, or one profession, without adopting another, I dissolve myself along absolute lines of flight, following the vectors that allow me stand outside of, for example, religion (thence able to draw from any religion, ignore religion, avoid overcoding by religion, and so on). Lines of flight can thus be seen as vectors of freedom, or at least freedom-from.

LONGITUDE: differential rates – 'speed and slowness' – of material elements of a body (260). As these rates immanently determine thresholds of change solely for the body in which they appear, longitude is an intensive property, rather than an extensive property subject to a metric or external and fixed measure. In other words, only experimentation can explore longitude, the bodily states up to and exceeding thresholds. Thus 'we don't know [in advance] what the body can do [until we try it out]'. Along with latitude, it composes the coordinate system for the cartography of a body on the plane of consistency (261).

MACHINE: in *AO*, a 'machine' is any connection of organs linking together flows in networks of desiring-production. In *ATP*, a machine is: (1) loosely speaking, any assemblage; (2) more precisely, the 'cutting edges of deterritorialization' that draw variations and mutations of an assemblage (333); or (3) any functional structure under the command of a higher unity (457). Machines in the third sense can be either imperial 'megamachines' (slave labor gangs: 428; cf. Mumford 1970) or 'technical machines' (457). DG emphasize the priority of 'social machines' as an assemblage linking bodies and regimes of signs over technical machines, which can only be used when linked with bodies to form parts of social machines (398). In other words, only the nomad war machine can integrate the stirrup and bow into the 'man-bow-horse' assemblage (391), although those elements [technical machines] might be taken up separately by different assemblages [social machines], thus forming different 'machinic phyla' (406).

MACHINIC: adjectival form for the operation of the machinic assemblage or machine (sense 2 under 'Machine', above): the 'synthesis of heterogeneity as such' (330).

107

MACHINIC ASSEMBLAGE [*agencement machinique*]: an actualized abstract machine maintaining consistency, that is, the teamwork of heterogeneous elements (71). In the process of stratification, the machinic assemblage is the 'surface of stratification' (40). In the organic strata, machinic assemblages are the various membranes of organisms (50). In territorial assemblages, that is, on the alloplastic stratum, the content is named the 'machinic assemblage of bodies' (88) to which is correlated, according to measures of reterritorialization and deterritorialization, a 'collective assemblage of enunciation' or set of order-words effecting incorporeal transformations of those bodies.

MACHINIC ENSLAVEMENT [*asservissement machinique*]: when humans form part of a machine [sense 3 under 'Machine', above] or functional structure (428; 457–8; 492). The great work gangs of imperial State construction projects form the most familiar case of machinic enslavement (428), but DG also point to the construction of cybernetic networks in which humans form nodes in an information-processing machine thus constituting a machinic surplus value (458), as when, for example, consumer purchasing information is fed back into manufacturing and marketing decisions.

MACHINIC PHYLUM: (1) There is a brief mention of an 'active' sense of 'machinic phylum', equivalent to 'destratifying transversality', as that which frees matter and taps forces to allow the meshing together of 'very heterogeneous elements' to achieve consistency or emergent effects in aggregates (335). (2) A more 'passive' sense of the machinic phylum occurs in the main discussion of it in *ATP* (406–10). There it is the set of self-ordering material processes inherent in material and enabling emergent effects. In the latter sense, we must distinguish the singular phylum and plural phyla. There are as many machinic phyla as there are 'technological lineages' enabled by tapping into the self-ordering forces of material (406). These are effectuated by 'assemblages' (cf. 'machinic assemblage') which are selections of singularities, hence actualizations or differenciations of the virtual (406). A machinic phylum is limned by artisans who follow the traits of materials and devise operations to bring forth new bodies with different affects (406; 409). A steel saber and an iron sword, for instance, come from different machinic phyla (406). The singular machinic phylum, in contrast, is the virtual limit case of intensive matter 'in variation, matter as a conveyor of sin-gularities and traits of expression' (409). Insofar as artisanal pro-duction relies on natural processes, the machinic phylum 'is as much artificial as natural: it is like the unity of human beings and Nature' (406; cf. *AO*: 4: man as 'the eternal custodian of the machines of the universe'). The virtual machinic phylum, matter in continuous variation, is composed of the 'unformed matters' which the abstract machine links to 'diagrams' of nonformal functions to form the plane of consistency (511).

MACHINIC SURPLUS VALUE: surplus value generated through the emergent effects of cybernetic assemblages extending beyond the workplace and spreading through all society in infor-mation-processing networks (458). While Marx restricted surplus value to the exploitation of the living labor power of human sub-jects working alongside technical machines, DG allow that the decoding exercised by capitalism frees capital to construct assem-blages of humans and information-processing machines that compose a new form of 'machinic enslavement'. This is a form of surplus value because the use of information generated by the analysis of consumer purchasing patterns (and/or TV viewing habits, voting behavior, etc.) and fed back into manufacturing and marketing processes puts people to work (assembles them into functional structures or 'machines' in sense 3 above) even when they are not officially 'working' (that is, exchanging labor power for a wage).

MACROPOLITICS. See Politics.

MAP [*carte*]: the set of instructions for the operation of an intensive consistency or rhizome (12). Maps are produced by the cartogra-phy that limns the longitude and latitude of a body (260–1). Maps are the multidimensional 'circuitry' of rhizomatic assem-blages that can be plugged into at any point and are connectable, via their lines of flight, to other assemblages. Since they are 'entirely oriented toward an experimentation in contact with the real' (12), maps are not tracings [*calques*], which only reproduce properties of stratified bodies. A map is also produced in study-ing transformational pragmatics of regimes of signs (119; 139; 146). Not to be confused with the 'diagram' produced by an abstract machine on the plane of consistency.

MARGIN: the zone within codes that is susceptible to decoding (53; 322). Postsignifying formations originate from the margins of decoding within the codes of signifying regimes (122).

MASS: following Canetti 1963, DG develop the notion of 'crowd' (Massumi's translation; DG use *masse* throughout) as a molarized aggregate with a leader and a group of hierarchized followers, each of whom is a paranoid subject who strives to be protected in the middle, to be average and normal. The edges of the crowd-mass are zones of vulnerability because they are subject to the packs [*meutes*] that prowl the borders between multiplicities. Crowd-masses are highly territorial, metastable, and fixed by a matrix of meanings intelligible as law to each mass subject (33). Contemporarily, the (presumably stage-managed) appearance of crowds was crucial in the 'Battle of Baghdad' in 2003: crowds appeared in Iraq State TV's video images of Saddam Hussein in public, while other assemblages called them into being in order to welcome the triumphal entry of foreign troops, to pull down statues of the despot, and so on. (In that last-named production, however, it was a single GI who covered the face of the despot with the American flag, thereby effecting the replacement of one icon by another.) However, DG will develop their own notion of mass as a molecular aggregate that flows (that flees molar norms), and hence is opposed to molarized classes and to 'crowds' (213–14). See also Politics.

MATERIAL [*matériau*]: 'molecularized' matter that displays traits linked to forces (capacities of self-ordering) (342–5). In other words, material is matter moved from equilibrium/steady state/stability to a far-from-equilibrium 'intensive crisis' state and thereby able to manifest the effects of virtual singularities as it crosses thresholds (or, indeed, in certain cases, to release a new set of singularities, new patterns and thresholds of behavior). Material is the object of artisans, who 'track' traits in order to map singularities to actualize effects of virtual attractors and bifurcators linked in the machinic phylum.

MATERIALISM: the ontological position held by DG, who claim that all production must ultimately be thought in immanent terms, either in the case of self-organizing bodies and assemblages, or when such a previously self-organized body becomes the organizing (overcoding) agent of a stratification process, so that it is transcendent with regard to the content (but still immanent to the entire production process of the world). DG's materialism is critical because it does not use the properties of actual strata or of intensive assemblages to predict the structure of the virtual multiplicities that subtend those strata or assemblages and the processes that gave rise to them. While materialism is often contrasted with idealism, the foil for DG's materialism is dualism, specifically a spiritualist dualism. Spiritualist dualisms have, because of an impoverished concept of matter as chaotic or passive, too hastily had recourse to a hylomorphic schema in which an organized transcendent agent is responsible for all production. The problem is how to account for the ordered and creative nature of bodies and assemblages, for, if matter is chaotic, it can't account for order, but, if it's passive, it can't account for creativity. DG's materialism avoids the 'forced choice' of matter's chaos or spirit's transcendent ordering by calling attention to the self-ordering potentials of material systems themselves, as outlined in the researches of complexity theory. DG can thus account for order and creativity in the world without the heavy ontological price of a dualism or the unacceptable phenomenal price of the denial of creativity as illusory, as in 'God's eye view' spiritualist transcendent determinism. Now since DG's materialism is not deterministic, they can also avoid any 'vitalism': life is not a mysterious element, but a property of certain material systems.

MATTER [*matière*]: DG have an analytic as well as an ontological sense of 'matter'. Analytically, matter is any input to a production process. Ontologically, all matter is 'alive', that is, endowed with self-ordering capabilities, but these capacities are hidden at 'equilibrium' (395) and after homogenization, so that such matter seems merely to receive passively a form in a hylomorphic schema. In such accounts of production, matter is chaotic (and hence cannot account for the order of bodies) or passive (a matter tamed by the laws of God or deterministic science and hence unable to account for the creativity seen in the genesis of new forms of bodies: the famous controversy over the alleged conflict of evolution and the second law of thermodynamics is a result of this thought pattern). Outside the homogenized and 'equilibrium'/steady state/stable condition, however, matter is a material endowed with (self-organizing and potentially creative) forces, and hence amenable to a 'following' by artisans that links its traits and singularities.

111

MECHANOSPHERE: the plane of consistency considered in its machinic aspect, that is, as a set of abstract machines enabling emergent effects within and among multiplicities, when those abstract machines are effectuated by machinic assemblages (252; 514).

MEMORY: DG distinguish two types of memory (15–16; see also 291–8). Short-term memory is rhizomatic, because it has not yet been sorted, classified, and stored. Recent events have not yet been accorded a valence or a decidability in some cases; in others, they consist of the bank of mutable solutions to problems where long-term memory cannot be an aid. Short-term memory is a sort of transshipment warehouse for the contorted, non-linear events that occur in the life of a body or assemblage. With distance and decidability attained (or when the body, even if unsatisfied, has resigned itself to an answer or been forced to decide), short-term memory morphs into long-term memory, which is arborescent and centralized, fixed and self-evident. 'Civilization' and 'Race' both thrive only on long-term memory; indeed, notable events are immediately classified by gatekeepers for their importance in terms of position on the tree-hierarchy; they are ranked, sorted, and filed, crystallized so fast these days that by the time historians reach critical distance, everything that didn't fit has already been left out. Short-term memory is the bank of schizophrenia; long-term memory the black hole of paranoia. See also Arborescence, Brain, Epistemology, Thought.

MESSIAEN, Olivier. French composer (1908–92). Messiaen is famous for his painstaking work in copying down bird song and transforming it into instrumental music. To formulate their key concept of the refrain and of rhythmic and melodic landscapes, DG drew from published interviews with Messiaen (548n11).

METALLURGY: prime example of a minor science because it works with traits betraying self-organizing processes of material. In other words, metallurgy brings to our awareness the life or creativity of matter when pushed into far-from-equilibrium intensive crisis states; it is a 'phenomenology of matter' (411). In metallurgy, the operations of artisans are always 'astride' thresholds of self-organization, and thus operate beyond the form–matter distinction: 'an energetic materiality overspills the prepared matter, and a qualitative deformation or transformation overspills the form' (410). In this way, 'metal and metallurgy bring to light a life proper to matter . . . the prodigious idea of *Nonorganic Life*' (411; italics in original). See also Holey Space, Machinic Phylum.

METAPHOR: DG deny vigorously and repeatedly that their work is metaphorical. By this they mean that their work is not dependent upon semantic effects caused by a transfer of a term from a literal to a figurative sense. In a Platonist scheme, metaphor is the transfer from meanings sedimented in language in the order of discovery (instances, copies) to those later discovered but prior in the order of being (forms). Thus the 'sense' of metaphor ('sense' here means 'direction': the French *sens*, like the German *Sinn*, retains the 'sense' of 'direction' among its 'meanings' [see Protevi 1994 and 1998]) is the transfer of sense (meaning) in a direction moving from sensible (first in the order of discovery) to intelligible (first in the order of being). When DG show that different actual or intensive registers of concrete strata or assemblages are grounded in an identical virtual abstract machine they are not relying on linguistic effects, but are undertaking an ontological demonstration of 'divergent actualization' or 'differenciation'.

MICROFASCISM. See Fascism.

MICROPOLITICS. See Politics.

MILIEU: the material field in which strata and assemblages are formed (49–52). A milieu is the 'soup' or the coded medium of particles-flows and the strata that gives birth to or at least supports a rhizomatic assemblage: a living being, a symbiont, or an ecosystem, for example. Milieus are drawn, with rhythms, from chaos; chaos (as entropy), with its 'ecstasies', still subsists as rhythm-chaos, the 'chaosmos', between milieus that themselves shift and change (313–14). Milieus are far from homogeneous (and far-from-equilibrium), and DG identify a typology, as follows:

> Every milieu is vibratory . . . a block of space-time constituted by the periodic repetition of the component. Thus the living thing has an exterior milieu of materials, an interior milieu of composing elements and composed substances, an intermediary milieu of membranes and limits, and an annexed [also 'associated'] milieu of energy sources and actions-perceptions. (313)

The human body's exterior milieu is the total of all materials accessible to it; its interior milieu is its organ systems; its intermediary milieu is the shell that surrounds it: the physical skin but also the various semiotic barriers by which the individual conceives of its 'I-ness' or individual identity. Its annexed or associated milieu is the materials that are useful or in use (clothes, food, speech, and so on) as well as the sources and source regions of those materials: the English language, such-and-such religion, the town in which one lives, and so forth.

The rhizomatic body is constantly changing milieus; indeed, territory is the living space or 'owned' space fashioned always at the intersection of milieus, carved from the milieus. Each stratum has a milieu; for example, the alloplastic stratum has the 'cerebral-nervous' milieu (64). But at the same time that 'high' characteristics such as consciousness are derived from the cerebral-nervous milieu, motility and other organism characteristics are part of the 'low': the 'prehuman soup immersing us' (64). Ultimately, the milieu of all milieus is the plane of consistency, the earth. Milieus, in geography, could be the first approximation of complex spaces, the sources for territories. DG mention markets and forests as milieus, where diverse territorialities are jumbled together; the rain forest is a milieu serving as the plane of consistency of myriad territorialities that draw from it and each other. See Figure 1.

MINOR SCIENCE: that science, employed by artisans, and operating by problematics, which is contrasted to Royal science (101–10; 361–74). Also referred to as 'ambulant', 'itinerant' (409) or 'nomad science' (361), minor science works by pushing systems to their intensive states in order to follow traits (indications of 'forces', that is, singularities or self-ordering capacities) in material to reveal their virtual structures or multiplicities (406). Examples of minor science given in *ATP* are metallurgy (404–15), hydrodynamics (363), and masonry (364–5). Minor science hence works by attending to material and forces rather than the matter and form couple of hylomorphism (364). See also Epistemology, Machinic Phylum, Problematics.

MOLAR: the technical scientific sense of 'mole' derives from chemistry, specifically from Avogadro's number, 6×10^{23}, the number of atoms in one gram of hydrogen. A 'mole' always contains this same number of particles, no matter the volume it takes up at any one combination of temperature and pressure values. The molar is 'the characteristic order of magnitude of the number of parti-

cles forming systems governed by the laws of classical thermodynamics' (Prigogine and Stengers 1984: 121n). And it is with equilibrium thermodynamics systems that the immense numbers
involved license the use of statistical measures so that non-average
fluctuations can be ignored as they are quickly 'damped out'.

DG's use of 'molar' (and its counterpart 'molecular') in *AO*
does not refer to the size of the particles, as if 'small' particles were
'molecular' and large ones were 'molar'. Rather, the distinction is
between different modes of order of a field or 'population' of particles of any size. Nor is the distinction necessarily that of 'individuals' (or 'local people') as 'molecular' and groups (or 'the
global') as 'molar', because what is seen as an individual at one
level of analysis can always be broken down into a population of
particles at another level of analysis. Rather, DG's use of 'molar'
refers to the ability to focus only on average behaviors in a field.
Thus, a field would be a 'molar individual' if it is organized with
reference to a standard or norm, so that the elements can be
ranked in terms of deviation from the norm and the field can be
seen to form a 'whole'. By contrast, a field would be said to be a
'molecular mass' if its order depended solely on local actions with
no reference to a center, standard, or norm. (We must distinguish
'order' and 'organization', since the critique of the term 'organism' [= body made into or seen as a centered, hierarchical whole]
depends on there being non-organismic, that is, non-centered,
forms of organic and social order.) A molar organization thus
requires the use of statistical analyses of large numbers of elements with regard to a norm. Further, DG assume that molar individuals have a 'becoming-molecular' (deterritorialization) that
must be constantly reined in by 'molarizing' or 'normalizing'
forces. 'Molarizing' social forces (in Foucault's terms, disciplinary
normalization) are thus those that want to treat people as
members of large groups and so measure behavior with reference
to the statistically derived norms of that group. A tax audit is a
perfect example: when one's deduction pattern sufficiently devi-
ates from what is expected for one's income group, then one must
justify such deviation. Furthermore, knowing in advance of the
possibility of such an audit increases the probability that members
of the population will behave normally.

ATP largely follows the *AO* treatment of molar and molecular,
but also correlates the molar–molecular distinction with that
between strata and consistencies. For example, the overcoding
'pincer' or second 'articulation' of stratification processes on the

inorganic stratum produces expression as the amplification of molecular processes of the content to a molar scale (41). This is another way of saying that equilibrium/steady state/stable systems are amenable to treatment by the assumption of homogeneous states and the average behavior of large numbers of particles. In the discussion of consistency, DG make it clear that the molar–molecular distinction is not that 'between the individual and the statistical' but that between types of order of populations of particles: 'the distinction is between two group movements . . . [1] toward increasingly equilibrated, homogeneous, and probable states [that is, molarization] . . . [2] toward less probable states [that is, molecularization]' (335).

MOLECULAR: the behavior of aggregates in far-from-equilibrium intensive crisis conditions, and operating solely by local action, in which the non-average behavior of particles must be taken into account because they may trigger significant, qualitative change in system behavior (335). In complexity theory terms, what DG call a 'molecularized' system is one in which chance fluctuations can move the system to a new attractor (what DG call 'relative deterritorialization') or even prompt the release of a new set of attractors and bifurcators ('absolute deterritorialization'). Molecularized matter is material, free to express creativity (345). Hence the 'imbrication of the semiotic and the material', where systems can 'sense' approaching thresholds, occurs in molecularized populations, that is, in assemblages displaying consistency (337). Because of the ability for the rare and non-normal, the deviant, to influence system behavior, it is only in molecular populations that becomings are possible (275). In the Olancho case study, human populations are highly molecularized due to the far-from-equilibrium, entangled nature of their landscape and semiotics; thus, their becomings are continually in process.

MOVEMENT: each of the ontological registers of actual, intensive, and virtual has a sense of 'movement'. Actuality: movement as the extensive characteristic of a unitary ('molarized') body shifting from point to point in striated space and hence an object grasped by the perception of an actual subject (381). Intensity: movement in the actual sense is contrasted to (intensive) speed (and slowness), the characteristics of molecular bodies in smooth space (381). Virtuality: DG differentiate extensive or actual movement from movement as virtual becoming or 'pure relations of speed

116

and slowness' (281). Finally, there is a sense of 'matter in movement' that is 'astride' the intensive and virtual: metallurgical operations (that push matter far-from-equilibrium into 'crisis' so that intensive states cross thresholds of self-organization) limn the machinic phylum, revealing matter (now converted into 'material') as a conveyor of (virtual) singularities arrayed in continuous variation (409).

MULTIPLICITY: the multiple treated in itself, as a substantive rather than as the attribute of a substance (8). On the plane of consistency, multiplicities are the virtual patterns and thresholds of systems, defined by singularities and laid out in diagrams by an abstract machine. An intensive multiplicity is an assemblage or complex system that cannot change past thresholds of intensity of flows (its speed and slowness) without a qualitative change in system behavior, that is, a 'becoming' (8). A multiplicity can be unified only by an overcoding process, which imposes upon the dimensions of the multiplicity a transcendent organizing 'metric' (8–9). A multiplicity is hence defined by its lines of flight or thresholds where qualitative change in the system will occur (9). Riemann and Bergson are said to have made contributions to the 'theory of multiplicities', Riemann in his theory of n-dimensional manifolds and Bergson with the distinction between intensive and extensive multiplicities; these concepts are then included in the concepts of smooth and striated space (482–6). Packs, becomings, rhizomes, and symbioses are multiplicities (248–52). (See DeLanda 2002 for extended analyses of Deleuze's notion of multiplicity.)

MUSIC: the French composers Olivier Messiaen and Pierre Boulez are major sources for the concepts of space in *ATP*. In the 'Refrain' plateau, DG extend music to the level of milieus and rhythms, tying it to transhuman expressions of territoriality and powers of deterritorialization, particularly through examples of bird song. Music, in a broader sense, is characterized by refrains that saturate not only the human stratum but also forests, deserts, courtship assemblages, and so forth.

NATION: the reterritorialization operated by the modern State on the deterritorialized territory, the 'land', and the decoded population, the 'people'. The nation is thus the operation of a 'collective subjectification' to which the State 'corresponds as a process of subjection' (456).

NOMAD SCIENCE. See Minor Science.

NOMAD SOCIETY: a social formation dedicated to maintaining its immanent relations in an intensive, far-from-equilibrium crisis state, as opposed to the desire of sedentary State societies to become stratified and stable systems. 'Nomadism' is also the name of a virtual singularity for the 'vector' or inhabitant of smooth space, the war machine, which shows up in many social registers: 'thinking, loving, dying or creating machines' (356). In this virtual sense, 'nomads' are said to have reterritorialized on deterritorialization itself (381), so that the 'nomad' is a name for absolute deterritorialization (384).

Nomad societies are organized by countersignifying regimes of signs or intensive numeration. Such organization prevents coding of territorial assemblages as well as the overcoding of the State by maintaining internal tension and power struggles (392). Note that the pure social formation of nomad society is an abstraction: 'the elements of nomadism . . . enter into de facto mixes with elements of migration, itinerancy, and transhumance' (420; see Miller 1993 and 1998 for a critical review of DG's use of anthropological sources regarding nomadism). The plateau of highest intensity for the nomad war machine (1227: the nomads of central Asia) had more recent analogues in the State-unfriendly mounted nomads of the Sahara (for example, the Tuareg and Tubu) up until quite recently, and to the North American Great Plains horse cultures up through the 1800s CE. DG utilize numerous accounts of nomadic societies and their war machines as these once related to States, to miners and black-smiths (holey space), to farmers, and to the smooth spaces that they themselves occupied. They use nomads to overturn and oppose the Western concept of settlement – of stasis in general – as the ideal to strive for. They oppose evolutionism to show that nomads (like 'primitives') always existed in relationship to settle-ments and to States (discussed, for example, by Ibn Khaldun). They distinguish nomads, who by their *nomos* (pastoral flock-distributing) occupation hold smooth spaces, not only from settled peoples and static spatial patterns but also from other types of movers: transhumants, itinerants, and migrants. (Trans-humants move back and forth, between points, while itinerants are wanderers who follow metallurgical matter-flows [409–10]; migrants leave areas subject to desertification in order actively to seek a new home territory [381].) In the contemporary world, there are numerous and growing mobile societies and semiotics, but no social formation traces that of the Steppe nomads strictly speaking, given that States have overcoded all terrestrial spaces in the world. Thus, the sites of creative activity outside the State appear now to be in the realm of holey space. While there is, in other words, no possibility of reproducing the nomad – a smooth space will not save us (500) – tunneling of all types – and the rhizome does this of course – holds great potential.

NOMADIC ESSENCE. See Essence.

NOMADOLOGY: the geography, geohistory, or logos of the rhizome and war machine, as opposed to history, the logos of the State: 'nomads have no history; they only have a geography' (393).

NOOLOGY: the study of images of thought. See Epistemology, Thought.

ONTOLOGY: the philosophical study of being. Deleuze and Guattari can be said to have a 'process ontology', which means they emphasize 'becoming' rather than 'being' (when the latter is thought of as enduring presence). As materialists, DG's ontology is dedicated to immanence rather than transcendence, and is hence a monism rather than a dualism. This commitment to an ontological monism might seem odd to readers of *ATP* who constantly discover binary distinctions (smooth space and striated space; nomadic and sedentary peoples; rhizome and tree; war machine and State apparatus; and many others). Such distinctions are merely heuristic, however:

> [W]e invoke one dualism only in order to challenge another . . . Each time, mental correctives are necessary to undo the dualisms we had no wish to construct but through which we pass. Arrive at the magic formula we all seek – PLURALISM = MONISM – via all the dualisms that are the enemy, an entirely necessary enemy, the furniture we are forever rearranging. (20–1)

We follow DeLanda in detailing three aspects of Deleuze's ontology: actual, intensive, and virtual. DG distinguish hierarchical and homogenizing strata (actual), consistent and heterogeneity-preserving assemblages (intensive), and the plane of consistency (the virtual field composed of diagrams or abstract machines that lay out the field of potential interactions with other things for a stratified body or intensive assemblage). Deleuze picks up the actual–virtual distinction from Bergson, and places it at the center of his ontology in *DR*. There, 'differentiation' names the process of creating new connections in the virtual realm and 'differenciation' is the process of differing that is the 'incarnation' or 'divergent actualization' of the virtual in the actual (for example, *DR*: 207).

OPERATION: an act performed by an artisan to actualize a singularity (406).

ORDER-WORD [*mot d'ordre*]: the 'elementary unit of language [*langage*]' (76), the order-word is a trigger of incorporeal transformation (79). Language is therefore not oriented to representation, but to experimentation or practical effect; order-words are assembled in a regime of signs, and intervene in bodies, as expression directing content in an assemblage: 'expressions or expresseds are inserted into or intervene in contents, not to represent them but to anticipate them or move them back, slow them down or speed them up, separate or combine them, delimit them in a different way' (86). Order-words belong to the genre of signs but are not equivalent to signifiers: 'Signs are at work in things themselves [*les signes travaillent les choses elles-mêmes*]' (87).

ORGAN: a term mostly associated with *AO*, an organ is a 'desiring-machine', that is, an emitter and breaker of flows, of which part is siphoned off to flow in the economy of the body. Organs are a body's way of negotiating with the exterior milieu, appropriating and regulating a bit of matter–energy flow. In psychoanalytic terms, organs are 'partial objects' not connected to a person, mere points of intensity of matter–energy. See also Body without Organs.

ORGANISM: a centralized, hierarchized, self-directed body, the 'judgment of God' (he who provides the model of such self-sufficiency), a molarized and stratified life form. The organism is an emergent effect of organizing organs in a particular way, a 'One' added to the multiplicity of organs in a 'supplementary dimension' (21; 265). The organism is the unifying emergent effect of interlocking homeostatic mechanisms that quickly compensate for any non-average fluctuations (below certain thresholds, of course) to return a body to its 'normal' condition (as measured by species-

wide norms; hence DG's sense of 'molar'). The organism as unifying emergent effect is a stratum on the Body without Organs
(BwO), 'a phenomenon of accumulation, coagulation, and sedimentation that, in order to extract useful labor from the BwO,
imposes upon it forms, functions, bonds, dominant and hierarchized organizations, organized transcendences' (159). The organism is hence a construction, a certain selection from the virtual
multiplicity of what a body can be, and hence a constraint imposed
on the BwO: 'The BwO howls: "They've made me an organism!
They've wrongfully folded me! They've stolen my body!"' (159).

While all actual or intensive bodies are 'ordered', that is,
contain some probability structure to the passage of flows among
their organs (only the virtual BwO, at 'intensity = 0', has removed
all patterning among its organs), the organism is 'organized',
that is, its habitual connections are centralized and hierarchical.
The organs of an organism are patterned by 'exclusive disjunctions', that is, series of virtual singularities actualized in such a
way as to preclude the actualization of other, alternative, patterns;
in complexity theory terms, an organism is locked into a basin of
attraction, or stereotyped set of such basins. As such a fixed habitual pattern locked onto normal functioning as determined by
species-wide average values, the organism deadens the creativity
of life; it is 'that which life sets against itself in order to limit itself'
(503). Like all stratification, however, the organism has a certain
value: 'staying stratified – organized, signified, subjected – is not
the worst that can happen' (161), although this utility is primarily as a resting point for further experimentation.

Constructing an organism out of a body (centralizing or
'molarizing' the body) is one of the three principal strata separating humans from the plane of consistency (along with signifiance and subjectivity). As a stratum, we can use the terminology
of form–substance and content–expression with regard to organisms, though we must remember that on the organic stratum,
content and expression must be specified at many different
scales: genes and proteins, cells, tissues, organs, systems, organism, reproductive community, species, biosphere. DG's discussion (for example, 42; 59) is often conducted in terms of
molecular and molar, but this is not very helpful if scale is not
specified first. At the level of genes and proteins, then, the substance of content, the materials drawn from the 'pre-biotic soup'
as substratum, are amino acids, and the form of content or
coding of these acids are amino acid sequences or proteins.

Expression, as we recall, is the putting of content to work, so the form of expression at this scale is composed of nucleotide base sequences, which specify amino acids, while the substance of expression, the emergent functional unit, is the gene, which determines protein shape and function. (Note that in this treatment we are overlooking the DNA/RNA relation, the dependence of genes on cellular metabolism, and the role of genes in intervening in the self-organizing processes of morphogenesis.) Skipping over several scales (cell, tissue, organ) for simplicity's sake, we arrive at the level of organic systems (for example, the nervous, endocrine, and digestive systems), where the substance of content is composed of organs and the form of content is coding or regulation of flows within the body and between the body and the outside. The form of expression at this level is homeostatic regulation (overcoding of the regulation of flows provided by organs), while the substance of expression, the highest level emergent unifying effect, is the organism, conceived as a process binding the functions of a body into a whole through coordination of multiple systems of homeostatic regulation.

OVERCODING [*surcodage*]: the overriding of heterogeneous codes in order to produce a unified substance, hence the operation of the 'form of expression' in the second articulation of a stratification process. 'Although the first articulation [that is, content] is not lacking in systematic interactions, it is in the second articulation [that is, expression] that phenomena constituting an overcoding are produced, phenomena of centering, unification, totalization, integration, hierarchization, and finalization' (41). In the inorganic strata, overcoding produces molar aggregates, while, in the organic strata, the overcoding of organs produces an organism, and, in the alloplastic strata, the overcoding of territorial societies produces a State. See also Signifying Regime.

PARASTRATA: sets of affects on the organic stratum produced by processes of coding and decoding. Parastrata enable the construction of assemblages linking an organism to 'associated milieus' allowing for 'respiration' or capture of energy sources, 'perception' or discernment of materials, and 'reaction' or fabrication of compounds (51). Such associated milieus are closely related to organic forms (the distribution of traits in a population) and react upon margins of decoding in the organism (54–5). See also Ecumenon, Epistrata, Strata.

PARTICLE-SIGN: released on the plane of consistency, particle-signs are prior to the distinction of content and expression (70); they are thus instantiated in the 'imbrication of the semiotic and the material' brought about by consistent assemblages (337).

PERCEPTION: (1) the subjective faculty of grasping the extensive movement of a unitary, molar body shifting from point to point in striated space; such a moving body is hence an (actual) object grasped by the perception of an actual subject (280–1). (2) The intensive faculty of sensing a becoming (281–2). Intensive movement or becoming has a seemingly paradoxical relation to perception. On the plane of transcendence, movement qua becoming is imperceptible, always above and below the threshold of perception as the capacity of an (actual) subject grasping the (extensive) movement of an (actual) object (281). In other words, the actual psychological faculty of perception as that which is attuned to actual objects with fixed properties can never grasp an intensive becoming. Once one has quit the plane of transcendence or organization, though, that is, once one has quit focusing on actual, fixed substances, and attained the plane of immanence or consistency, intensive movement or becoming is precisely what is perceived with an intensive, immanent, molecular faculty performing 'a whole rhizomatic labor of perception' (281–3). The changed perception available by the careful attainment of the plane of consistency through practices of destratification is only imitated and often botched by the careless use of drugs (282–6).

PLACE [*lieu*]: although DG do not have a technical discussion of place, the concept of place as a site of concentration or coagulation of forces, a stopping-point along a trajectory, or the event of emergence of a haecceity when it is tied to a location is present in *ATP*. In any hierarchical system – that of the State, for example – places are primarily fixed locations predetermined and overcoded by forces of striation. Thus, places are assigned qualities and roles, and fix reality: the temple, the house, the village. Movement is only possible *between* places. In smooth space, by contrast, places are mere points that may shift and change as intensive relations of elements of an environmental haecceity change (262). Places in smooth space arise from the crossing of nomad trajectories or the shifting of sand and vegetation, and so forth (381–2).

In the 'Refrain' plateau DG also discuss the 'deeper' power of places, in particular sacred places, following the descriptions of Mircea Eliade (1996) and others. Here, they see sacred places as barely veiled stratified sites covering over entangled knots of (intensive) earthly and (virtual) cosmic forces into which humans believe themselves capable of tapping (321). Places of this nature are necessarily centers for pilgrimage, and escape the grasp of specific State claims to them as territory (we would cite the case of the Temple Mount/Dome of the Rock in Jerusalem as well as the Ayodhya Hindu/Muslim temple/mosque conflict in Gujarat) that can be owned and parceled out. This then allows the absolute – the deterritorialized, the power of the creation of being, and so forth – to have an abode, or at least a site whence it can be called forth. No coincidence, then, that intensely sacred places have great importance in presignifying and signifying regimes; in the latter, they are segmented and are not allowed to resonate (hence 'primitive' societies do not impart world religions) whereas in State religions just the opposite occurs. Meanwhile, sacred places have little to no meaning in smooth space. There is, of course, a rich literature on sacred places in geography.

PLANE OF CONSISTENCY [*plan de consistance*]: an immanent field enabling exchanges between multiplicities in either the virtual or intensive registers. Constructing a plane of consistency requires overcoming habitual patterns or hierarchizing agents (in other words, it is constructed by deterritorialization or destratification), in order to enable the formation of heterogeneity-preserving emergent structures ('consistencies'). In other words, a plane of consistency is a field of experimentation for constructing immanent and horizontal relationships: 'rhizomes', 'war machines', and so on.

In the virtual register, the plane of consistency is a 'rhizomatic realm of possibility effecting the potentialization of the possible' (190), an immanent virtual field subtending morphogenetic processes ('machinic assemblages') and enabling the production of, and transverse communication among, bodies and assemblages. Since multiplicities are composed of series of singularities (laid out by 'abstract machines' that join unformed matters and non-formal functions to mark off the patterns and thresholds of material systems), the 'possibilities' of actualizing assemblages are 'potentialized': a machinic assemblage must be able to push a system past a threshold to trigger a singularity or process of self-organization.

Now since each process of relative destratification/deterritorialization draws a (relative) plane of consistency, there are many intensive planes of consistency reached by relative destratification/deterritorialization. THE (virtual) plane of consistency, or the plane of all the relative planes, in contrast, is reached by absolute deterritorialization. While intensive assemblages meet on the various relative planes of consistency, virtual multiplicities are the 'matter' of the virtual plane of consistency (72). A plane of consistency (or THE plane) is always 'flat', that is, possesses only the number of dimensions of the assemblages or multiplicities that inhabit it, thus ensuring the necessity of immanent (ethical) experimentation and evaluation (266; 509). The flatness or immanence of the plane of consistency is opposed to the (moral) judgments enabled by recourse to a transcendent 'plan(e) of organization' (265).

A variety of things is 'inscribed' on the virtual plane of consistency: (1) haecceities or events, that is, 'incorporeal transformations apprehended in themselves'; (2) nomadic essences, which are 'vague yet rigorous'; (3) continuums of intensities, or 'continuous variations' [machinic phyla]; (4) becomings; and (5) smooth spaces (507). As such, the virtual plane of consistency is the arena of 'nonorganic life' or creativity (507), as well as the arena for ethical selection: 'what is retained and preserved, therefore created, what consists, is only *that which increases the number of connections* at each level of division or composition' (508; italics in original).

DG seem also to relate the plane of consistency to the concepts of quantum mechanics as the following quotes reveal: 'the unformed, unorganized, nonstratified or destratified body and all its flows: subatomic and submolecular particles, pure intensities, prevital and prephysical free singularities' (43).

> There is no doubt that mad physical particles crash through the strata as they accelerate, leaving minimal traces of their passage, escaping spatiotemporal and even existential coordinates as they tend toward a state of absolute deterritorialization, the state of unformed matter on the plane of consistency. (55–6)

See Murphy (1998) for a reading of DG in relation to Bohm's realist quantum mechanics. See also Body without Organs, Cosmos, Earth. See Figure 1.

PLAN(E) OF ORGANIZATION [*plan d'organisation*]: Massumi adopts this typological convention to bring forth the secondary meanings of the French word *plan*: beyond the geometrical 'plane' (the primary sense of 'plane of consistency' above), there are the senses of 'plan' (for a project), 'blueprint' (for a building or machine), or 'map'. In common French usage, a large-scale map of a city is a *plan*, as opposed to the *carte* of a neighborhood posted outside a subway station. This sense of 'map' [*plan*] as a finished product that merely reproduces the actual or extensive properties of the city, is closer to 'tracing' than it would be to the processes of 'cartography' (laying out the longitude and latitude of an intensive body) or 'diagrammatics' (laying out, by an 'abstract machine', the virtual singularities subtending intensive morphogenetic processes). These secondary senses of *plan* are included in 'plan(e) of organization', which is that transcendent plan/blueprint/tracing by which one produces goals of perfect development which form the pre-established standard to which things are submitted in judgment and ordered by the forms of representation: identity, analogy, opposition, and resemblance. Subjectivity as the centralization and command of affect is thus the product of a plan(e) of organization (265). Insofar as the plan(e) of organization imposes a pre-established standard it is always in a 'supplementary dimension' with regard to its products, as opposed to the 'flat' plane of consistency, which possesses only as many dimensions as the multiplicities 'drawn' on it (9; 266). See also Immanence, Transcendence.

PLANOMENON: the abstract machine on the plane of consistency, and so opposed to ecumenon, the abstract machine on a stratum (50).

PLATEAU: a 'region of intensities' without reference to a transcendent goal. DG offer their own clear definition of the term: 'A rhizome is made of plateaus. Gregory Bateson [1999] uses the word "plateau" to designate . . . a continuous, self-vibrating region of intensities whose development avoids any orientation toward a culmination point or external end' (21–2). (Bateson's example is a Balinese approach to sexuality that avoids climax.) See also Rhizome.

POINT: the relation of point to line changes relative to the manner of forming space one adopts. In the most general terms, the point is the origin of a line, according to arborescence, which thereby enforces a submission of line to point (293); by contrast, there are no points, only lines in a rhizome (8). In terms of social formations, a migrant moves from point to point, while, for a nomad, a point is only a relay along a trajectory (380). In 'psychological' terms, the origin of a 'mental reality' or relative line of flight in the passional or post-signifying regime of signs is the 'point of subjectivation' (129). In epistemological terms, axiomatics block all lines and subordinate them to a punctual system (143). In physical terms, a unitary body in extensive movement travels from point to point in striated space, while a nomad body possesses an intensive 'speed', so that it can 'spring up [*surgir*] at any point' in the field that it 'occupies' (381).

POLAR ICE: a type of smooth space that DG also refer to as 'ice space' or ice desert (382; 574n28) and liken to the sand desert. It is inhabited by nomads who rely on close readings of relations between environmental factors – haecceities constituted by the movement of air, the creaking of ice, the local characteristics of snow. Ice space is thus 'haptic', 'sonorous', and 'tactile' (382; the same applies to the sea, steppe, and desert) and is opposed to the 'visual space' of (for example) agropastoral landscapes.

POLITICS: the regulation of the interchange of molar segmentation and molecular flow: 'everything is political, but every politics is simultaneously a macropolitics and a micropolitics' (213). 'Everything' is meant literally here: DG mention a 'politics of science' (143); a micropolitics of the 'threshold of perceptions' at the intersection of the stratified and intensive, the perception of becomings (213; 281); political questions of hierarchical stratification and consistent assemblages are germane even in analyzing 'two tendencies of atomic matter' (335). Everywhere there are bodies politic. Now the great question of (ordinarily conceived) politics is always: underneath the molar categories of man and woman, white and black, straight and gay, right wing and left wing, what is happening? The lines of flight of molecular becoming are not captured by Marxist thinking, bound to the notion of 'contradiction' between the great molar classes of 'bourgeoisie' and 'proletariat' (216). Instead, we must think the interchange between molar class and molecular mass: classes are the 'crystallization' of masses, but masses are 'constantly flowing or leaking' from classes (213), something which always made party officials very nervous. Politicians make molarized, binary choices, but the success or failure of these moves depends on 'an evaluation of [molecular] flows and their quanta' (221), so that 'politics and its judgments are always molar, but it is the molecular and its assessment that makes it or breaks it' (222). Our everyday political language is full of biological and geological metaphors for this micro-macro relation: politicians must constantly 'keep their finger on the pulse of the public' or watch out for the little tremors that become 'seismic shifts' or the little trickles that become 'tidal waves' of 'changes in values' (216) and so forth. A whole industry of molecular focus groups grows underneath the molar polling apparatus: polls ask about stances toward molar representations ('do you approve of the President?'), while focus groups use a variety of means to look for trends in the ever shifting patterns and triggers in populations of bodies politic, such as measuring physiological reactions to how long the flag is shown in a political advertisement. Because of the way molecular flows and lines of flight are the primary constituents of social machines, 'resistance' is not a primary political category for DG, because resistance is always aimed at molar categories and power structures (530n39). This emphasis on the molecular flow of micropolitics does not, however, necessarily entail a neglect of traditional macropolitics of representation, of lobbying for axioms (462). In the vexed discussion of becoming-woman DG write: 'It is, of course, indispensable for women to conduct a molar politics, with a view to winning back their own organism, their own history, their own subjectivity', even while warning in the next breath that 'it is dangerous to confine oneself to such a subject' (276). See also Fascism.

POSTMODERNISM: this term is not used by DG. We feel it is a misapplication to call them postmodernists, if that is taken to mean a concern with slippage or excess of meaning from the free play of signifiers. If one takes modernism to be characterized by centralized and hierarchical state bureaucracies administering molar subjectivities, then DG can easily be called 'anti-modernist'. But in this case one must distinguish *AO* and *ATP*. Written in the aftermath of May 1968, *AO*'s motto is 'destroy, destroy' (*AO*: 311). Written after the beginnings of the neo-liberal revolution of the 1970s, *ATP* is much more cautious. There, DG make a provisional judgment that a bit more flow would be useful in some cases, but that a simple a priori judgment in favor of flow is just that, an a priori judgment, and hence nothing but a moralism, a too-simple 'reversal of Platonism' as nothing but a change of moral standards, rather than an immanent ethical stance 'beyond good and evil'. Rather than being postmodern moralists in favor of flow, DG in *ATP* are cautious experimentalists, always demanding careful immanent (ethical) evaluation of the life-affirming or life-destroying character of assemblages.

POSTSIGNIFYING REGIME: the semiotic of escape, of betrayal, of turning away. DG use the Mosaic account to show how the flight of the Israelites encapsulates the postsignifying pole whereby ('barbaric', imperial) rule by an absolute Sun-God was abandoned, to be replaced by an authoritarian, uniter-of-the-tribes, prophetic turning toward the One God; the Word and the Book – the arborescent text, and graphic representation in general – become the ultimate authority, replacing the Face of the despot (127). (The post signifying regime is later mixed with the signifying regime to form State Christianity and its Christ-face [176].)

The postsignifying regime is the milieu for the formation of the autonomous subject who strives for representation, who experiences love as passion (more than as filial, for example), who doubts, who is rational and conscious. Time, in the postsignifying regime, is inescapably linear and evolutionary; the signifying sign constantly flees the black hole; and it is the line of flight that charts the course of the vanguards of the postsignifying regime – missionaries, explorers, scientists, traders – who, however, serve only to anchor the striated spaces of States that follow in their wake or shadow them. The line of flight of the self-declared autonomous subject/group thus implants signifiance and subjectification in 'barbaric', 'primitive', and nomadic societies and spaces. In 2003 we observed the implanting of the mixed signifying/postsignifying regime in Iraq, as a 'war of liberation' was waged to depose a Despot who by the US account reigned over a paranoid landscape saturated by his own face. Iraq was liberated from the Despot, only in order to be occupied by a much more powerful State apparatus aiming to grant it 'freedom and democracy' and thereby install it fully within the global smooth space of capital and security from which the post-1991 sanctions and Baathist party social infrastructure (centralized, hierarchical, 'modernist') had isolated it.

POWER (*pouvoir*): transcendent form-imposing or overcoding ability. Power as *pouvoir* is that which forms organisms, or strata more generally, and sets goals by limiting the possible directions of flows in pre-determined patterns. Power centers inhabit the intersection of molar segmented lines and molecular flows and regulate their interchange (224–7).

POWER (*puissance*): the ability of a material system to form new affects, that is, to exercise the creativity inherent in life (256).

PRAGMATICS: in the 'Postulates of Linguistics' plateau, the name for DG's language philosophy. A pragmatic treatment of language sees order-words as triggers of material production. In the 'Regimes of Signs' plateau, four components of pragmatics are laid out: generative, transformational, diagrammatic, and machinic (145–6). See Regime of Signs.

PRESIGNIFYING REGIME: the semiotic of the 'primitive' or territorial society that is directly indexed to the earth and to the non-human – or at least, more so than the other regimes DG discuss. (The presignifying regime is detailed in *AO*; a mere sketch of it is given at *ATP*: 117–18.) This semiotic is pluralistic and polyvocal and cannot be conquered by the signifier. Words and speech form only part of the weave of presignifying signs; 'body language' is important because signs are emitted corporeally (the face is blocked, trivialized, masked, or discarded) through tattooing, scarification, painting, and dance. Communication includes the non-human as well as the human (animals and plants speak). Signs do not attain the power of signification and circulate only jerkily, thus not falling into the trap of self-evident meaning that is applicable in all places and at all times in the signifying regime. Names can be eaten; statements can be used up and discarded.

The State is able to effect the resonation of presignifying spaces, to overcode them, and also to obliterate them, which can to some extent be done by effacing the presignifying landscape and peopling it with signifying icons. Probably the very fact that the presignifying regime indexes clans directly to the earth and contains numerous sacred places that serve as conduits from the plane of consistency to the strata means that no amount of erasure of physical terrain features can do away entirely with this semiotic. In the case of the Americas post-1492, a common tactic was the cooption of sacred places by the postsignifying friars (vanguard of the signifying regime), such that 'primitive' people were 'swindled' into going to church because it was built on top of the sacred. The Christ-face and the Virgin stared back at them; Christianity became syncretized; and the presignifying regime went to lurk as an intensive territory coiled up within the obvious, extensive landscapes of the West.

PRIMITIVE SOCIETY: DG derive their discussion of 'primitive' (*AO*: 'savage') society and the presignifying regime of signs from ethnological accounts of Clastres, Lévi-Strauss, Mauss, Leroi-Gourhan, and others (see Miller [1993 and 1998] for a critical account of DG's use of anthropology). Primitive society is not facialized, but rather corporeal, and bodies are indexed directly to the earth; semiotics are inscribed directly onto the earth in 'a kind of geodesy' (388). Black holes are everywhere, but they do not resonate; indeed, the entire 'project' of primitive societies is to prevent accumulation (via anti-productive practices such as the potlatch) and prevent striation from without, even while they are highly segmented and striated internally (440). The primary mechanism for maintaining the 'anti-State' of Clastres's 'society against the State' (1987) is through the opposition of tribal territory and clan lineage. Primitive societies are outside States which they anticipate in warding off (hence 'presignifying' is a misnomer if the 'pre-' is taken developmentally) and DG represent them as agriculturalists, in rhizomatic relationship with the forests, and as enemies of the nomads. According to DG's formula, primitive societies have always been constituted in relationship to States even as they fend them off; by their capture, they give birth to the State as extended land. *ATP* takes the non-evolutionary, complex mutualistic approach of 'geohistory' (*WP*: 95) to replace any idea that the primitive is a 'stage' of evolution or development. 'Primitive' swidden (slash-and-burn) agriculture, mixed with gathering and hunting and fishing lifeways, mixed in some areas with pastoralism, side-by-side with States or within them: this entanglement has characterized at least the last 7,000 to 10,000 years of human existence.

PRIVATE PROPERTY: the idea that land can be owned privately blossoms within the striated space of the State that has already overcoded all presignifying territories, colonized all smooth spaces (destroying the nomads as well as making the desert bloom), and plugged up holey spaces as much as possible (388; 441). The State, of course, retains the absolute 'depth' of the space onto which private property is imposed, and also profits continually, through taxation (442). Private property alters radically human relationships to the earth, because the State is always the intermediary. Private property allows for faux-smooth spaces such as the 'commons' of nature reserves, wildernesses, and even city parks and roadways.

PROBLEMATICS: the opposite pole to axiomatics and Royal science, hence the procedures of minor science. At *LS*: 54 Deleuze cites Proclus as distinguishing in geometry between a problematic figure, defined by what it can do, and a theorematic figure, defined in terms of its essence. Thus in Archimedean geometry, a line is the least curvature, whereas by contrast, in Euclidean geometry (an axiomatic system) a line is the shortest distance between two points. We can call this the level of 'intensive' problematics. The field of virtual problematics is attained by the distinction between singularities in the differential vectorial field and trajectories plotted by integration (see *LS*: 104; DeLanda 2002: 71; Smith [forthcoming]).

PRODUCTION: In *ATP*, there are three schemas of production: hylomorphism, artisanal production, and what we call 'machinic production', which corresponds to the universal sense of 'desiring-production' given in *AO*. Due to the principle of critique, the properties of a product are no clue to the characteristics of the production process that gave rise to it. See also Desiring-Production.

PUBLIC SPACE: the opposing partner of private property in the dualistic configuration of the State's striated space. The concept and necessity of the public/private dualism arises as the State profits from terrain that becomes commodity, while still owning all the space it encompasses. Private property is essentially a lease, or the figure on the ground of perpetual State ownership. Where private individuals or corporations or other non-State bodies do not own land, it is seen as public space, but this is in many cases simply the most 'marginal' land (the forest, the desert, the glacier). In the case of Honduras, at Conquest presignifying territories became the domain of the King of Spain in the 1500s; as time went by, land grants (*sitios*) were awarded to private groups, towns were founded and given *ejidos*, the Church gained massive estates, and tribute-paying Indians were awarded titles. The least-accessible and least-arable land remained the property of the

King unless it was titled, all the way to 1821. Upon independence, all such land automatically became *tierra nacional* (national land, owned by the Republic) and, despite continuing land-titling to groups and individuals, much of the most mountainous and inaccessible land still retains this designation. Recently, national lands have become protected public lands (national parks and forest reserves). See also Presignfiying Regime, Territory.

REDUNDANCY: the state of being repeated. In the signifying regime of signs, redundancy takes the form of a frequency of signifiers, while in the postsignifying regime redundancy is the resonance of subjectivity (132). The face, formed at the intersection of signifiance and subjectivation, is doubly redundant (168).

REFRAIN [*ritournelle*]: this term is at the heart of DG's discussion of territory, milieu, and landscape, interwoven as these are with bird song and other musical expressions. A refrain is a 'block of content' (299) that serves as the organizing principle for a territory – that which in the territory establishes a link or bond between a body or an assemblage and the Cosmos, earth, and/or milieus. It is crafted from rhythm (horizontal axis) and melody (vertical axis), drawn from chaotic and cosmic forces, and essential to the establishment of a home or abode. Any body, possessing a refrain, can use this refrain as protection as that body wanders out on 'lines of drift' (312): the refrain becomes the sonorous shell of the body, and accompanies it through whatever relative de- and reterritorialization it undertakes.

The basic example of the refrain is that of the territorial birds (not just Passerine 'songbirds', and not just 'songs' but also calls), that sing to mark off their territories from others of the same species, and carve them out from the milieu of the forest (for example). Avian territories are drawn and constituted by the refrain that is itself a becoming-earth of the bird. For example, to claim a soundspace, understory rain forest birds emit series of hollow hoots and other sounds that are adapted to the qualities of that space (*Formicariidae*, the New World antbirds, for example). The refrain not only creates and holds the territory, but also becomes the motif or repeatable theme of a landscape. It is portable, as mentioned above, and therefore the refrain can be carried to alien milieus that can be territorialized as it is expressed there, even as it undergoes continuous variation. The refrain is the repeated block of code that catalyzes matter,

133

summons forth a landscape and a world, and 'fabricates time', the 'a priori form of time' (349). DG use Robert Schumann (a schizophrenic) to call for the deterritorialization of the refrain 'as the final end of music, releas[ing] it into the Cosmos' (350).

Beyond music, 'the refrain may assume other functions, amorous, professional or social, liturgical or cosmic: it always carries earth with it' (312). The refrain is the 'I am' that allows the human being to think of itself as an independent consciousness (repeat: 'I am free', over and over again; repeat the mantra). The refrain can also be the territorial motif of an entire empire, essential to the spatial conquests of that empire and to the continued obedience of imperial subjects (Rule, Brittania!). Refrains are also the repeated little mottos that prop up empires, formulae muttered over and over: 'God Save the Queen'; 'weapons of mass destruction'; and so on.

REGIME OF SIGNS: a form of expression considered by itself, as a semiotic system (111). To isolate a regime of signs one must abstract the form of expression from the form of content and from the substance of expression that always accompany it and with which it forms a territorial assemblage. (Recall that a territorial assemblage is composed of a machinic assemblage of bodies [substance and form of content] and a collective assemblage of enunciation [form and substance of expression; the latter is made up of the social institutions that effectuate the incorporeal transformations of the relevant order-words making up the form of expression or regime of signs].)

Although an actual society never instantiates a pure regime of signs, DG do discuss four ideal types of regimes of signs (presignifying, signifying, postsignifying, and countersignifying); they are always careful to stress that there are many more than these four, and that they are always mixed within assemblages (119). Any system, any State, any society, and certainly any landscape will contain relatively dominant and relatively latent regimes of signs in a complex mixture that can be studied by what DG call Pragmatics or schizoanalysis (139, 145–6). 'Generative pragmatics' studies the internal structure of an actual regime, creating a 'tracing [calque]'; 'transformational pragmatics' studies the ways that regimes can change from one to another, or mix and create new regimes, creating a 'map [carte]'; 'diagrammatic pragmatics' studies the relation of unformed matters and nonformal functions in the abstract machine subtending regimes of signs, creating a 'diagram'; 'machinic pragmatics' studies the effectuation of the abstract machine of a regime of signs in machinic assemblages, creating a 'program' (146).

In the Olancho case study, we show that each space constituted by a land use assemblage (cattle ranching, for example) can be analyzed in terms of its own unique regime of signs, which contains elements of the four regimes in *ATP*, but through Pragmatics can be mapped as the semiotic proper to 'ranching space'. A possibility for materialist, problem-solving geography is to map complex spaces by way of their regimes of signs, and thereby partially to comprehend the ways that these spaces can generate territories across broad regions that can hold sway in any given landscape, relate to each other, create conflict and/or alliances, and so forth.

REPRESENTATION: the duplication or tracing in mental images of the things composing the world, or, more broadly, the doctrine that knowledge consists of such tracing. Deleuze consistently maintained a critique of the domination of representation in Western philosophy. Representation operates on the level of actual products, duplicating their extensive properties in words and arranging these properties according to the principles of identity, analogy, opposition, and resemblance (Deleuze 1995: 29). Deleuze, by contrast, prefers to investigate the intensive morphogenetic processes that give rise to these products, and the virtual multiplicities that structure those processes. The critique of representation is carried into DG's treatment of linguistics in *ATP*. An isolated word or set of words does not represent to a consciousness an isolated pre-existent thing or set of things. Rather language is composed of order-words, that is, triggers of incorporeal transformation and via them certain processes of material production in bodies and assemblages.

RESONANCE: the process of echoing (vibration) that produces amplifying effects through positive feedback loops (DeLanda 2002: 160). In inorganic strata, resonance is the amplifying communication between molecular content and molar expression such that the molar expresses the molecular interactions in their 'statistical aggregate and state of equilibrium existing on the macroscopic level' (57). In a 'passional' or postsignifying regime of signs, redundancy takes the form of a resonance of subjectivity in its black hole, that is, the self-reference of linguistic 'shifters' such as '*moi= moi*' (133). In the political-economic register, the State is a 'resonance chamber' (224, 433), as opposed to the frequency established by towns (432).

RETERRITORIALIZATION: the process of forming a new territory, following (and always together with) deterritorialization. Reterritorialization is never a return to an old territory, and even if a body similar to what was deterritorialized or fled from is reconstituted, it is not the same body, not the same State, not the same discourse, not the same species. See also Line of Flight.

RHIZOME: a decentered multiplicity or network, roughly synonymous with 'consistency' or 'war machine'. DG list six principles of a rhizome: connection (all points are immediately connectable); heterogeneity (rhizomes mingle signs and bodies); multiplicity (the rhizome is 'flat' or immanent); 'asignifying rupture' (the line of flight is a primary component, which enables heterogeneity-preserving emergence or 'consistency'); cartography (maps of emergence are necessary to follow a rhizome); and decalcomania (the rhizome is not a model like the tree, but an 'immanent process') (7–14). There can be a rhizome from which one extracts a piece and plants elsewhere; the piece is also a rhizome and continues to bud. Two multiplicities can form a rhizome with each other or become each other; this is the primordial example of the wasp and the orchid (12). 'Rhizomatics' is the study or the practice of the rhizome; the 'rhizosphere' is the zone of contact between two rhizomes, or between a tree–structure and a rhizome (DG derive it from an ecological term denoting the zone of contact of plant roots, microorganisms, and other soil elements).

The reference to the subterranean nature of the botanical rhizome is intentional in DG's use of the term, because it is meant to evoke the hidden network quality of interlinked forces that have adapted to resist the striating forces of the surface and air, and particularly the hierarchized State. Now, in all cases rhizomes are always partially hierarchized and striated, just as hierarchies (tree-structures) are partially smooth. But the essential quality of the rhizome is its 'flatness': it can never be overcoded in a dimension supplementary to its own. Its constitutive bodies or packets of particles-signs can move in novel ways from point A to point B without going through any hierarchical steps or imposed barriers. Thus, the rhizome possesses the power to emerge into striated space at any point. Also, because it has no centralized organization, it cannot be eradicated completely: it has multiple lines of flight, so escaping forces can always reestablish themselves elsewhere, and bud to form new rhizomes. The rhizome itself, as subterranean matter, is a holey space, but as such is the content for a (surface) smooth space (the smooth space is created at the tips of the buds of the rhizome, for example).

The mantra of the rhizome is 'and . . . and . . . and' without beginning or end (always interbeing, intermezzo). Examples of rhizomes are rife in *ATP*: the unconscious is a rhizome but also the river, the fire ant, kudzu, mycorrhizal fungi, gossip, sexuality, the rain forest, and, on another level, it is the milieu of things, of beings ('knots of arborescence'), the fabric weaving together plateaus. To this list we might add any 'terrorist' force with worldwide cells (the post-9/11/2001 'Al Qaeda' as it is officially portrayed, for example) that cannot be eradicated because of its decentralization. Another example is the Internet, a rhizome that allows non-hierarchical worldwide actions such as simultaneous global protests; the Internet's instantaneous communication that bypasses movement through a command structure allows flat connectivity between any two or more users in a completely decentralized community of users. In the case of the Internet, a holey space of completely mixed semiotics, the safeguards are the 'firewalls' that block 'spyware'. The Internet at present is a weakly striated rhizome that, while a force of creativity and resistance, also breaks through the walls of supple spatial segmentation and invades the privacy of every user, potentially to benefit the power of the State apparatus and certainly to benefit globalized corporations. Because an individual computer user-unit has value as a subject (as a consumer or as a suspicious character, for example), the clear alternative for the user is to erect firewalls that block flows, that filter the desired forces from the predators, spies, spammers, and other swarms that populate the Internet's 'dark space'.

RHYTHM: primordial constitutive element of milieus as they relate to the Cosmos. DG call the 'chaosmos' the interlocking relationship or space of rhythm and chaos (in this usage NOT the deterministic chaos of self-organizing systems; rather, entropy), the border zone between the two intervals in a differentiated system (the chaosmos of night and day, or of living and dying). Rhythm itself is intensive, not extensive, and it is the condition of spacing by intervals, the condition of difference, but not of repetition, which is a feature of the territorial motif. Rhythm and melody together form the refrain, which as motif (and in combination with other motifs) draws the landscape and the territory.

RIEMANNIAN SPACE: non-Euclidean space named after Bernhard Riemann (1826–66), a mathematician and student of Johann Gauss, who himself dabbled in geodesy (earth-measuring) and worked with Alexander von Humboldt; this is important in that it establishes a partially geographical lineage for non-Euclidean geometry. In the 'Smooth and Striated' plateau, DG use Riemannian space as the mathematical model for smooth space, though one certainly does not have to understand or apply non-Euclidean geometry to the earth to understand smooth space. Characteristics of Riemannian space cited by DG include its patchwork quality, its heterogeneity, and its capacity for continuous variation, all of which are characteristics of smooth space (485–6). By contrast, Euclidean geometry functions at the very basis and origin of the State, as evidence by the State's absolute need to bound a homogenized set of overcoded territories with a polygon and to crisscross it with vectors frozen into boundary lines and other lines of rigid segmentarity. See also Holey Space, Smooth Space, Striated Space.

ROYAL SCIENCE: DG base their notion of Royal science ('major science') on the positivist interpretation of classical mechanics. Royal science operates by the extraction of constants from variables of extensive properties and the formation of laws expressed in linear equations for the relation of independent and dependent variables (109; 369). Royal science has as its goal the formation of an axiomatic. See also Minor Science, Problematics.

SCHIZOANALYSIS: the study of bodies politic from a materialist (165), 'anti-Oedipal' (18) perspective: 'the body is the only practical object of schizoanalysis' (203). Schizoanalysis is equivalent to 'rhizomatics, stratoanalysis . . . nomadology, micropolitics, pragmatics, the science of multiplicities' (43). It can thus be applied to the relation of abstract machines and assemblages (513), to experimentation with rhizomes (251), and to the Body without Organs (165), its original target in *AO*.

SEA: 'the archetype of smooth space' (480), occupying a central role in the history of the State, for it was the first space to be striated during the colonization of the planet by the European powers. Indeed, without the superficial striation of the sea (via geodesy and coordinate systems), the global reach of empires would have been impossible. By contrast, the Imperial reach of Rome included the striation of the Mediterranean, but not beyond. The same could be said for the seas that surrounded imperial China; in both cases, sea power was not effectively extended across the oceans. DG's analysis of sea space draws heavily from Paul Virilio, but we can also cite the importance of Mahan (1987 [1890]) as an exemplar of the materialist approach to history; Braudel's work also includes and inspires the material history of the sea. A recent geographical work in this vein is Steinberg (2001).

Prior to striation, the sea was smooth even where it became the abode of humans, because those 'primitives' who voyaged upon it successfully (most notably and spectacularly, during the settling of Polynesia) attained detailed localized knowledge of specific qualities of the water, to the extent that location could be established by taste (salt content, for example), currents, flora and fauna, wind, and so forth (cf. 'haptic space' [382]); this was an empowering system opposed to the helplessness that Europeans felt until they developed a way to plot both longitude and latitude and (unlike Columbus) get the size of the earth right.

Such historical events as the 1588 defeat of the Spanish armada of course mark the shift or bifurcation in control over the world sea, and the eventual unquestioned British domination of the high seas only gave way finally in the twentieth century to the US. Shipping channels, chokepoints (Bab-al-Mandeb, Straits of Hormuz, Panama Canal, Gibraltar, and so on), deepwater ports, and small oceanic islands used as military bases (Diego García, Guam) are nodes in the striation of the sea, and DG also point out that the sea has to be striated to effect control of the air. Here, we see the importance of the aircraft carrier. However, the total control of the sea returns it again to a smooth space in that Virilio's 'fleet in being' is capable of acting autonomously at any point to subjugate the land more completely (480). At the same time, the holey spaces of the undersea serve, through the nuclear submarine, as the ultimate check on the land.

SEGMENTARITY: the compartmentalization of human existence, and by extension of space, achieved but controlled in the presignifying regime of the 'primitive', and rigidified in the modern State (210). Segmentarity is binary (either/or: gender, age, class,

139

place, and so on), circular (concentric rings of 'my-ness' extending from the bed to the home to the neighborhood, and outward), and linear (the striated journey in time and/or space) (208–9). Segmentarity is resisted in the countersignifying regime and in any patch of smooth space within striated space (in any space that emphasizes rhizomatic connections, boundary-crossing, and heterogeneity). Segmentarity is achieved by the drawing or following of lines that create functions for spaces and times: here you will sleep, there you will eat, over there you will defecate. The line of molecular segmentarity is supple and can be modified: one may sleep on the sofa, or drive to work on an alternate route, and probably not get into trouble. However, rigid lines of molar segmentarity achieve the overcoding and striation of society and space: here is the sidewalk for walking, there the street for driving, over there the park for (certain types of) assemblies; laws at all levels draw lines in space between what can and cannot be done. Smooth spaces of the city (cf. 'Walking in the City' in DeCerteau 1984) are attempts to erase molar segmentarity, but given that permanent buildings and street plans themselves are created by segmentation of space, achieving anything other than slight ruptures in striated space is probably not possible. More likely, one sleeps on a park bench and is arrested or ignored: 'trespassers beware!'

SEMIOTIC TRANSFORMATION: the way by which one regime of signs is deterritorialized and then reterritorialized into another, or any regime of signs or mixture is destroyed altogether (the latter case is called diagrammatic transformation, or return to the plane of consistency). Pragmatics is the study of these transformations (139–40). Examples given include: analogical transformations to the presignifying regime; symbolic transformations to the signifying regime; strategic transformations to the counter-signifying regime; and consciousness-related transformations into the postsignifying regime. For example, any presignifying piece or form of music must be transformed semiotically to be appealing to the postsignifying regime of the Western subject, to a certain extent at any rate. As it becomes an element in Western music, or is made attractive to a Westerner, it takes on unmistakable characteristics, one of which, at least in popular music, is the dominance of the line of melody over any other aspect and the dominance of the Theme over the variations and the message over the rhythm – imagine how, for example, African drumming,

Balinese temple music, Tibetan monk chant, or Tuvan throat-singing would and could be made over into 'catchy' Top-40 tunes (difficult, but not impossible, transformations, given 'Roll over, Beethoven!'). Semiotic transformations on a massive scale occurred during colonialism, and continue today through globalized media: *Baywatch* and similar US TV shows, along with Hollywood films, have done much of the work. Not to be confused with 'incorporeal transformation' effected by order-words.

SIGN: an element that triggers a material process in a properly attuned body: 'signs are at work in things themselves' [*les signes travaillent les choses elles-mêmes*]' (87). Although in *ATP* DG want to restrict 'signs' to linguistic elements (but not to signifiers: 65), Deleuze had earlier called for a notion of 'signal–sign' systems in all physical processes at the edge of self-organization (*DR*: 20; *LS*: 261; cf. DeLanda 2002: 76; 207n67). We have employed this wider sense of 'sign' in the text. Thus we interpret the 'imbrication of the semiotic and the material' characteristic of the way signs trigger material processes as not limited to human social systems, or even to organic systems, but as appearing whenever an assemblage achieves consistency (334–7). Whatever one's stance regarding the utility of using 'sign' beyond the linguistic and human registers, DG are clear in criticizing the 'imperialism' that would equate all signs with signifiers, and they distinguish indexes as territorial signs, symbols as deterritorialized signs, and icons as signs of reterritorialization (65).

SIGNIFIANCE: a neologism meaning 'signifier-ness', and denoting the construction of meaning by the reference of signifiers to each other to form chains and circles. In the signifying regime of signs and mixed regimes containing signifiers, signifiance is a limitless process of constructing meaning (112), so that priests and psychoanalysts will always have more work to do.

SIGNIFIER [*signifiant*]: the treatment of signs in a signifying regime of signs. Signifiers are coupled to signifieds in the linguistic theory of Ferdnand de Saussure. DG do not deny the 'existence' of signifiers; they are real products of signifying regimes and also codetermine the semiotics of mixed postsignifying regimes. Rather, DG criticize the 'imperialism' of 'signifier enthusiasts' who use a simplified word/thing model to treat all signs as signifiers and hence reduce the differences among the many different regimes of signs (66). Signifiers are deterritorialized from the territorial signs of 'primitive societies' in an overcoding imperial regime and set loose, repeating themselves in an 'objective frequency' (132), but are reterritorialized on the face (115), which guides their interpretation (117).

SIGNIFYING REGIME: the reign of the signifying sign that refers only to another sign in the circular trap of the signifier (the syntagmatic axis: sign to sign); the master signifier of this regime is the Despot, the Sun-God, the all-seeing, all-knowing, and so on (the paradigmatic axis: sign to signifier). Paranoia, needless to say, is the normal condition of those trapped within signifying regimes tending toward purity, and the mania for interpretation – as 'interpretosis' – is its 'disease' (114). Symbols are the conduits for signs from level to level and circle to concentric circle of being and perfection; *à la* Kafka, the Castle is necessarily unattainable. Everything means, and meaning, of course, must be interpreted by 'high priests'. In the signifying regime, nothing is ever exhausted. Everything circulates, but, ideally, nothing escapes of its own volition. This circularity is the reason why the Despot and the hierarchy seek eternal power: everything is accounted for, and nothing new is needed; those who resist are criminalized, locked up or banished (to return, perhaps, as heroes and liberators). To seem to be something one is not – to deceive – comes about as a natural byproduct of an extremely paranoid regime and society, and so this eventually becomes the way by which this semiotic's grip is loosened (never destroyed: the State will always be with us). Meaning, because and as it is seen to be all powerful, becomes meaningless, which plunges the signifying regime into relative chaos: 'the Answer was a lie! All lies!'.

Ironically, the Signifier itself is nothing, a black hole, a void or even the Wizard of Oz, but its fragility or nothingness – its monstrous lie – is covered over by the projection of a Face, its substance, not only plastered everywhere on city walls, but also watching, everywhere, the movements of the Imperial subjects, and even engraved into the landscape. At a certain level, every State is signifying, even though the State, like Christianity, is a mixture of the signifying regime and the postsignifying (independent, passional, subjectified) regime. Much of the tension between modern and postmodern modes of thought and critique are between the modernist, humanist, postsignifying project of human freedom, and the postmodernist claim that freedom is illusory within the signifying regime that it sees as 'using' the postsignifiers. The binarity of these two claims is actually complementary and ultimately only feeds the circle, but there is never just an either/or, because other semiotics and other mixtures are always at work as well. The Signifier can be a trap, but can always be blown apart, subverted, escaped from; it is a whole attractor and in some epochs a nearly inescapable black hole at the center of its basin of attraction, but it is hardly the be-all and end-all it claims and is claimed to be.

SIMONDON, Gilbert. French philosopher (1924–89). DG cite Simondon (1995) as the source of their critique of hylomorphism. Simondon's critique of hylomorphism pinpoints its social conditions. As Simondon puts it: 'the hylomorphic schema corresponds to the knowledge [*connaissance*] of someone who stays outside the workshop and only considers what goes in and comes out of it' (1995: 40). Simondon refines his analysis of the social conditions of hylomorphism by showing that it is fundamentally not just the viewpoint of the observer outside the workshop, but that of the master commanding slave labor: 'What the hylomorphic schema reflects in the first place is a socialized representation of work ... The technical operation which imposes a form on a passive and indeterminate matter is ... essentially the operation commanded by the free man and executed by the slave' (1995: 48–9). See also Artisan, Form, Minor Science, Royal Science.

SINGULARITY: a mathematical object indicating the change in direction of a line representing the derivative of a function modeling the behavior of a system. Mathematical singularities are established by differentiation in the vector field prior to integration, which establishes trajectories; the discussion of this 'ontological difference' in Lautman (1946) was important for Deleuze in distinguishing the virtual (singularities) from the actual (trajectories) (see *LS*: 104–5). Singularities indicate self-ordering capacities of systems and thus are used to model virtual multiplicities, that is, the patterns (attractors) and thresholds (bifurcations) of intensive processes subtending assemblages. Impersonal and pre-individual in the virtual field, singularities are 'captured' or 'imprisoned' in actual strata.

SMOOTH SPACE [*espace lisse*]: the space of intensive process and assemblages, as opposed to the striated space of stratified or stable systems (479), although in constant interchange with it, so that it is in fact probably better to speak of 'smoothing' and 'striating' forces (474–5; 481). In this sense, smooth space is the substance of expression of which the nomad war machine, the smoothing force par excellence, is the form of expression (416). Smooth space operates in the landscape, in mathematics, in music, in thought, in politics, in religion, and so forth. DG borrow the term, along with 'striated space', from Pierre Boulez (518n22; see Campbell 2000). Below, we describe smooth space outside the realm of music. The plane of consistency, as a 'flat multiplicity' without supplementary dimensions and occupied by series of singularities (an 'accumulation of proximities') distributed across it so that 'each accumulation defines a *zone of indiscernability* proper to "becoming"' can also be described as a smooth space (488; italics in original). In contrast, we can also say that (intensive) smooth spaces are 'inscribed' on the plane of consistency (507).

Emergent properties, intensive becomings, occur only in smooth space. The possibility for symbiosis, for mutualism, for a food web and ecosystem, and finally for forests, seas, prairies, and so forth, is predicated on smoothing, not striating forces. When viewed as isolated entities, organisms can themselves be seen as stratified and located in striated space, but not the complex webs of forces known as ecosystems that have no centralized organization, no climax or end point, but only continuous variation and rhizomes. Forces of destruction – fire, for example – also impart smooth spaces, and humans to the extent that they adapt to ecological and other processes can be said to create *at most* striated disruptions of the smooth spaces of nature. In the case of fire-fallow (swidden) agriculture, the 'best fit' to the smooth (the long-fallow swidden) is the becoming-forest that in the end case striates the forest only in the sense of temporarily controlling it.

The nomads of the central Asian steppes serve as the primordial exemplars of producers and occupiers of smooth spaces, and by extension the environmental component of 'classic' smooth spaces (steppe, sea, desert, polar ice, air) are preconditions in *ATP* for the harboring of rhizomatic forces that smooth and that destroy or attain uneasy peace with the localized striations of 'primitive' space and destroy (via the war machine) the striations of imperial State apparatuses. Smooth space is uncontrollable by definition, because it disappears as it is overcoded. It can be encircled, but as its qualities are made static they recede under the force of striating order. Relatively smooth spaces contain points – as events, haecceities, affects – linked by vectors, rather than a segmented order of places that give rise to the necessity of movement. Smooth spaces contain localized landscape features in continuous variation, and navigators of smooth space, bereft of any iconic or facialized landscape, must pay attention to the minute visual as well as sonorous, olfactory, and tactile qualities that shift subtly from point to point, if they are to be able to thrive there. Patches of smooth space enclosed by striated space are constituted by free relationships of molecular bodies in local motion: the street of the dance party can become a smooth space even if bounded on all sides by the striated, segmented space of the city. The space of the shantytown, and of the urban poor in general, swells as a smoothing force of what the State inevitably calls 'chaos' breaks down the rigid segmentarity of cities. (In Tegucigalpa and across Latin America, we have the ongoing 'war' between ambulant street vendors and city administrations, who heeding the sedentary businesses continually seek to rein in the power of rampant 'black market' [informal economy] capitalism to sell at any point, rather than only in taxed and controlled market spaces.) Work is a striation of the State, so free action, its opposite, can carve out a smooth space. Childrens' play, and their actions in general, for example, can smooth the most striated space, even if children seek to reproduce tiny, striated spaces. Smooth space does not have a long-term memory with all that that entails, so only microhistories are possible, and microsociologies.

As noted in other entries, not smooth space but rather holey space is posed by DG as the space of counter-action to striation. Smooth space, indeed, has become the provenance of the State security forces that can descend on the land at any point after gathering surveillance information and are not bounded by territories or by segmented lines in general (467; 480); of course the effect of the global smooth space of securitarian intervention is the discovering of 'terrorist' enemies everywhere: 'a macropolitics of society by and for a micropolitics of insecurity' (216). Dancing in the street, molecular deviation of all sorts in smooth spaces, falls right into the hands of 'control society' (345; cf. Hardt and Negri 2000). Furthermore, capitalism, as practiced by multinational corporations, uses 'machinic enslavement', that is, 'a complex qualitative process bringing into play modes of transportation, urban models, the media, the entertainment industries, ways of perceiving and feeling' to create 'a new smooth space' (492). Thus 'never believe that a smooth space will suffice to save us' (500). Indeed, the tank achieves the smoothing of the most striated space: it can disregard segmentarity altogether, but only to do the will of the State.

SPACE: although *ATP* never explicitly enters into discussion of 'space' per se, without the 'striated' or 'smooth' adjectives, we can say that there is no Space with a capital S as something that precedes bodies and awaits them as a container. Just the opposite: the body or assemblage in question is co-constituted along with the space it occupies. In so far as an actual body or assemblage is the locus of varying ratios of smoothing and striating forces (intensifying and equilibrating, deterritorializing/decoding/destratifying and reterritorializing/re- or over-coding/restratifying, forces) 'space' is itself always a mix of smooth and striated (474–5; 481). If we bring to bear some complexity theory terms, we can say that a full statement of 'geophilosophy' would be that all bodies on the strata occupying a striated space arise through the congealing or cooling of an intensive process forming a smooth space and subtended by the singularities inhabiting the virtual plane of consistency ('phase space' or 'state space').

SPEED AND SLOWNESS: [*vitesse* and *lenteur*]: in the discussion of the characteristics of intensive differences in internal material flows, speed and slowness are united as the longitude of bodies (260), one of the components, along with latitude (affects) in a cartography. In this case, slowing down can be just as effective a means of deterritorialization or destratification as speeding up, for it is the shift of the intensive differential rates of change that wrenches a body out of its old habits, that frees it from the basin of attraction of a singularity (56; 270). However, in the discussion of the characteristics of vectors (e.g. nomads) in a smooth space, speed and slowness are opposed as *celeritas* and *gravitas*, that is, as the least deviation opposed to the laminar:

> Laminar movement that striates space, that goes from one point to another, is weighty [*grave*; this can also mean 'serious' in addition to its relation to 'gravity'; cf. Nietzsche's critique of the 'spirit of gravity' in *Zarathustra* 3.11]; but rapidity, celerity, applies only to movement that deviates to the minimum extent and thereby assumes a vortical motion [*une allure tourbillonnaire*], occupying a smooth space, actually drawing smooth space itself. (371)

146

In this sense, speed can be opposed to movement as the intensive opposed to the extensive (381).

SPINOZA, Baruch. Dutch philosopher (1632–77). Spinoza is the author of the *Ethics*, a study of the world as a single substance with infinite modes. Such a rigorous construction of a plane of immanence makes him one of the major influences on Deleuze, who devoted a large work (Deleuze 1992 [1968]) and a smaller handbook (Deleuze 1988b [1970]) to explicating him. As with Bergson, although his implicit influence can be seen everywhere in the book, in *ATP* Spinoza is mentioned relatively infrequently. The *Ethics* is called the 'great book of the BwO' (153) for posing the question of the connection of bodies on an immanent plane, while the sections of the 'Becoming-Intense' plateau devoted to affect are entitled 'Memories of a Spinozist' (252–60). A final homage to Spinoza in *ATP* is the use of the 'geometric method' Spinoza used in the *Ethics* in the 'Theorems of Deterritorialization' (174–5; 306–7), and in plateaus 12 and 13 on the war machine and 'apparatus of capture' of the State). DG are unbridled in their praise of Spinoza in *What Is Philosophy?*, calling him the 'prince' (*WP*: 48) and even the 'Christ' of philosophers (*WP*: 60). See also Immanence, Plane of Consistency.

STATE APPARATUS: the machinic assemblage for effectuating, in the social register, the abstract machine of overcoding or stratification (223; 513). The constant danger of the State is its tendency to 'identify' with the abstract machine of overcoding and become totalitarian (223). The date for the plateau 'Apparatus of Capture' is 7000 BC, which DG broadly identify as the time of emergence of the ancient, Imperial State that came to effect and to perfect the goals of the paranoid signifying regime. The State in *ATP* is no abstraction: it is an apparatus or complex mechanism whereby alien and rogue semiotics and machinic assemblages are captured and overcoded, engulfed by a transcendent force that striates all reality: space, time, body, culture, nature. Every State has an apparatus that effects both the capture of an exterior and its continued existence through the recapture of fleeing interior elements. Even with the current power of other semiotic regimes we are still as subject to the *pouvoir* of the State apparatus as at any time during the past 9,000 years. Obvious proof of this is the nation-state system that overcodes the planet, such that it is not only simply impossible to carve out a non-State anywhere, but also all attempts to achieve independence from existing nation-states result in the establishment of yet more nation-states; regardless of the proliferation of non-State actors and even globalization, the State is still the 'only conceivable' way by which the earth can be organized by humans. DG, of course, are strident critics of the State and call for a new earth or something like it in all their collaborative works – in this they are geo-anarchists working against State socialism as much as against smooth capitalism and striated 'free' State existence.

DG call striation one of the 'fundamental tasks' of States (385), given that the State apparatus must operate to transform the earth [terre] of primitive society (or even the ground [sol] of nomads) into land [terre] (441). They show that the State, though it did not originate in one place, is a universal and unavoidable feature of human existence, and indeed has formed everywhere in relationship to nomads as well as 'primitives' (360; 429–30). What a State apparatus cannot striate, it retains as a smooth space for communication and transportation of the war machines of capitalistic conquest. It may still be that everything in existence exists on the terms of the State, particularly, of State or Royal science (and State philosophy, whether Plato, Aristotle, Kant, or Hegel); we might presume that the current era of globalization is a precursor to a stronger one, two, or three mega-States, rather than a break-down of the nation-state world in favor of decentered corporate/tribal networks. One way or the other, the State apparatus's fundamental operations remain constants. The war machine, the cutting edge or expansive wave of smooth space as it smoothes striated space, was long ago appropriated by the State apparatus, though civilian control of the military and the hesitancy of the most powerful contemporary States to deploy the military internally (next to or in place of the police) indicates the still uneasy and incomplete nature of the capture of the nomads' war machine. The role of the military nomads, today, is to wage war using the smooth global spaces, but still at the whims of the State apparatus.

The State apparatus can act directly on any stratum of human society, any regime of signs, and any ecosystem. It has and is the force and power to overcode anything, to put anything to work, to turn anything into stock. However, all the diverse, molecular spaces must be made to resonate, to come into some sort of harmony, to obey some type of universal refrain (usually having to do with the absolute beneficence of the leader-Signifier or

Principle); the State is an 'intraconsistency' (433). Once resonating, the overcoded territories can be stratified and organized in numerous ways, segmented and striated to the limits of human tolerance. State apparatuses operate in a supplemental or higher dimension than their subjects, and thus are able, parasitically, to oversee, to control, and to siphon the surplus that is necessary for their survival. DG describe several forms of States that have come about, and in many cases there has been little or no pretension to universality among these States; just the opposite has often been the case. However, the worldwide machines of capitalism, 'American democracy', and Protestant-work-ethic Christianity have returned us to the pretenses of the archaic, universalizing State: 'Capitalism has awakened the Urstaat, and given it new strength' (460). This was written before the fall of the Soviet Union, so is even more pertinent to today's conditions.

Despite the deeper unity of 'the State', DG recognize that individual States are determined in large part by the geographically-dependent needs and flows of world capital at any given time, and also that States are differentiated because of this into North and South, East and West, center and periphery (455; 464–6). There is, in other words, a 'natural order' or organizing principle that would necessarily thrive in a dimension supplementary to States, that striates them through capital – this, we could assume, is the Empire of Hardt and Negri (2000). See also Earth/Land, Signifying Regime, Striated Space, Territory.

STEPPE: the environment or milieu of the countersignifying nomad, and the primordial smooth space. Here, DG are influenced by the central Asian steppes as source areas for the 'true' nomadic war machines – those of Tamerlane, Genghis Khan, et al. – that never appeared to 'understand' the State or the value of the signifying regime. However, they also use 'steppe' in the Geology of Morals plateau (60–1) in a broader sense of the plains upon which humans are thought to have evolved when we descended from the trees and emerged from the dense forests along the Great Rift Valley. According to this account, humans became deterritorialized as we stood upright, gazed and scanned the horizon, and developed the hand and leg (from paws). In other words, the steppe served to deterritorialize humans and free them from the highly territorialized forest milieu (172). We would argue that humans were also able to act upon the land and create the plain as a smooth space through the use of fire (thus the steppe only created us as we created it). It is unclear whether we emerged from dense rain forests or from an already patchy savanna mosaic, however, so it may be more a matter of degrees than DG suggest. Other effects of human occupation of the plains included the formation of speech and indeed of a 'supple larynx' with very different qualities than that which would have been required inside the sound space of the forest (62). Generally speaking, DG see forest as pure milieu, and therefore the plains or 'steppe' as our first 'world', where the earth was for the first time deterritorialized and humans could effectuate lines of flight (172).

STRATA: actualized systems with homogenized components operating at or near equilibrium/steady state/stability; hence the result of the process of stratification. Strata are formed in a process of 'double articulation', which draws matter from milieus and organizes it to produce stable structures (40–1). Strata are not primary constituents of the world, but are 'residues': 'The question is not how something manages to leave the strata but how things get into them in the first place' (56). Because of this residual status of strata, 'resistance' is not a primary political category for DG (530n39). Although all strata display a 'unity of composition' they are nonetheless 'shattered' by 'epistrata', or stable states of bodies arising through processes of territorialization and deterritorialization (50), and 'parastrata', or sets of affects arising through processes of coding and decoding (52). In terms of the difference among strata, DG discuss three main types: the inorganic, the organic, and the alloplastic, each of which displays a characteristic relation of content and expression. In the inorganic strata the molecular interactions of content are amplified to form molar aggregates in the process of 'induction' (60). In the organic strata, both content and expression are molecular and molar in the process of 'transduction' (60). In the human region of the alloplastic strata, content becomes technological and expression linguistic, giving rise to 'translation' (62).

STRATIFICATION: the process of creating strata by 'double articulation'. The abstract machine of stratification works by content–expression or territorialization-coding-overcoding, and operates in any register from geological to organic (speciation) to social (effectuated by the State apparatus) as the way to appropriate matter–energy flows from the earth and build a layer that regulates

the flow. DG use geological terms in discussing the four components in the double articulation of stratification (40–1). The first
articulation is 'sedimentation', which determines (1) a substance
of content, that is, the selection of homogenous materials or
matter from a subordinate flow in a milieu (= territorialization),
and (2) a form of content, that is, the depositing of these matters
into layers (= coding). The second articulation is 'folding', in
which there is (3) a form of expression, that is, the creation of new
linkages (= overcoding), and (4) a substance of expression, the
creation of new entities with emergent properties. (DeLanda crit-
icizes the link of 'sedimentation' and 'folding', claiming rightly
that it is geologically more correct to have 'cementation' as the
second articulation, with 'folding' occurring at a different spatial
scale [1999: 290n82].) See Figure 2.

STRIATED SPACE [*espace strié*]: space marked by striae (striations);
metric or measured space. Just as smooth space is the product of
intensification, striated space is the product of stratification, especially as effectuated by the State apparatus (385; 441). However, as
good Deleuzoguattarians, we should not stay on the level of products. Although nominally opposed to smooth space, striated space
is in such constant interchange with it, that it is in fact probably
better to speak of an interchange of 'smoothing' and 'striating'
forces (474–5; 481). Like 'smooth space', the term comes from
Boulez, but 'striation', a geological phenomenon first detected by
Louis Agassiz in 1840, was primordially the scratching of the
earth's surface by continental glaciers. Given that DG refer to the
earth qua plane of consistency as the 'Glacial' (40), it is reason-
able to suspect that they were in some way comparing the effects
of the State to that of the ice sheets, though this seems more
playful than central to their portrayal of striated space.

In the above entry on smooth space, we claimed that 'nature'
in general is constituted by smoothing forces, at least at the level
of the ecosystem. This is not to say that only humans striate: any
organism striates milieus to achieve territorial organization.
Human systems, however, attempt to achieve a particularly crude
type of striation, and strive, via the signifying regime, to striate the
earth completely. Presignifying regimes only striate the local, and
continually ward off being striated from their exterior (440).
Striation results from stratification, the overcoding, centralization, hierarchization, binarization, and segmentation of the free
movements of signs, particles, bodies, territories, spaces, and so

Figure 2 The system of the strata

Stratum	Scale[a]	Example[b]	Notes	Epistrata and Parastrata
Inorganic	Sedimentary rock	SC: particles FC: sedimentary layers FE: cementation SE: rock	Molecular Formed matters Molar Functional structure	EPISTRATA (stable states) and PARASTRATA (opportunities for expansion) develop by induction or physical contact; crystals (e.g.) replicate rather than reproduce.
Organic	Genes and proteins	SC: amino acids FC: proteins FE: nucleotide base sequences SE: genes	Double articulation of content and expression must be specified at different scales, only two of which are indicated here.	EPISTRATA: stable intermediate states below thresholds regulating relations: (1) between exterior milieu and interior elements; (2) between elements and compounds; (3) between compounds and substances; (4) between substance of content and substance of expression. Epistrata form the thresholds and patterns of organs and thus establish the qualitative internal differences in the internal milieu. Epistrata are established by the ratio of relative deterritorialization and reterritorialization.
	Organic Systems (Nervous, Endocrine, Digestive . . .)	SC: organs FC: regulation of flows FE: homeostatic regulation SE: organism as emergent process		PARASTRATA: affects of an organism or the capacities to form assemblages or associated milieus allowing for: (1) respiration or capture of energy sources; (2) perception or discernment of materials; (3) reaction or fabrication of compounds. Parastrata are established by coding/decoding/transcoding and are responsible for the distribution of traits or organic forms in a population. Thresholds of parastrata establish events of speciation.
Alloplastic	Social Machine	SC: bodies FC: actions and passions	Technological content: hand – tool = machinic assemblage of bodies.	EPISTRATA: tolerated variation in behavior.
		FE: regime of signs SE: social institutions effectuating incorporeal transformations	Linguistic expression: face – language = collective assemblage of enunciation.	PARASTRATA: affects of the social assemblage.

Notes:

a. It's vital to distinguish scale. As we have repeatedly noted, DeLanda points out that DG conflate levels of scale by putting 'folding' as form of expression when the topic is sedimentary rock. (Folding occurs at the scale of mountain ranges.) DeLanda also stresses in a personal communication to the authors that DG's discussion of the organic stratum is confused because of their bringing examples from different scales to bear: genes and proteins, cells, tissues, organs, and systems are all different scales, with the organism as the emergent effect of unifying all these scales. Reproductive communities and species must also be considered, however, as part of the organic stratum, as well as the interweaving of the organic stratum with the processes of 'nonorganic life'. There are also many scales to be considered on the alloplastic strata, although we present here only DG's notion of 'social machine'. We should remember, however, that the point of DeLanda's criticism of DG's Marxism is their eagerness to leap to this level without demonstrating the emergence-producing mechanisms at intermediate scales: between subjects and social machines lie many interweavings of families, institutions, cities, nations, and so on.

b. Each stratum works by double articulation: Substances of content (SC) = materials extracted or selected from a substratum; Form of content (FC) = the statistical ordering of those materials ('coding'). Form of expression (FE) = functional connections among those statistically ordered materials ('overcoding'). Substance of expression (SE) = the emergent whole.

on. Striated space is first gridded and delineated, then occupied, by the drawing of rigid lines that compartmentalize reality into segments, all controlled to a greater or lesser extent through a nested hierarchy of centers (and researched in the geographic pursuit known as 'spatial analysis'). Thus striated space, because it is composed of centers, is productive of remoteness, of the entire idea that there are places of more and of less importance. Striation imparts the 'truth' that 'place' is an immobile point and that immobility (dwelling) is always better than 'aimless' voyaging, wandering, itinerancy, and of course nomadism, which at best are either temporary vacations, but, if insisted upon, pose grave threats to striated space. Nevertheless, to repeat, as we do many times in this book, smoothing and striating are processes, and cannot achieve complete actualization on the ground. Real spaces and landscapes are entangled – constituted by mixtures – though it is important to underscore that States and other agents of striation often do much damage by their attempt to striate everything absolutely (even and particularly thought). But here a simple example will suffice: if one goes from point A to B by the quickest and most efficient route, one is fully striated if one does not even consider going any other way, or by any other than the quickest means. One recognizes the smooth qualities inherent in all spaces as one dwells upon the journey, wanders, takes back roads, and eventually gets out and walks, but not along the berm (cf. DeCerteau 1984).

As noted in the entry 'Forest', DG see the supposed vertical striations of the forest as a precursor of agriculture, but we see this only as the case in the 'tame', non-primeval forests of Europe that came about long after the destruction of long-fallow swidden regimes that under low population densities do not striate the forest at all. In any case, the settled agriculture that eventually removes so-called 'primeval' forest is the basis for the striations of the State: for example, taxing and putting to work of the peasants, and draining excess labor for monumental projects. Sedentary agriculture itself striates the land to an extreme extent, and, even without the State, towns take advantage of this, then cities, and so forth. Though agriculture and the peasant striate space, they are not necessarily forces for imparting it beyond their own neighborhood (though States move them about to do so). The city, arising eventually from networks of human settlements, is what allows the striation of a larger territory; the inter-linkage of striated spaces imparted by cities eventually summons forth the emergence of the State, and, as we have it today, the pre-eminent power of sovereign States to striate their own spaces has given way, via capitalism and military might, to a worldwide space of Empire that operates through a smooth space to achieve ever-more-homogeneous striated space.

As a final note here, we need to emphasize that striated (and smooth) can be features of non-geographic assemblages (desire, music, and cloth, to cite examples from *ATP*) and so are not restricted to spaces of interest to geographical pursuits at the scale of the human or the landscape.

SUBJECT [*sujet*]: the product of the process of subjectification. DG's notion of the subject as product does not deny the agency of sub-jects, but does locate them as only an intermediate level of struc-ture, the emergent effect of an assemblage of stratified organs constituting the focal point of an organism, but in turn 'subject to' [see Subjection] the constraints of social machines. In the postsignifying or 'passional' regime of signs (127), as well as in the capitalist axiomatic (457), there is a division between the subject of enunciation and the subject of the statement.

SUBJECT OF ENUNCIATION [*sujet d'énonciation*]: in the passional, postsignifying regime of signs (127), or in the capitalist axiomatic (457), that which issues from the 'point' of subjectification. The subject of enunciation is the active, subjective 'I' (the lover, the prophet, the capitalist) who names things or issues orders and so constructs a 'mental reality' to which the subject of the statement must conform as if to a 'dominant reality' (129).

SUBJECT OF THE STATEMENT [*sujet d'énoncé*]: in the passional or postsignifying regime of signs (127) or, in the capitalist axiomatic (457), that which is named or commanded (the beloved, the people, the worker), and thereby 'bound to statements in confor-mity with a dominant reality' issuing from the 'mental reality' constructed by the subject of enunciation (129).

SUBJECTIFICATION [*subjectivation*]: the process of producing sub-jects on the basis of a regime of signs or 'collective assemblage of enunciation' (130). The whole of *AO*, following a critique of the Freudian model, is a reconstruction of a machinic process of sub-jectification implicit in desiring-production. In *ATP*, subjectifica-tion is not a process of ideology, but a regime of signs, a collective or social assemblage linking bodies and order-words. In the passional or postsignifying regime of signs, 'anything' can serve as the 'point of subjectification' or the organizing point for the construction by a subject of enunciation of a 'mental reality' (a *Weltanschauung* or 'world-view') to which is submitted, as if to a 'dominant reality', a subject of the statement (129). In subjectification, the (active, commanding) subject of enunciation and the (passive, obedient) subject of the statement recoil into each other, as in the identity of the Kantian legislator-subject, who is more free the more the dictates of the moral law one gives oneself are obeyed. In such cases there is no longer a need for a transcendent center of power, as subjectification is the self-application of power [*pouvoir*], making oneself conform to a normalized standard (130; cf. Foucault 1977). The capitalist axiomatic also serves as the 'point of subjectification', with 'capitalists' as the subjects of enunciation and workers the subject of the statement (457).

SUBJECTION [*assujettissement*]: the process of 'subjecting to' (linking a subject to) a technical machine. Social subjection operates within the modern nation-state as the correlate of subjectification (457). Under subjection, workers 'willingly' labor alongside technical machines, as opposed to contemporary machinic enslavement in which people are often unwitting parts of a great technical-social cybernetic machine generating machinic surplus value (456–9).

SUBJECTIVITY [*subjectivité*]: the characteristic ability of subjects to construct, or follow, a 'mental reality' (129). Subjectivity forms a resonance chamber in the 'passional' or postsignifying regime of signs (132).

SUBSTANCE: formed matter, that is, homogenized and coded material composing a functional structure (41). As the 'substance of content', a substance is selected from an 'exterior milieu' and forms the beginning of a process of stratification. The 'substance of expression', the end result of a double articulation or process of stratification, is a new entity with emergent properties. When caught up in a new overpowering stratum, such a substance forms a new substance of content.

SUBSTRATUM: the source of matter for a stratum (40), serving as its exterior milieu (49). As the matter of a stratum consists of substances or formed matter composed in another stratum, the sub-stratum is not composed of the unformed matters of the plane of consistency, and thus is in no way 'inferior' to the stratum to which it is submitted; to think otherwise is to risk a 'ridiculous cosmic evolutionism' (49). Furthermore, there is no fixed order to the strata, so that 'one stratum can serve directly as a substratum for another without the intermediaries one would expect'; in addi-tion, 'the apparent order can be reversed, with cultural or techni-cal phenomena providing a fertile soil, a good soup, for the development of insects, bacteria, germs, or even particles' (69).

SURPLUS VALUE [*plus-value*]: basic Marxist term for 'profit' adapted by DG in a variety of ways. In the organic strata, the 'transversal communication' of DNA via viral transfer or 'sym-biogenesis' (Margulis 1998) yields a 'surplus value of code' (53). In the social strata, surplus value of code is the gain in prestige in tribal societies from occupying a privileged position in the circu-lation of debts, as well as being the pleasure of the eye evaluating the pain of punishment (*AO*: 191). Imperial taxation, although proceeding from an overcoding, is also a surplus vale of code (E. Holland 1999: 66). Capitalism, however, derives a 'surplus value of flow' (*AO*: 226), the 'quantitative differential between the flow of money invested in factors of production . . . and the flow of money returning at the end of the production-consumption cycle' (E. Holland 1999: 67). Contemporary capitalist systems also generate a machinic surplus value through the construction of cybernetic assemblages (458).

SYMBOL: a deterritorialized sign that stands 'outside itself' to stand for something else, pointing to another sign within an assem-blage, or pointing away from an assemblage or a stratum and inviting a voyage to another assemblage or stratum, or even to the plane of consistency (112). It should be noted that DG derive their taxonomy of signs from Charles Sanders Peirce (531n41), though they change Peirce's conceptions as they claim that he was unable to escape the trap of the signifier: they call him the true originator of semiotics, but more closely follow Louis Trolle Hjelmslev. See also Icon, Index, Sign.

TENSOR: a complex mathematical object derived from differential calculus, tensors define the transformations its components are capable of given transformations of its coordinate systems.

Tensors are said to describe the 'nonformal functions' by which an abstract machine forms the diagram of an assemblage (511).

TERRITORY [*territoire*]: the 'becoming' or 'emergence' (316) of the interaction of functions and expressive markers (315) producing the feeling of being at home [*chez soi*] (311). Territories are fashioned from parts of milieus, and composed only of those milieu materials that have meaning and function for the territorial assemblage. Territories intermingle in landscapes; deterritorialization and reterritorialization are the movements of escape and capture from one territory to another or new territory on the strata, or to and from the plane of consistency. Territories contain that which is owned or used, actually or in reserve.

   The milieus utilized by territories are the following: the interior milieu is the zone of residence (the home, shelter, or abode); the exterior milieu of the territory is its domain; the intermediary milieu is composed by the (usually mobile) limits or membranes separating the territory from others (constituting the border or boundary); the annexed milieu, which contains the energy reserves of the organism and may be spatially distant from the domain (314). Territorial organisms achieve the expression of territory through marking; indeed, the mark brings about the territory. Examples among animal species are numerous. Marks (DG call them 'signatures') are organized as indexes, the semiotics of territories. Though DG draw heavily from Konrad Lorenz, they disagree that aggressivity is what establishes territory, and seek instead to show that territory derives from the needs of the domain and the abode, essentially what the refrain carves out as a comfort zone from chaos and the earth/Cosmos (315–16). Territories are fashioned as necessities to establish the maximal distribution of individuals of the same kind within a milieu and regulate access to spatially distributed resources.

   Territory, to DG, is primordial, not the species. Territory can bring about species and assemblages, which in turn have to escape territories to effectuate needed changes. Thus, courtship assemblages demand the intermingling or even explosion of territories in neutral zones DG call the 'interassemblage' (333). Similarly, the Natal or source of a territorial assemblage is by necessity outside of it (being the source of numerous side-by-side territories, it cannot be located in any of them) and here DG discuss the 'pilgrimages' of salmon and the 'long marches' of spiny lobsters off the Yucatán (325–6). They note the guidance coming from 'deep' forces such as the earth's magnetic field and the sun, completely outside the territories but common to them all, and thereby cementing the relationship of territories with the Cosmos. In other words, deterritorializing and destratifying movements are necessarily tapping into the intensive forces of the earth and the virtual forces of the Cosmos, machinic phyla inscribed on the plane of consistency. (Following Mircea Eliade's 1949 study of comparative religions, DG see territory as the separator or mediator between the forces of the earth and Cosmos, and the forces of Chaos or entropy. Religion, a great territorializing force of humans, draws from the milieus of the earth to control and fend off chaos.)

Humans, like many other animals, are territorial (though there are also 'milieu animals'), but diverse human assemblages and regimes of signs differ from each other in the ways that they deterritorialize milieus and form their territories. For example the very notion of territory for the State is tied to reserves of land [*terre*] (441), but, in contrast, for the nomad, the land [*terre*] becomes ground [*sol*], a thin support allowing a mobile territory (381). Though territorial assemblages are important in human existence, the primary components of them, as with any assemblage, are lines of flight (88–9; 539n39). Thus territories are not the permanent standards they appear to be (although they may have very long life-spans and quite violent defense mechanisms). Territories appropriate only fragments of milieus, and though any analysis can start with territoriality and the relationship between territories, the outside must also be thought of, and we could just as effectively begin a geographic account from the vantage-point of the landscape; in the Olancho case study, we propose 'complex spaces' as the generators of territories that were mixed within landscapes on the strata. See Figure 1.

THOUGHT [*la pensée*]: although the brain is rhizomatic (15), 'noology', or the study of the form or 'image' of thought, shows that thought can take a State form, that is, stratified, linear, overcoded, centralized, hierarchical, and so forth (375–6), taking up the tree and root as a 'sad image of thought' (16). Such a contrast of the rhizomatic brain and arborescent thought recalls one of the main themes of Daniel Dennett's *Consciousness Explained*: 'Conscious human minds are more or less serial virtual machines implemented – inefficiently – on the parallel hardware that evolution has provided for us' (Dennett 1991: 218). The State provides a 'form of interiority' to thought (thought as capture and domestication of the represented contents of the world); as such, State thought uneasily juxtaposes an 'imperium of truth' (the logically ordered results of thought, operating by capture, foundation, myth) and a 'republic of free spirits' (the free critical investigation proper to thought, operating by contract, legislation, logos) (375). Noology also shows, however, that thought can perform rhizomatically: it can be a 'war machine', adopting a 'form of exteriority' (377). Such 'outside thought' (376), putting thought in a smooth space (377), is not, however, an 'image of thought', but a 'force that destroys both the image and its copies, the model and its reproductions, every possibility of subordinating thought to a model of the True, the Just, or the Right' (377: cf. 20: the rhizome is not a model in the way that the tree is a model; rather, it is an 'immanent process that overturns the model'). See also Brain, Epistemology, Memory.

TIME: we may distinguish three types of time in *ATP*, aligned with each of the registers of DG's ontology: the actual, the virtual, and the intensive. Chronos is time of actual or stratified bodies, paired with striated space in measuring extensive movement; it is 'the time of measure that situates things and persons, develops a form, and determines a subject' (262; 381). Aion is the time of the virtual realm, the plane of consistency, 'the indefinite time of the event', a 'simultaneous too-late and too-early' (262). It is 'the time of the pure event or of becoming, which articulates relative speeds and slownesses independently of the chronometric or chronological values time assumes in the other modes' (263). In other words, in Aion, a bifurcation – as a virtual phase transition considered in itself, not as actualized in any one instance where one could mark the commencement of the process in Chronos – can never be located by temporal metrics. That is to say, an actual pot of water can be said to begin boiling at such and such a time, but what can one say is the temporal location of 'boiling' considered in itself, as an event? Finally, 'haecceity' is the time of the intensive: in an environmental assemblage, spatio-temporal determinations are no longer attributed to a subject, but achieve an impersonal individuation as 'dimensions of multiplicities' (263). In other words, intensive time and space are not containers for bodies, but elements of an event that includes bodies: 'It is the entire assemblage in its individuated aggregate that is a haecceity ... [bodies] cease to be subjects to become events, in assemblages that are inseparable from an hour, a season, an atmosphere' (262). The distinction between Chronos and Aion is also described in terms of a distinction, drawn from Boulez, between 'pulsed' and 'nonpulsed' time (262–3; 267; 317).

TOWN [*ville*]: created by roads and flows, the town produces the countryside and invents agriculture (481). DG discuss towns in relationship to Braudel's discussion of the genesis of capitalism (1985: 432–4). Towns arise anywhere that flows on the land, or at the border of land and sea, need to be rechanneled, profited from, taxed, and regulated. Consequently, towns impose a frequency on commercialized flows. As products circulate, towns arise; as towns arise, concentric rings of agropastoral settlement develop that are striated by the towns, necessary to the success of growing numbers of people who do not grow their own food (to give an obvious example). In many cases, towns arise 'on purpose' at chokepoints or break-of-bulk points and populations gather to feed off the flows that of necessity are channelled–through the Bosporus, along the Silk Road, or down the Mississippi River and its tributaries.

Towns are imbedded in networks and are deterritorialized from their surroundings, to the extreme in those maritime communities that depend most on the sea and little on the land. As geographers have of course studied in fine detail, the functions of towns within market economies and within hierarchized networks dictate certain minimum and maximum distances between each – the hexagonal pattern that results, however, precedes the State and is rooted in the original nodes of settlement implanted in smooth space. Thus, in Honduras, the basic pattern of towns was established by the Spanish in the 1500s and prevails today, with few substantial differences – the sites that were held, which in some cases were on or near indigenous towns, were those that had to be held to impose a striated space following the Iberian model. In a separate example, in the Mississippi Valley, as early as La Salle (1681–2 expedition), the French imperial State established outposts in smooth space at the obvious points, places (like the Arkansas Post) at or near the confluence of major rivers; others (like Baton Rouge) were necessary for control of the main river as they sat high up on bluffs. LaSalle, in essence, and Western explorers like him, laid down the blueprint for settlement geographies based on ideas of where trade would be most fruitful and where military control would be easiest. Later, towns grew up at logical places along land routes, along railroads, at junctions of railroads and rivers, at points where the products of the Midwest reached the Great Lakes (Chicago), at interstate intersections, and so forth.

Balancing this, and following Braudel, DG also stress the resistance of towns to overcoding by States and imperial centers – 'flat' networks of towns appear to have been sufficient in the European Middle Ages, each a local center of striation, each balancing the next (434). See also Frequency, Smooth Space.

TRACING [*décalquer*]: the act of representation, the mimetic reproduction of the properties of an actual substance in an image, a *calque*. Copying without changing in nature, gathering up, sorting, and classifying – the methods of accounting and bureaucracy – are ways of tracing, as opposed to the making of maps [*cartes*], which creates (12). See also Decalcomania, Rhizome.

TRAIT: on the intensive register, that is, in material, traits are indications of singularities, or self-ordering processes that provide opportunities for intervention by artisans. Traits are aligned with operations in a machinic phylum (406). Intensive traits of content are 'implicit forms that are topological rather than geometrical, and that combine with processes of deformation: for example, the variable undulations and torsions of the fibers guiding the operation of splitting wood' (408). Intensive traits of expression are 'variable intensive affects . . . for example, wood that is more or less porous, more or less elastic and resistant' (408). In the virtual register, the plane of consistency, traits of content are unformed matters or intensities, while traits of expression are nonformal functions or tensors (511). See also Minor Science.

TRANSCENDENCE: in philosophical usage, the act of being above or beyond something else either empirically, that is, in space or power [*pouvoir*], or ontologically, in mode of being (for example, the supernatural or extramundane character of God in many theologies). Absolute ontological transcendence is thus perforce dualist. For DG, whose ontology is dedicated to immanence or monism, all transcendence must be considered empirical and hence relative to that which is transcended or overpowered. Thus the transcendence of expression is relative to content for agents of overcoding in processes of stratification. (By contrast, expression is not transcendent relative to content in an assemblage, but is intertwined with it [90; 337].) Relatively transcendent agency is reified in the doctrine of hylomorphism as the process of imposing a form on chaotic matter. A plan(e) of organization, as providing a blueprint for the construction of form, that is, the construction of exclusive disjunctions establishing a restricted set of singularities for a body, operates as a plane of transcendence (265). The (relative) transcendence of the whole to the parts, of a subject to the set of desiring-machines or 'network of finite automata' (18) of which it is composed, is simply an emergent effect operating in a supplementary dimension (cf. 21: 'the multiple . . . to which One is added').

TRANSCENDENTAL: Kant began the 'transcendental turn' in philosophy with the *Critique of Pure Reason*, which set out to determine the universal and necessary conditions of possibility for the unified experience of rational beings. In DR, Deleuze transforms the transcendental inquiry into a search for the genetic conditions of real existence, which leads him to distinguish the actual and the virtual in his ontology. Somewhat confusingly for non-initiates, philosophers in the transcendental tradition precisely search for immanence as opposed to transcendence. This is made clear in a rightfully famous passage in *AO*: 'In what he called the critical revolution, Kant intended to discover criteria immanent to understanding . . . In the name of *transcendental* philosophy (immanence of criteria), he therefore renounced the transcendent use of syntheses such as appeared in metaphysics. In like fashion we . . . [seek to] rediscover a transcendental unconscious defined by the immanence of its criteria, and a corresponding practice that we shall call schizoanalysis' (*AO*: 75; italics in original). Despite this legacy, DG do not use the term 'transcendental' in *ATP*, though there is no reason not to say its toolbox of concepts could receive a grounding in transcendental inquiry in the sense of a demonstration of their immanent character.

TRANSCENDENTAL ILLUSION: in DR, the 'transcendental physical illusion' is the burying of the intensive under the extensive (Deleuze 1995: 228) and the virtual under the actual (244). In *ATP*, the idea that hylomorphism is a form of production is revealed as an illusion by the critical notion of artisanal production (408–9).

TRANSCODING: also known as 'transduction', the processes by which milieus interrelate in a 'rhythm' or 'co-ordination of heterogeneous space-times' (313).

TRANSVERSAL COMMUNICATION. See Decoding, Surplus Value.

VARIATION, CONTINUOUS: the characteristic of the series formed by singularities making up virtual multiplicities on the plane of consistency (109; 511). Establishing continuous variation among variables, as the operation of minor science or problematics (for example, metallurgy: 411), is thus opposed to the extraction of constants, the operation of Royal science or axiomatics (103).

VIRILIO, Paul. French architect and philosopher (1932–). Virilio's work strongly influenced DG's thinking on nomads, space, and speed and slowness. For the Virilio–DG link, see particularly 558n63 on *Speed and Politics* and 559n65 on the 'fleet in being'.

VIRTUAL: the component of Deleuze's ontology determining the modal relation of possibility or potentiality vis-à-vis actuality for complex systems; the virtual provides a way of talking about the phase space of systems, the patterns and thresholds of their behavior. Non-actualized attractors, that is, those in a virtual condition, can only be glimpsed in complex systems pushed into far-from-equilibrium crisis by manipulation of their intensive variables. The virtual realm is called the 'plane of consistency' in *ATP*, and is populated by multiplicities, which provide the structure for intensive morphogenetic processes composing bodies and assemblages and actual strata.

VOYAGING: not a worthwhile endeavor if it is one's primary way of searching out the 'new earth' elsewhere: one is always reterritorialized, particularly if one seeks out the presignifying that dwells in some other place (hence, the futility of giving up the modern world to go and live with a 'primitive' society) (188–9). In contrast, DG laud the 'voyaging in place' body experimentation (159) on lines of flight that sets up de- and reterritorializations that would contribute to the construction of the new earth, as it needs to be established right here, within striated space, by way of smooth space and/or holey space. See also Line of Flight, Nomad Society.

WAR MACHINE: the machinic assemblage that effectuates the abstract machine of creativity in the world by forming a smooth space which maintains social formations in a far-from-equilibrium or 'intensive crisis' condition (223; 422). As such, the war machine is the counterforce to the State's stratification machine, which forms hierarchical, centralized, and overcoded social formations.

The State has always attempted to incorporate the war machine as the army, yet this defeat is the moment of the war machine's proliferation:

> Could it be that it is at the moment the war machine ceases to exist, conquered by the State, that it displays to the utmost its irreducibility, that it scatters into thinking, loving, dying, or creating machines that have at their disposal vital or revolutionary powers capable of challenging the conquering State? (356)

This is no dialectics or romanticism; the creativity the war machine effectuates is not the sublated opposite of State capture nor a demonic gift given to rebels, but the ability, via minor science, to tap the 'forces' or powers of self-organization and emergence in material; in other words, the war machine is that which effectuates 'Non-organic life' (411). In the contemporary world, the existence of the war machine is completely taken up by its own process of productive material creativity, both social and technological at once:

> [T]he war machine's form of exteriority is such that it exists only in its own metamorphoses; it exists in an industrial innovation as well as in a technological innovation, in a commercial circuit as well as in a religious creation, in all flows and currents that only secondarily allow themselves to be appropriated by the State. (360)

Because of the emphasis on creativity, 'war is like the fall or failure of the war machine, the only object left for the war machine after it has lost its power to change' (230). The worst case for the failed war machine occurs when it 'has constructed itself a State apparatus capable only of destruction. When this happens, the war machine no longer draws mutant lines of flight, but a pure, cold line of abolition' (230); DG's target here is the Nazi regime.

In the standard-setting case of actual historical 'nomads', DG derive the term from the effects the central Asian steppe military bands had on the settled, agricultural civilizations of China, the Muslim world, and Europe. The historical war machine of the nomads was brought near 'perfection' by the almost entirely anti-State, countersignifying destruction of the Mongol hordes, burning, raping, and looting their way across striated spaces. The nomadic war machines were captured by States and one way or the other many settled down. In the case of the Vikings (insofar as they effectuated a war machine, as opposed to simply being raiders who returned home with their booty whenever they could), they became Normans, and their deterritorializing force, which in the case of their nomad existence 'reterritorializes on deterritorialization itself' (381), fell under the control of sedentary forces and was reterritorialized on the conquest of territory, as in the Crusades (220), although this is of course not without a deterritorializing effect on the religious institution that attempts to control it (384). Universalizing religions – Christianity and Islam being the two most notable and successful in this case – can thus be thought of as war machines in their own right, parallel to their existence as State religions (383). Islam's effect on medieval India, for example, was one of disruption and chaos, of smoothing as it redistributed the possibilities of human freedom, and hammered at the Hindu caste system by preaching the equality of 'brotherhood' under God. Christianity was a war machine as it did very similar things, particularly in the Americas. As war machines, the world religions have worked in the service of State apparatuses but are at low-level war with these as well – 'war', of course, being much more and else than bloodshed.

The affects of war machines are the suite of tools/weapons that allow them always to maintain 'intensive' speed, that is, to occupy a smooth space by being able to intervene immediately at any point in that space (381). Hence the function of the State-captured war machine, as incarnated in today's global security forces whose 'force projection' and surveillance capacities strive to create and maintain a global smooth space. Needless to say, these forces go hand-in-hand with globalized capitalism, a war machine in its own right that forms a smooth space (466). In contrast, as much as the capitalist axiomatic strives to 'conjugate' the creative flows it liberates (that is, to have technological and social innovation reterritorialized on private property relations), there are always 'connections' of such flows (autocatalysis, the ability to 'accelerate their shared escape' [220]). The war machine formed by such a connection of flows, which 'has as its object not war but the drawing of a creative line of flight' (422), aims at 'revolutionary movement', that is, 'the becoming-minoritarian of everybody/everything [*tout le monde*]' (472–3).

WHITE WALL. See BLACK HOLE/WHITE WALL SYSTEM.

WITTFOGEL, Karl August. German historian and de facto historical geographer (1896–1988). Wittfogel is famous for *Oriental
Despotism: A Comparative Study of Total Power* (1957) in which he
highlighted the (now controversial and contested) role of State
power in constructing 'hydraulic societies'. DG, in a move that
might seem somewhat naïvely Orientalist, follow Wittfogel's
models in their often seemingly caricatured portrayal of 'the East'
and its Despots, both of them in the footsteps of Marx and
Montesquieu (564–5n9). Although DG affirm that 'there is no
going back on Wittfogel's theses on the importance of large-scale
waterworks for an empire' (363), they do acknowledge that some
parts of Wittfogel's work have been 'refuted' (19). Although they
do not enter the details of this refutation, when we do, we find
they affirm some of DG's central theses on the State. Butzer
(1976 and 1996) shows how control of the Nile floods arose as a
complex adaptive, decentralized, village-based system, and was
later overcoded and controlled by the State. Butzer thus directly
contradicts Wittfogel, who stresses the State as the origin of large-
scale water works, and confirms DG's theses that the State stratifies
without producing consistencies. (The State need not be the
origin of large-scale waterworks to recognize their importance; it
should be said, however, that the State's interest in hydraulics is
preventing turbulence in channeling water in aqueducts and so
forth, while the 'hydraulic model of nomad science and the war
machine . . . consists in being distributed by turbulence across a
smooth space' [363].) Butzer's entire geographic oeuvre may be
read profitably for its complex adaptive systems approach to
understanding spaces and spatial transformation in both the Old
World and the New World (primarily Mexico). The cultural ecological approach to geography, in general, is closely related to the
Deleuzoguattarian materialist project, though it lacks the latter's
breadth and depth. (Structuralist and poststructuralist *political*
ecology is less closely related to geophilosophy in that it too closely
follows the alloplastic stratum and various semiological conventions at the expense of fuller, nonlinear treatments of the earth.)

WORLD: a deterritorialized milieu (172), the 'culmination' of the
'associated' milieus (51), or even the set of affects of an animal
(257). The prime example of 'animal world' or *Umwelt* is that of
the Tick, as studied by von Uexküll (1965) and taken up at 51 and

257 (see also Ansell Pearson 1999). DG will specify that the 'scientific world' is a *Welt*, as opposed to the animal *Umwelt*, since the former is more highly deterritorialized, the 'translation of all of the flows, particles, codes, and territorialities of the other strata into a sufficiently deterritorialized system of signs, in other words, into an overcoding specific to language' (62).

ZONE OF INDISCERNIBILITY: the transitional zone, limitrophe zone, or zone of variation (101). The zone of indiscernibility (see also 'Border') is not only the fuzzy zone of encounter, but also the margin wherein becomings occur that affect each dialect in the encounter. Although first proposed in the discussion of minor languages, which are distributed across a smooth language space, DG also say that in a broader sense zones of indiscernibility are found between singularities in any smooth space. By contrast, the major language 'swoops down' from a transcendent position, striating minor languages and turning them into dialects within a Language that has hard-and-fast boundaries between it and the next.

ZONE OF PROXIMITY: the 'neighborhood' zone (272–3; see the note on set theory at 542n55). The zone of proximity is the milieu in which particles may have 'favorable' encounters: in which desire is possible. The zone of proximity is the zone where becoming can happen. It is the rhizosphere where no hard boundary can exist.

Appendix: Case study – entangled spaces and semiotics in Olancho

In this section we demonstrate how the tools of *ATP*, as we have explicated them in the text and in the Glossary, can allow us to map the transformations of entangled complex systems in a particular region. Drawing on Bonta (2001),[75] we supply enough details to approach an understanding of certain complex spaces – and to assert that spaces *are* complex – through painting rather broad strokes where many would no doubt prefer pointillistic detail. The full study in Bonta (2001) supplies these details, so below we cite selectively only certain key secondary sources; the account is also constructed from an array of archival sources as well as Bonta's ethnographic fieldnotes covering the period 1991–present.

We will produce the elements of a Deleuzoguattarian cartography of Olancho. Thus we will not so much disentangle its extensive 'strata' (for example, separating human from forest, peasant from rancher) as offer proof that landscapes have resilience and power as long as the spaces that spawn them remain or become tightly entangled; we strive to keep them that way as much as possible, and tease them apart only for simplicity's sake. Spaces may be subject at any one time to a ratio of more or less intense smoothing or striating forces, but through a process of protecting their entanglement (the *enredo*: the concrete mixture of complex spaces we find in any given landscape), many such spaces can ward off the overwhelming State-sponsored striation that so often threatens them.

We are selectively profiling the province of Olancho in eastern Honduras, in which the chief striating threat is not so much a monolithic State per se as a State that may come to favor one land use over all others, one economy, one semiotic, one corporation, in any one place. The State achieves the 'order' and 'organization' of its hinterlands so that certain assemblages may more perfectly extract resources, steal land, and oppress or banish existent land users.[76] What we outline is a way to understand and characterize spatial heterogeneity in a 'far-from-striated' (thus far-from-equilibrium) region. We submit that spatial heterogeneity (favored by the coexistence of myriad complex spaces) provides resilience and 'freedom' as it allows the possibility of decentered network-alliances ('rhizomes') that can preserve immanence and resist overcoding, and just plain do a better job at guaranteeing self-governance, human dignity, adequate use of 'natural resources', and other presumably desirable situations in which the State, to judge by the region's geo-history, has tampered almost wholly unsuccessfully. The Olancho case might draw comparisons with other far-from-striated regions of the planet, though we urge caution in that respect.

We start with Bonta's (hereafter 'the researcher's') quandary that led him to study Deleuze and Guattari in the first place: little to no agreement exists among inhabitants of Olancho (and those who study them) over the following spatial issues:

- Rights to land. Profound disagreement and conflict exist over who or what owns just about every rural place.
- Deforestation. Intense disagreement over who or what is responsible for the removal of trees that was commonly agreed upon to have contributed to the disastrous consequences of Hurricane Mitch in 1998.
- Aesthetics. Lack of agreement on whether an attractive landscape looks like a pasture, a forest, a beanfield, a coffee farm, or a reservoir.
- Whether the individual and family, or the municipality, or the province, or the State, or a corporation, or God, or the entire society as a whole, can be exclusive owners of a property, or in what combinations and by what mechanisms can ownership be established and respected.
- Which of the mutually contradictory land-related laws are applicable, in a society lacking a local court system capable of interpreting them to the satisfaction of the land users.
- What constitutes 'development' (*desarrollo*)?

The researcher found that everybody tended to think of their own group as correct in questions regarding space, even though there was a vague idea floating around that at the bottom all space belonged to 'Honduras' (*la nación, la patria, nuestro país*). But even there, many environmentalists asserted the world–space quality of the rain forest: these might be in Honduras, but they were primarily global property. At the other end of the spectrum, many Olanchanos belittled 'Honduras' and claimed priority for local and regional identities.

Though the researcher opted to take the stand that heterogeneity was desirable and that striation that abrogated sociospatial rights
was bad, he still sought to understand each 'spatial identity' (for
example, *yo soy ganadero, yo soy cafetalero*: haecceities) on and by its
own terms, mapping the space that it occupied as fairly as possible.
Parallel to full treatments of land uses and other factors in determining how and why spaces were so contentious and segregated, the
researcher sought out the 'mixture', where they are entangled semiotically. Public meetings, for example, revealed a cacophony of spatially polarized stances clamoring for recognition and rights, each
voice repeating the refrain of a different space, all packed into a relatively tiny area.

Bonta stayed with the common geographers' conception of 'the
landscape' as a jumbled-together segment of the earth's surface, not
just visual but tactile, olfactory, sonorous, containing evidence of
human dwelling but also of the non-human – an everything, in
others words, that obviously contains a multitude of territories and
structures and is traversed by and productive of the flows and block-
ages of divers systems at all registers.[77] Humans' attempts to achieve
a one-to-one match between their own land uses and the totality of
the landscapes that they occupied became a central issue of research
– how do spaces become manifested as territories across landscapes,
and, more crucially, what are the mechanisms by which spaces
extend themselves at the expense of other spaces, and eventually
deny even the possibility that other spaces have any 'rights' to
occupy the landscape at all. Certain issues that served as exemplars
of spatial conflict in Olancho included the territorial imposition
of development project space, hydroelectric project space, and
national park space, and how these became deterritorialized as they
were fragmented and drawn into heterogeneous landscapes.

What was needed was a definition of 'spaces' – properly speaking,
in the plural – that would help explain not only the incessant jostlings
of human-made territories but also the way that non-adjacent territories took on similar characteristics. How, for example, is it possible
for there to be a 'coffee farm' that, though varying from place to
place and region to region, is easily recognizeable as such – as part
of 'coffee space' – across Latin America and indeed anywhere that
coffee is found? Why do cattle ranches, for that matter, resemble
each other both in the New and Old worlds, despite centuries of
divergence? It became necessary to move back from what one finds
out there in the landscape to the 'machinic assemblages' and 'collective machines of enunciation' that brought about the 'stratification'

of complex systems in such a way as to allow for a 'universal' and a 'particular' to codetermine each other. There are different but related 'machines' producing each space; otherwise, a single apparatus such as the State would have been capable of harmonizing land uses through having overcoded them and striated them within a logical, single system. A region operating in far-from-equilibrium crisis is the best way of describing what researchers find in so-called 'developing countries', quite unlike the case of 'developed countries' where striation has been so effective in achieving one-to-one matches between processes and landscapes. (Land users in 'advanced' countries do indeed vie with each other for dominance in particular landscapes, but not to the degree of 'disorganized' Honduras. Perhaps that's the point of being 'developed': settling into basins of attraction.)

The entangled spatial issues listed above reveal that people in some way actually inhabited different spaces even while standing next to each other in the same landscape. There was no a priori 'Olancho Space' that then got broken down into smaller side-by-side, nested-hexagon spaces; you didn't walk from one space to another as much as move through varied degrees of becoming across the landscape. Coffee farms were being taken over by cattle; beans were taking over forest; forests were taking over ranches; Hurricane Mitch had stripped away cattle pastures, beanfields, coffee, and forest alike.[78] A 'space', then, became the room filled by the workings of a complex system at the extensive, intensive, and virtual registers. If one were 'plugged into' the cattle-ranching assemblage, one was to a large extent predetermined and at the very least codetermined by a complex system quite different than that of one's neighbor, who was plugged into the complex system of coffee farming – or of peasant farming, conservation, development, logging, and so forth. One was an 'actor' in that complex system's space – an enactor of its space – wherever one went. Inasmuch as one (and one's cattle or coffee bushes or beans) 'made space', one territorialized one's assemblage somewhere in some landscape. One carved out a territory to provide room 'demanded' by one's assemblage. But because individual human bodies are the nexus for myriad forces that traverse them, they are easily put to work for different complex systems at the same time. The human profession-identity (I am a rancher and also a farmer) marks the various haecceities or becomings that are hyphenated as long as they are practicably combinable. Thus, we have mayor-loggers (an individual becoming-mayor, becoming-logger), rancher-conservationist-teachers, peasant farmer-ranchers, rancher-logger-coffee growers, and so on ad infinitum. Individuals, then, have the power to create spatial alliances, to draw even conflictive spaces together in part because of the very rhizomatic qualities of their own body-systems as indexed to different territorialities. They can be partisan to coffee space + ranchland + protected forest + . . . In other words, while territoriality sorts out and places side-by-side partisans of the same space to a certain extent, it does not preclude the co-existence of various spaces in the same landscape: the 'machinic orchestra' referred to in *ATP* (see 'Refrain' in the Glossary). The non-human constitution of spaces and territories sometimes precludes this (beans can't grow in pine forest because the soil isn't right), but in general humans have the capacity to transform and re-smooth their landscapes by transmuting their spaces, drawing new 'planes of consistency' for them: indeed, one can argue that this is going on all the time.

We name 'complex spaces' the spaces occupied by complex systems; they are therefore practically infinite, and yet for a given spatial conflict (land use, in the case of Olancho) can be reduced to a finite set. What matters in the final analysis – because cattle will never become coffee, and both have their place in the landscape – are the ways that the spaces can connect to each other and become entangled if they are not already. What we see as primordial is the idea that complex spaces are endlessly dynamic and can maintain the far-from-equilibrium crisis conditions that are more resilient, diverse, and empowering than the unsuccessful homeostatic spaces dreamed up by the monolithic State, spaces-as-landscapes that settle into their separate homogeneous basins of attraction and are so hard to escape from by those inside. What we have tried to understand, then, is the 'deterministic chaos' that possesses localized order but no overall striation, is constantly in disarray, but that is always birthing new haecceities and allowing for rhizomes to preclude the establishment of centralization and hierarchization. Stratifications and striation, in other words, but no overcoding Order principle.

Each space is qualitatively different – they are not variants on one theme, but come about through vastly divergent processes. Each has a geohistory that must be engaged on its own terms. Each is territorialized in the landscape by means of human and non-human 'agents' guided by a certain set of instructions, tendencies, trajectories: lines and segments, in terms of *ATP*. Each is organized differently with respect to their powers and needs to smooth and to striate materials. Each contains its own semiotic, its own 'regime of signs' that at first approximation can be understood in terms of *ATP*'s four regimes (presignifying, signifying, postsignifying, and countersignifying) but should be more accurately understood as containing a concrete mixture of these. Each complex system deterritorializes forces of the earth and cosmos and puts them to work in a different way, stratifying them in different sequences, drawing from elements common to them – on the physico-chemical, geological, biological, and human strata – but for different purposes. To be precise, the types of 'land use' complex spaces we are seeking to understand here are deterritorialized elements of non-human spaces ('nature') created by non-human complex systems ('forces of nature'): it is usually a case of the interweaving of complex systems rather than the tapping of hitherto-untapped 'raw material' that has not yet been territorialized. The land-use complex systems are drawing from, for example, a forest space that is highly rhizomatic and in far-from-equilibrium crisis, a network of milieus and territories creating products drawing from different strata simultaneously. 'Rain forest space' is a complex space in its own right – with or without humans – and indeed may be the finest example we have of the working of a far-from-equilibrium crisis system so heterogeneous, so fast-moving, so interwoven that it has created the greatest diversity of coexistent life and territories possible within the absolute constraints of the planet. Rain forest space's extreme diversity of forms, for example (take the example of numbers of species per unit of land area – in the western Amazon basin lowlands, highest in the world), increases as disturbance factors increase, up to a threshold of disturbance (characterized, for example, by extreme fragmentation) whereby the hollowed-cube dimensionality of forest space collapses and surface area decreases: the Sierpinski Sponge is replaced by a slightly-more-than-two-dimensional striated plane (pasture or rows of banana trees, for example).

Land use complex spaces can be dated in their penetration of a new landscape, and in their overcoding of that landscape. In the case of Honduras, we can gain a relatively good idea of when these dates are. Through historical geographical research we can establish when a certain complex system or vanguard of that system, perhaps the smoothing force of a 'war machine' – cattle, for example – enters a region and begins to effect the landscape changes necessary for the establishment of a new space. For Olancho, we have little data to support the idea that a State was present there – undergirding and overcoding the whole region, as States always do – before the 1520s; this is different from other places in the Americas at Conquest, but, as Deleuze and Guattari state, radically decentered non-State ('primitive' or presignifying, in this region) polities defined themselves by their power to ward off States and any form of outside striation, so Olancho in that sense had been 'successful'. Ethnohistorical evidence, the basis for interpreting what was going on before 1492 in Honduras, and up until 1600 (lacking any large-scale archaeological digs as yet), points to a landscape of decentered polities (Newson [1986] calls them 'chiefdoms') that warred and traded with each other and were weakly penetrated by the forces of the Aztec empire. Hernan Cortés and Pedrarias Dávila, two conquistadors who struggled against each other to impose the Iberoamerican State in eastern Honduras in the 1520s, had little success in striating most of the region, as there was little way to introduce the concept of the State: what had been so successful in the Conquest of Mexico, and of the Nicarao in Nicaragua, failed miserably in such non-State and presumably anti-State regions.[79]

We have, then, 'instantaneous' semiotic and thus material transformations demanded by the Spanish in Olancho in the period 1525–1600. All that existed automatically became the property of Spain, and specifically of the King and the Christian God. All landscapes were underlain by these principles, and overseen by them as well. Furthermore, Olancho took up its dutiful place on the remote margins of the Spanish empire, far down the power hierarchy that became anchored and structured thus: (1) Spain; (2) Mexico (Mexico City); (3) Central America (capital ending up at Guatemala City, eventually); (4) Provincia de Honduras (capital ending up at Comayagua, eventually); (5) outlying 'partidos' such as Olancho. Consequently, Olancho became a 'remote' and 'backward' region.

A universalizing space that lagged slightly behind this new State space in Olancho was that of the Church, which had to striate minds and bodies in a somewhat more subtle but lasting way. While colonial administrators sought to carve out the State, Franciscan friars sought to extract Indians from the yet-unstriated spaces out of reach of God and Spain (in the case of Honduras, the Mosquito Coast, and in general, in Central America, the Caribbean litorral where transport was by canoe, swamps abounded, and conquerors' horses were all but useless). Thus, one can track the conflicts and alliances between Church and State spaces – both universalizing, both colonizers of the mind and body together – to the present day. But land use spaces, through which wealth might be created, and by which the goals of all spatialized human-guided complex systems might be achieved, were and remain the most powerful encompassing 'containers' for human populations, and testament to this is the pride by which many people in Olancho today and throughout the historical record first mention their land use spatial identities and last mention being 'Hondurans'. Control over space, throughout five centuries, was the way to power, security, and importance in Olancho. The researcher is never quite clear as to whether the land users feel themselves primarily as embedded in the hierarchies of the Church and the State, or rather as – in the case of ranchers, particularly – masters of all they survey, at the center of their worlds, for whom the Church and State are annoying disturbances where they are not convenient (for example, when Catholic priests and State entities side with land reform movements). One more thing might be said on this theme: people see themselves as participants in political and cultural spaces of the municipality and the province as well as the *nación*, but in a land-focused society where what is local takes precedence over what is not, pride in place – an evidence of the power of place, or, by other phraseology, a strong sense of place – is most intensely felt at the 'level' of the town and outlying territory (municipality), less so at the level of Olancho, and least at 'Honduras'. Nationalism, in other words, has historically been less important than regionalism and localism. Because of their fierce independence (or just the poor striation effected by the Church and State), Honduran spaces have not easily been brought into the type of 'resonance' that can lead to the 'macrofascism' produced by a paranoid State apparatus, a resonance that would bring the chaotic hinterlands into direct obedience to the center and under a single semiotic of command-and-obey.[80]

For Olancho, the 1500s also brought cattle ranching to a region that possessed plains that had been maintained as wide-open agricultural and hunting spaces to feed dense pre-Columbian populations. Though most Indians were enslaved, died of disease, or fled, cattle – a nomadic 'war machine' unleashed into the abandoned striated horticultural spaces – kept the plains open. Cattle served as the agents for the achievement of a highly smooth 'cattle space' that, by way of the introduction of the animals and use of fire, rapidly multiplied itself across not just land-grant hacienda territories but across the entire available terrain of the drier parts of the province, unable to penetrate only isolated highlands and the lowland humid forests to the east. The phenomenon of wild cattle creating open or at least semi-open landscapes, and the idea that where cattle were located belonged to the rancher (helped by the conversion of the few thousand remaining tribute Indians themselves to cattle ranchers par excellence) created the popular image of the essence of Olancho as cattle and grass – not vegetable gardens (that cattle trampled often, to the dismay of horticulturalists), and certainly not dense forests. Spanish landholders received limited land grants from the Crown and sold them to each other, to Indian towns, to the Church, but they had already claimed, extralegally, most of the drylands, as far as the eye could survey, for cattle space. Later ways and dates that cattle space advanced were through the introduction of aggressive African grass rhizomes (late 1800s), the extirpation of the peasant land take-over movement (24 June 1975, through a high-profile massacre), and the following of logging and coffee roads into the humid forests (1970s–present). Cattle space came to saturate Olancho's very sense of place – expansive, green pasture dotted by cows, the wide-open plains cited numerous times by outsiders and by local authors; cowboys and riding in general revered; the ideal meal a big steak; all the sounds (the cattle call as the primary refrain of the space) and the pungent smells; even the way that cattle take precedence today over cars on highways. Fences in cattle space partition off one territory from the next, or are (often vain) attempts to keep cattle out of other spaces, but they never signify that cattle space is reaching an absolute boundary (cattle can, basically, thrive absolutely anywhere once heavy forest is removed, regardless of soil type, rainfall, or other parameters).

Ranchers deploy cattle to effect takeovers of other territories, for example, the deterritorialization of coffee space. Cattle let loose in a coffee farm can be disastrous, so coffee space has to be fenced and gated. The cow is so much the vanguard of the spatial takeover by the rancher that its very presence may be a threat in, for example, the spaces of small farmers.[81] But there are serious threats to cattle space today, due to the becoming-environmentalist society's now generalized dislike of burning (the way to get fresh and healthy grass and browse) and a preference for more shade trees and less-open pasture. Cattle ranchers, and their space, are currently embattled and at a loss as they find that what had before been the norm is being increasingly criticized.

The locally striated spaces of agriculture coevolved since Conquest, but are today characterized by New World crops (maize and beans; Old World wheat never worked out). Swidden agriculture (fire-fallow rotation) which presumably arose independently at different spots around the globe remains the preferred way of growing food for local consumption. The Spanish conquerors were ranchers and hacienda owners, not farmers, so cattle space only allowed agriculture in its interstices (plantain groves along rivers, for example) or out of sight (in the humid forest where cattle couldn't/wouldn't go). To striate the wandering Indians, the Franciscan friars tried some Iberian techniques (for example, agriculture in only one place, not dispersed across swidden plots, which the friars couldn't comprehend). Many Old World fruit varieties (mangos, for example) were introduced and multiplied rapidly, while chickens and pigs became integral in the constricted smallholder landscapes of tribute Indians and emerging rural classes of mestizos and mulattos (the mix is known as *campesino* today), but we suppose that the major transformations in agriculture came about through tribute paying (channeling excess production outward) and through the introduction of a mercantile capitalist system that produced lack and even famine though did not bankrupt the region altogether, given that farmers continued to (and still) hunt wild game, gather wild plant products, and fish. Partial socioeconomic dependency on the spatial hierarchy described above was established quite early, and would one day give rise to the need for 'development space', the space built on the concept that the way to erase the socioeconomic and intellectual 'backwardness' of a region was not through erasing its hierarchical position, but by educating the poor to use what they had more sustainably.

Other agricultural spaces involved capital-intensive production by large landowners, and have achieved a certain success on the plains, but other than coffee have not replaced the smallholder swidden spaces in the mountains.

Coffee plants were introduced to Olancho in the early 1800s, but 'coffee space' really began to achieve status competitive to other land uses in the 1900s, and continued to increase in importance up to the 1990s. It may be internal to smallholder space or to large landholdings; in some cases, coffee is grown on reclaimed cattle space. Coffee farms in Olancho are usually forests striated by rows of plants and, where they are not used solely for local consumption, inextricably linked to the world market. The maintenance and ownership of coffee space is tied directly to market forces, and, when world prices are high, it is an emancipatory (even 'get rich quick') space for smallholders. But coffee space has nothing like the semi-autonomous agency of the cow to keep it intact, and grows back quickly to 'real' forest if not maintained. Because coffee space's very morphology is tied to availability of capital (it can't be maintained if you can't afford to pay for its upkeep), it is extremely high maintenance and by consequence easily bought by landowners farther up the socioeconomic hierarchy and transformed as necessary. Capital-intensive transformations usually include thinning of forest cover and replacement of traditional, low-yielding plants with high-yield, sun-loving varieties. Coffee space can easily be transformed from its 'forest' mode to its biotic 'desert' mode (sun-grown bushes saturated by agricultural chemicals).

By virtue of the geology, climate, and anthropogenic fire history of Olancho, large swaths of landscape are covered by pine woods on top of soil almost always completely useless for agriculture of any type. They are maintained by burning and provide sources of firewood and timber for small farmers, as well as watersources and grass. Pine woods, thanks to their ubiquity on so many hilly surfaces (they grow poorly on the plains), became the province's scenic but sterile backdrop (what was on the hills in the background in the mental landscape painting of 'typical' Olancho, where cattle dominated the foreground) and historically were seen as impoverished and of little practical use, and therefore available to whomever occupied the plains. They were titled to a certain extent for the use of dry-season *retiros* (seasonal pastures) during the transhumance of cattle from the plains and back, but other uses were always allowed. However, their casual use for products such as pitch and timber, old as the Spanish occupation in terms of importance for the world market, intensified with the introduction of 'timber space' in the mid- to late twentieth century. Previously, well back into the 1800s, Olancho's hardwoods were extracted wherever they might grow, and forest space was penetrated and then abandoned by logging companies in search of mahogany and other species. But the wholesale transformation of Honduras's vast pine woods into timber space – semiotically transforming each and every pine tree in Honduras into 'timber', and marking everything else within the space as useless clutter (for example, trees that 'gobble up' shade are called 'wolf trees' in forester parlance) – was achieved finally in the early 1970s through laws and government institutions, a national forestry school, and foresters to serve as the promoters. Timber space became even more important as hardwoods were logged out from accessible areas, and inaccessible rain forests were locked up inside parks (1980s–present). Hardwood extraction was eventually criminalized, and pine woods as timber space are currently at threat of reclamation by other spaces (by villages, as watersheds; by environmentalists, as habitat) despite what foresters and loggers see as their 'obvious' and even divinely ordained qualities as an easy and regrowable source of wealth.

'Development' (*desarrollo*), which we take to be any seemingly self-evident process of unfolding the potential of a society and space (all space, but some in particular more than others), is a notion easily traceable to the late colonial period in Honduras, thanks to reforms in Spain and certain 'progressive' governors such as Ramón de Anguiano (1997), who wrote in 1801 that Honduras's potential was being 'wasted' because of the 'lazy' Spanish overlords, but could and should be tapped into. Development became the unifying goal of the Honduran nation-state (1821–present) as its founders and more progressive leaders aspired to the ideal that a perfect state of society and space exists that can and must be striven toward, and may even be reachable some day. Measures of development vary, but the underlying truths, that one who claims to be in favor of development believes, are that tradition is wrong or imperfect, material poverty is bad, education and the work ethic are good, and a powerful outside force (capital, 'experts', 'America') can and should come in and set things right, or at minimum oversee, consult, or advise, bringing the wisdom of a country or region that has already become developed.

By the 1850s, outsiders and many of its own residents judged Olancho as being in need of development. Urban citizens knew what things were like elsewhere, and wanted to catch up. 'Enlightened' folk welcomed roads, bridges, modern buildings, the telegraph, new educational and agricultural methods, and so on. Development projects in the modern sense, however, really began to penetrate Olancho only in the 1950s, and are pervasive today, though there are still many areas that have not been occupied by one. The idea of development, in general, saturates the human dimensions of all landscapes (everything human-related can be developed), but development projects limited in time and space occupy certain landscapes to turn them into exemplars, the local territories of 'development space', localized manifestations of a worldwide complex system that seeks to transform the 'hearts and minds' as well as the pastures and coffee farms of the entire planet, making them produce more and/or better.[82]

Development practitioners see the need to make examples out of certain landscapes, to fashion them into facsimiles-in-miniature of what the global development machine can achieve. A development organization's territory thus takes on certain strong qualitative differences from 'normal' ('disorganized') landscapes, and effects in a certain way an iconographic space. New, colorful signs point to development icons: outhouses, communal gardens, women's cooperative sewing circle meeting places, health clinics, schools, bridges, irrigation systems. Donor names and amounts in both dollars and lempiras for each icon are often printed right on the sign.

Agents of development space are, these days, often local people themselves who have been (re)educated to believe that in all cases non-developed human space is irrational, that all everyday space is 'naturally' irrational and backward. Solutions, however (except in the mostly finely attuned development agencies), must come from elsewhere, or at least must be repackaged in a way that allows the agents to measure the indicators marking the progress of their space toward development quantitatively (which is itself never an achievable space – one is only ever 'on the way' to it). Sustainable, Green Revolution, NGO-led, Church-based, government-driven development: all are variations on the Theme of Development which has changed little in substance in over a century. To the extent that development is the necessary condition of modern, globalized humanity, and is cited as desirable by people themselves, for all spaces except the inside of the untouchable zones of 'conservation space' (see below), it is not as invasive as when it seeks to bring about development space that is a 1:1 match to the otherwise heterogeneous landscape. The microfascistic power of development lies in its attempt to forbid or at least belittle any other type of space from emerging within its domain.[83] These days, even the State withdraws to let the Development Project do its work; where it can, the State chips in and hitchhikes to political ends. Development space is the only space in Olancho with universalizing pretensions toward human spatial practice, and the only space wherein the human landscape is brought toward perfection (conservation space tries to do this in a parallel venture, with 'nature').

Development space is supposed to outlive its Project, but from what we have seen it is quickly reclaimed by the chaos of jostling spaces, and only echoes remain. Those who have inhabited the diaphonous, multi-year territory of the Development Project are supposed to have carried it off elsewhere, little war machines which will introduce Development into other landscapes, will work to overturn the irrational tenets of undeveloped spaces everywhere. This is called the 'multiplier effect'.

At this point it helps to step back from the mixture and think about the 'natural environment'. Heterogeneity is 'built in' prior to human alteration of landscapes. Thanks to the differentiating powers of 'nature', the earth has been stratified into surfaces, sediments, chemicals, minerals, vegetation, and so forth in such a way that not all spaces can be territorialized everywhere. To that extent, timber space, for example, can exist only where there are pines which in turn are limited by several environmental factors that humans can't modify, even by fire; timber space could therefore never take over everywhere the way cattle space could. Seeing this, spatial planners and managers often seek to allot each space its 'potential' local territories and go from there, not recognizing that univocal spatial identities are the exception rather than the rule, and in any case what happens in one space always affects another, plugged as they all are into flows of capital, cultural networks, the State, and so on. The planner's project is to 'sort things out' to make them function better, usually indicated by a two-dimensional map that has a hard time portraying spatial complexity. Planners, who gaze at the rural from the standpoint of the urban, use the 'natural environment' to impose that most hegemonic of territories, the protected area.

Urban space in Olancho – a tiny part of the whole – is a conduit whereby the rural landscape is channeled outward to the nation and the world, and whereby the nation and the world can penetrate the local. Towns therefore contain headquarters of government agencies, development projects, and so forth; they contain Internet cafes and post offices; they have accumulated much better goods and services than outlying areas; they are market, education, and religious centers. They mix the spatial identities and politics of land-use spaces to such an extent that they are, following *ATP*, more coagulations of the flows of capital and ideas rather than the source of these – they are nodes that arose from a rural landscape, some having arisen, through necessities of physical geography, earlier even than the Spanish conquest (see 'Town' in the Glossary). But however beholden are urban spaces to rural spaces, they are also zones of isolation from the countryside, and collect people whose spatialities are but roughly attuned to the exigencies of land use. Environmentalism typically found lodging in urban areas among people divorced from the necessities of sustenance and free to practice non-land-based trades and hence with the luxury and mindset to posit environmental guidelines for the use of the entire landscape, based partly on what looked pretty from a distance and, increasingly, on what makes most sense for the harmony between conflictive spaces and the benefit of both human and non-human populations alike. Thus, environmentalists fostered hostility toward cattle space that favors pasture over forest cover, toward coffee space that poisons and degrades forest, timber space that commodifies trees, and smallholder space that creates 'deforestation'. Urban dwellers, who don't have to know the intricacies of why it is done, simply see 'deforestation' as the cause of destroyed watersheds, a perceived rise in temperatures due to change in microclimate, and few to no animals any more.

Forest space, even among some who depend on altering it for the maintenance of their own space, has gained a premium value in contemporary Olanchano society. Landscape ideals now include forests where before only open savanna would do (elderly Olanchanos tend to think of uncontrolled vegetation as 'rank' and 'dirty'). Though this is not completely an outside implant, the effect of over a decade of intense environmentalism in schools, development projects, on TV, and in political campaigns cannot be discounted. Forest was not previously disliked, but in the past there was more of it in the places it was supposed to be (the *montaña*), whereas today the most visible areas close to towns are, not unsurprisingly, highly deforested, so urbanites are forced to gaze at smoking hillsides on a daily basis. Hurricane Mitch in 1998 poured so much rain on Olancho that hillsides collapsed, unchecked rivers flooded, and hundreds of people died; people noticed that deforested hillsides tended to collapse more than forested ones, while deforested floodplains did a poor job of slowing down and channeling floodwaters as they emerged from the mountains to the plains. Four years later, annual heavy rains in the mountains continued to cause disastrous flooding because Mitch – perhaps a 1,000-year flood event – had carved open river channels and removed vegetation allowing for faster flow and less retention. Bonta's field research came in the wake of Mitch, and, because the hurricane had laid open the landscape to its seams, the evidence for the damage done by decades of deforestation was incontrovertible in Olanchanos' minds. Environmentalism jumped into the mainstream with astounding force, so that *campesinos* began to call themselves environmentalists and mean it, while agricultural development projects stopped ignoring the necessity for development spaces to contain forested watersheds. Industrial ventures factored environmental concerns into their impact statements and mitigation projects. This was the milieu in which the spatial issues listed at the beginning of this study were raised.

When environmental awareness is awakened, it becomes spatially and temporally focused ('we need to do something here and now!'), rather than remaining, like 'development', a general principle, applicable anywhere and everywhere. Thus, we arrive at 'conservation space', usually effected as a polygon with a name such as 'national park' or 'biosphere reserve'. In general, conservation space in Honduras is achieved through an archipelago of 'protected areas'. These began as 1980s implants from out-of-country, based on the US model but with a certain margin of human landscape called the 'buffer zone'. Conservationists pursued adamantly what they presumed to be 'untouched' forest space and proceeded to 'lock it up' via presidential decrees, laws, and 'presence': basically, Peace Corps volunteers and Honduran park guards, biologists, and others, who went around and talked about the existence of protected areas ('See that forest over there? It's now a park, and it has rules that must be obeyed'). The agents of conservation space strained to achieve its actualization through convincing people that what they had thought of as either part of their own spaces, or as part of a yet-untransformed *pura montaña* (virgin forest in the US conception) belonged to the nation and to the world: rain forest, eternal store-house of biodiversity, source of pure water and plants that could possibly cure cancer. For you but also for all Humankind: don't be selfish! Don't cut it down!

Now, forest space in Olancho belonged in theory to the State anyway, though some forests that were still *pura montaña* had been surreptitiously territorialized by *campesinos* and others, as private woodlots reserved for possible future tree removal. But by conservationists' conceptions, forest space in Olancho was either 'empty' (contained no indigenous users) or Biosphere Reserve-grade, meaning that indigenous groups like the Tawahka Indians were recognized as hunters and gatherers and were allowed to continue such 'non-damaging' practices within it. However, in the case of protected areas such as the Sierra de Agalta National Park,[84] conservationists were able to (re)claim it entirely as national territory and proceed to remake it in the image of conservation space.

Through the use of the buffer zone concept, they were able to promote a zone of contact between land-using humans and Nature, and try to achieve sustainable development there (that is, stop deforestation by persuading land-users to adopt 'land-friendly' practices), while making the forest space itself off-limits to all localized land uses, but useful as a pure reserve of water and biodiversity, and accessible only to ecotourists and scientists. The decree protecting Agalta was issued in 1987, and small teams of conservationists and becoming-conservationist foresters, farmers, and others, in the employ of the State and development organizations, set about trying to achieve conservation space – the 'perfect' park out of the US text-book, or even something better – based on the idea that true forest space should be entirely free of human influence and only then could regain its prehuman magnificence. Now, obviously conservationists had overlooked several important facts: all forest space was already territorialized by humans in the sense that they used it and claimed it, just not necessarily for farms and ranches; they hunted and gathered in it; they were accustomed to transforming it into human landscape; it was embedded within municipal territories that had claimed it for hundreds of years; it was being used as refuge for clandestine practices (in the 1980s, the Honduran State made some rain forests off-limits because they believed them to be hideouts for Marxist guerrilla 'terrorists'). Locking up precisely the land that is fated for transformation to land-use spaces was sure to create serious problems, because the forces that propelled the expansion of territories into relatively unused forest space could not simply be blocked, and the buffer zone slowed things down only a little. At first, the national park was synonymous with the worst fascistic tendencies of the hated State and hated US 'gringo' presence. It went directly against the radical land reforms of the 1960s that had resulted in massacres of *campesinos* in the 1970s. The State had declared rain forests barren zones that were free for transformation on a first-come, first-serve basis; *campesinos* who were tired of being abused while trying to seize cattle space turned increasingly to forest space – which abounded in Olancho in the 1970s – and streamed into the province. Left alone for only a few years, they were suddenly informed after 1987 that they were illegally within a park 'nuclear zone' and must leave.

Conservation space never achieves its own perfection, and is always felt as lack. Conservation space is drawn from a set of instructions for an untrammeled Nature; it strains to reach the perfection of the prehuman and is thus in that sense not a land-use space at all, but some sort of ahuman, non-capitalized, non-'degraded' source that can only serve to renew humanity (or at least those of the ecotourist variety, and water users) but cannot be sullied by base human land uses (here we of course recognize that many protected areas are not so harsh on humans, but in the case of rain forest surrounded by *mestizo* land users who deforest, the dichotomy is stark; indigenous people, by definition, are 'stewards' and their presence within conservation spaces is more acceptable). Conservation space in this example is thus actually a plane of consistency for conservationists, which explains why many conservationists of our acquaintance appear incapable of accepting any human space as anything but inferior when compared with the perfection of untouched Nature (again, this feeling manifests itself in only some conservationists, usually those unaware of or wilfully ignorant of the complex interlinkages of human and nonhuman).

185

So far we have laid out a brief typology and geohistory of spaces. What follows is an example of the transformative entanglements of these same spaces, at least as they are unfolded within landscapes. To restate what we started out with, the very existence of interwoven complex spaces tends to favor the packed, jumbled, and 'chaotic' non-equilibrium crisis conditions of landscapes to the (ideal, for us) extent that no one system can seize control and overcode the landscape for only one spatial regime. Striation by a monolithic State, in other words, remains illusory, thus the State cannot pave the way for parasitic capitalistic assemblages that, in essence, (re)colonize the heterogeneous landscape to siphon off as much of its contents as possible for the enjoyment of people elsewhere, at the lowest possible price to investors. The Deleuzian 'new Earth', by contrast, is based on the localized disruptions and alliances that guard against 'total' Conquest by Empire or *any* straitjacketing, hierarchizing machine that fits places into non-dynamic molds within an 'unfair' system of differential access to the world. However, the new Earth should not warp local territories into some anti-outsider envelope, but rather foster myriad local-global connections as well as dynamic access at all points to emergent forces.

There will always be localized striation (even agriculture does this) just as there will always be limited conflicts between territories (anti-State societies may or may not be peaceful), and this is not the place to pass ethical judgment on these.[85] If deterministic chaos, multiple centers of limited power, abundant invention, maximal biodiversity – the full, relatively equitable mixture of striating and smoothing forces – can be present in the landscape, then the State can be fended off and people can go about the business of returning the Earth to a world of post-State, post-polygonal spaces. This, anyway, was the conclusion that Bonta reached based on the fact that in Olancho the State or any universal striating force had become replaceable by 'sustainable development', which in the 1990s became the radical idea that the local was preeminent and the State was necessary only for favors (being, in practice, far from monolithic, as Graham points out in *Paper Arrows* [2002]). Complex spaces and the land-users that enact them do not require the State any more or less than they need any foreign power to come in and set them straight. Empowerment, in other words, is available everywhere (and certainly not just through 'development space') – this, in any case, is another way of phrasing what many people in Olancho came to believe *desarrollo sostenible* meant.

When a hydroelectric company sought to gain acceptance for a dam project that was to be located in the Sierra de Agalta National Park, it cited its love of Nature, of the park, of the forest, and promised to protect these more effectively than the State was able to do. The State had encouraged the hydro company to do this precisely because the State, being fragmented, worked both for and against the interests of each and every space (some State policies favored small farmers, while others worked against them, for example). The people – ranchers, *campesinos*, townspeople, teachers, conservationists, coffee farmers, and so forth – were quick to perceive that the company was 'using' the park as a 'way in' to an already fully-occupied landscape. An 85 per cent majority of local inhabitants were not about to let an alien spatiality destroy natural landscape features by flooding a forest and ruining a major waterfall, nor decimate human livelihoods by restricting access to some land uses (coffee farms) and destroying others altogether (water for cattle, ecotourist money paid into local pockets for the privilege of gazing at waterfalls), and by moving or removing dwellings (erasing the landscape altogether). The company was a sort of war machine of globalization, a test to see how well fast-moving, small hydro project initiatives could colonize un-industrialized rural landscapes in 'undeveloped' parts of Honduras. Dam projects provide the electricity necessary for further capital investment projects in remote areas, so they necessarily have to precede further industrialization (including agro-industry). Large dam projects in Olancho had already been proven impossible because of environmentalist and native land-rights campaigns, so the forces of globalization (known in Central Americas as 'regional economic integration')[86] put on environmentalist masks and attempted to insert their war machine more subtly. The open secret of the company was that it believed that the entire local landscape in Olancho was underdeveloped because it was not industrialized, and that none of the spaces – neither cattle, nor coffee, nor grains, nor timber – had a preeminent right to occupy a drainage basin that was 'destined' for use by Man in a more rational way.

This end-of-millennium threat was countered by a rapidly-growing alliance that gained new adherents at public meetings and across the Internet as it became understood that the project was but the vanguard of a new approach to space in Olancho, that would first smooth and then re-striate following a new order. The Sierra de Agalta National Park, once an enemy as well, was used as a shield against the hydroelectric company, because by its legal constitution it could not be the site of an industrial project. The tightly interwoven family networks of Olancho, which crosscut the land-use territorialities to a large extent, also served to strengthen more quickly the counter-project rhizome that added on adherents with each one's simple acceptance that industrialization of this type was wrong and damaging despite all the jobs that were promised and the modernization that supposedly would follow. The disastrous environmental and social situation of the modernized, industrialized Caribbean Coast region of Honduras, well known to the people of Olancho, gave the lie to the supposed benefits of the type of modernization promised by the hydro company. For the movement's leaders, success at keeping the project out became a matter of bringing diverse and usually heavily-at-odds spatial interests into some sort of Gordian knot that would cripple the company's designs.

Showing their desperation, the tactics used by the new space's agents included harassment of activists and eventually assassination. Elements of the Honduran State apparatus – its Cobra special forces, its congressional energy committee, its Environmental and Natural Resources Ministry – allied with the company on the side of Order and Development, so eventually the dam did get built, but the alliance that had partially fended off the company (preventing its worst excesses) was successful in that it began to link with other rhizomes (particularly, one that involved Catholic priests and land-rights activists arrayed against logging companies) in an Olancho-wide environmental justice movement that claimed trees, parks, and environmental self-determination as its prerogatives. The State could get involved as a participant but the land users themselves called for the 'democratic' application of sustainable development principles in an effort to reorganize all spaces in the province. State agencies that didn't shape up were to be overhauled or dismantled.

In 2003, the burgeoning movement's decentered cells (linked to and strengthened by activist movements outside Olancho by this time) called for a ten-year ban on all for-profit tree-cutting in Olancho, the removal of timber companies and hydroelectric projects from the landscape, and in general the right for autonomous municipalities to choose how they wanted to develop their resources, after they had had time to study all the existent laws and the benefits of protecting habitats, or flooding landscapes, or whatever scheme that was being foisted upon them.

It was the very complexity of the landscape that befuddled all actors, and kept power from becoming concentrated in any one space. The existence of a national park had been the easy way in for a hydro company helped by a government ministry that saw the park as 'its space' to dispense with as it pleased. What led to serious concessions by the company, and what fed an ever-growing rhizome, was the fact that proponents of all spaces felt threatened (except those who stood to gain from favors imparted by the company) by a simplifying and striating force that sought to replace each and every heterogeneous space with a single, new and improved, homogenous space. The mixture, it turned out, was preferred, and it was the mixture that provided the most strength of resistance.

In an approach to this entangled situation inspired by the geophilosophy of *ATP*, there can be no intent to 'sort things out' or 'make everything work right'. It is our contention that the entangled, heterogeneous landscape, because it is best at resisting homogenization, is already the 'solution' inasmuch as it can, where power relations begin to be evened out (where smallholder space comes to hold territories sufficient for the social welfare of its inhabitants, for example), commence a 'power-sharing' arrangement in which spaces become increasingly imbricated as the very diagrams of the complex systems themselves are reconfigured. The spaces certainly do not need to meld into one space (and probably never have existed that way in any case), given that cattle and coffee plants just don't mix, and you can't grow beans in a pine forest. It is not a matter of erasing difference but rather the opposite, of letting difference erase rock-solid identity, taking down a few notches the arrogance of spatial identities that, like so many ranchers and corporations, are willing to harm and even to kill those who challenge their territorial pretensions and the natural supremacy of their spaces.

What good is it to 'do' a geography of a relatively 'minor' region like Olancho, a tiny cog in a world landscape which comprises so many more 'important' regions? Perhaps we can say that we seek to do 'minor geography' because the margins, being more disorganized zones, are much more productive of change. Olancho may have played its own irreplaceable part in world systems, but the same could be said of anywhere. But doesn't this make 'anywhere' always worthy of study, not as 'anywhere' (the case study that proves the Case) but as unique and not interchangeable? Your 'typical frontier region' Olancho is not that at all, because there is no such thing. We do not pretend that everything important to the 'new Earth' arises through local interactions or solely at the scale of place-haecceities;[87] molar forces that set capital and air and news and hurricanes in motion are equally important and we cannot neglect one at the expense of the other, for the local and the global are in chiasmatic embrace. In the case of Olancho, it was more a matter of investigating a region where no one semiotic has achieved dominance, and least of all that of the State – where non-equilibrium crisis processes are not as buried or congealed as they are elsewhere.

We hope that this brief summary of Bonta's research cast in the light of the first part of this book, and read along with the Glossary, can suggest certain potentials for geophilosophically attuned research elsewhere. As a final note, and as important as anything that precedes it, the research described was enabling to the 'subjects' involved in it, in so far as Bonta was and remains a participant in the process of spatial entanglement and emancipation. He has sought to put to work the precepts of this entanglement – the understanding of dynamic heterogeneity as a desired framework within which to operate – as a geographer within and outside Olancho, and particularly in the full service of the 'new environmentalist' rhizome. We hope that our own ways toward the new Earth, via complexity, remain faithful to the calls of 'minor geographers' from Kropotkin to Harvey and on to the political ecologists, that 'what geography ought to be'[88] is anything but a service to the State and to multinational corporations, and, if this refrain is repeated, then geography can become the shelter for the vast diversity of everything else.

Notes

1. INTRODUCTION

1. Together they wrote four books. In 1972, they published *Anti-Oedipus* (DG 1984), subtitled *Capitalism and Schizophrenia*, a rip-roaring attack on the tame Marx–Freud synthesis that was the grail of post-war French left intellectuals but that was exposed as bankrupt by the 'events' of May 1968 in Paris. In 1975, it was *Kafka: Toward a Minor Literature* (DG 1986), an influential work in cultural and literary criticism. In 1980 they published *A Thousand Plateaus* (DG 1987), volume 2 of *Capitalism and Schizophrenia*. In 1991 they completed their collaboration with *What Is Philosophy?* (DG 1994), in which they attempt to delimit the respective relations of philosophy, science, logic, and art. Although it is only in the last work that a sustained reflection on the term 'geophilosophy' appears, the use of geophilosophical terms and concepts is common throughout their collaborative work. In this book, we concentrate on *ATP*, but make reference to the others, as well as to Deleuze's single-authored works, when appropriate.

2. Two points need to be made here. (1) It is very difficult to say when a scientific field has coalesced to the point it can receive the name of a 'theory'. Thus pinning down a birthday for 'complexity theory', and hence determining what exactly is the proper name for the science that Deleuze was reading in the 1960s in formulating his ontology in *Difference and Repetition* will have to await detailed work in the history of ideas, specifically, an intellectual biography of Deleuze. While this detailed historical work has not begun in any real sense, we can at least say that Deleuze's ontology maps the world in a way that fits the results achieved by that science we now call 'complexity theory'. (2) The various scientific communities investigating these fields also use the terms 'nonlinear dynamics' and 'complex adaptive systems'. Although we explain below a way to distinguish these terms from each other, for simplicity's sake we use 'complexity theory' throughout most of the

191

book as a generic term for these investigations, because it has gained a certain popular currency as a catchall phrase. We should, however, always distinguish complexity theory from chaos theory. While chaos theory treats the growth of unpredictable behavior from simple rules (and so might remain within the strictures of positivism, that is, need only commit itself only to an epistemological stance toward models), complexity theory treats the question of the emergence of relatively simple functional structures from complex interchanges of the component parts of a system, and hence entails an irreducible ontological commitment (see Silberstein and McGeever 1999 for a detailed treatment of these issues). In particular, we should note that while 'nonlinear dynamics' is often used as a description of chaos theory rather than complexity theory, it is also often used in a generic sense for nonlinear mathematical modeling of complex systems, which may exhibit (only) deterministic chaos (that is, they hit on fractal attractors and work through that region of state space in unpredictable and non-repeating ways), or complex emergence (they form 'habits', that is, relatively simple patterns of attractors and bifurcators). There are now many popularizations of these fields available. For chaos theory, see Gleick (1987) or Kellert (1993); for complexity theory, see Prigogine and Stengers (1984); for a survey of both fields, see Cohen and Stewart (1994).

3. We use 'register' rather than 'level' here to indicate the ways in which the inorganic, organic, and social interact (calcium and iron in bones and hemoglobin, 'global warming' from fossil fuel burning, and so on) and to avoid what Deleuze and Guattari warn against as a 'ridiculous cosmic evolutionism' in the system of the strata (*ATP*: 49).

4. We are well aware that sophisticated semiologies, which would combine Peircean and Saussurean theory to produce a typology of signs other than signifiers, would not be subject to such criticism. We have found little recognition among these semiologists, however, of the notion of 'triggering' so important to Deleuze and Guattari's notion of signs.

5. In the 'Geology of Morals' chapter of *ATP*, Deleuze and Guattari, in an attempt to undercut the 'imperialism of language', warn against using the term 'sign' to discuss events on the physical and organic strata. In this restricted sense, signs occur only on the alloplastic stratum, with the extraction of a 'regime of signs'. However, this restriction is only made to protect us from the worst mistake, which is to equate sign and signifier (*ATP*: 65). In our book, however, while fully acknowledging the need to distinguish sign from signifier, we would like to use 'sign' in an extended sense to refer to critical thresholds in any physical, organic, or social system, thereby recuperating the sense of 'sign' developed at Deleuze 1991: 261 (see also DeLanda 2002: 76–7 and 207n67). While Deleuze and Guattari are worried about the 'imperialistic' becoming-linguistic of nature, we feel this worry is outweighed

by the utility of such an extended sense of 'sign' in emphasizing the naturalization of language. What Deleuze and Guattari will call the 'essence of language' (the 'order-word') is precisely the triggering of material processes; the order-word thus performs the same function for a social system as the crossing of a critical threshold in an intensive process does for physical or organic systems.

6. But they can do so only under far-from-equilibrium, 'crisis' situations. This is precisely why functionalist accounts of structure, when based on a hidden assumption that social systems are 'equilibrium' systems, cannot see individual agency. In equilibrium thermodynamics, it is completely acceptable to discount individual trajectories and to deal only with average measures of large numbers of trajectories. (In fact, such a 'molarizing' treatment is the only proper method for dealing with equilibrium systems.) However, it is precisely in the crisis situations into which some complex systems enter that individual, non-average, rare trajectories can trigger either a shift in system from one attractor to another or even the creation of a new set of attractors and bifurcators.

Note on terminology: technically speaking, 'equilibrium' is only well defined for thermodynamic systems, those with a huge quantity of elements (a 'mole' is the minimum threshold). For other systems, physics speaks of 'steady state' systems, while biology will use the term 'stability'. Economics, in contrast, will use the term 'equilibrium' but, while it has important resonances with the thermodynamic concept, it has its own definition. The important point is that in all these systems, like in equilibrium thermodynamic systems, the system stays within a single basin of attraction, no matter how complex the attractor governing that basin and the resultant behavior patterns. Presuppositions for modeling these systems are that components are homogeneous and that non-average behaviors can be discounted. (In the case of biological and social systems with heterogeneous components, the repetition of stereotyped behaviors provides the homogeneity required.) Functioning social and organic systems are by definition not in thermodynamic equilibrium, but when they are said to be 'stable' their habitual homeostatic mechanisms function to the extent that external shocks and internal fluctuations below a certain threshold are recuperated ('damped out' is the equivalent thermodynamic term) and the system quickly returns to 'normal'. While these stable systems are analogous to equilibrium thermodynamic systems, we do not believe it is useful to call their relations 'metaphorical', because of the strong linguistic component of the latter term. We deal with this issue in several places in this book.

7. While structural social thinking is often opposed by agency thinking, it is also opposed by methodological individualism. However, rational choice theory, which has become the leading school of methodological individualism in the social sciences, should not be seen as an

example of agency thinking. There are both realist and positivist approaches to rational choice theory, both of which propose human behavior as determined – not by social structures, to be sure, but by psychological laws. In the case of the realists, these are assumed to be naturalist laws determining the behavior of human organisms. In the case of the positivists, the determinist universe of laws is merely a heuristic posit to allow further research. As positivists, they see themselves as merely constructing models to account for social phenomena and make little or no ontological commitment to whether there 'really are' rational agents at work in the world. They merely seek to explain social phenomena by constructing models as if there were such agents. This ontological modesty on the level of theory does not prevent the real effects of rational choice theory, which occur when it is used to design policies that produce social conditions in which agents are constrained to act according to the predictions of . . . rational choice theory. We continue to explore this issue in subsequent notes.

8. The 'society of mind' thesis deals only with the composition of a 'cognitive architecture' of abstract functions, as Varela (1992) stresses. Later in this fascinating article he makes the case for brain-level cognitive multiplicity by recourse to neurological findings. Other more recent accounts are of course available, but we cite Varela for this short sketch of the fascinating breadth of his concerns, linking Buddhist thought with contemporary neuroscience and both analytic philosophy of mind and 'continental' phenomenology. For other treatments of the 'embodied mind' see Varela, Thompson, and Rosch 1991, Clark 1997, Juarrero 1999, and Lakoff and Johnson 1999.

9. Here DeLanda (1997) is essential for thematizing the necessity of intermediate social levels, because Deleuze and Guattari have the unfortunate tendency of leaping immediately to the global social level, what they call the 'socius' in *AO*. The abruptness of the move to the level of 'capitalism' forms the basis of DeLanda's critique of Deleuze and Guattari's Marxism, which in his point of view violates Deleuze and Guattari's own principles of demanding a 'bottom-up' morphogenetic account for each individual in a 'flat ontology'. See DeLanda 1997: 266–7 and 331n7, as well as DeLanda 2001, 2003, and Thanem, DeLanda, and Protevi (Forthcoming).

10. At the risk of disinterring a thankfully buried dead horse for more beating, let us return briefly to the late and unlamented 'Science Wars' of the 1990s, specifically Sokal and Bricmont (1998). In general, Sokal and Bricmont's warnings against the sort of chatter that declares a 'revolution against Newton' are very well founded. The history of the relation between linear models and nonlinear models is quite complex and is not at all capturable by the term 'revolution'. It is true that for a long time linear models and those (simple equilibrium) areas of the world amenable to linear analysis held pride of place, while nonlinear phe-

nomena were marginalized or explained away, and that today linearity or equilibrium is often seen as a special case and nonlinearity and far-from-equilibrium systems the majority of cases. However, we cannot forget that some natural and social areas of the world have actually been rendered more homogenized and normalized (by genetic modification and by disciplinary practices) and hence more amenable to linear modeling. In any event, the fact that Sokal and Bricmont are correct here is no reason to accept their treatment of Deleuze and Guattari, and that for two reasons: they don't uphold the standards for a good polemic, and they polemicize at all. To produce a good polemic you have to reconstruct the context in which the attacked authors make their claims, but this is precisely what Sokal and Bricmont fail to do. Their remarkable chapter on Deleuze and Guattari in *Fashionable Nonsense* largely consists in the presentation of extended quotation juxtaposed with out-of-hand dismissals, which simply assert that Deleuze and Guattari's discourse is 'utterly meaningless', and so forth. But even if they had polemicized well, the genre of polemic is not very helpful, for, at base, a polemic tells you not to bother to read X. But to see if that is sound advice, you have then to go ahead and read X! In other words, the genre of polemic is beset by a fundamental 'performative contradiction'. So go ahead and read Sokal and Bricmont and see if you think we're doing them justice when we say they don't do Deleuze and Guattari justice.

11. See Wickens 1986 and Dyke 1989. This interest in using nonlinear dynamics as a model for a general field of biosociality continues in DeLanda (1997), and with great precision and brilliant insight in physics, chemistry and biology, coupled with an absolutely maddening political naïveté concerning 'the market', in Kauffman (1995) and (2000). Kauffman completely misses the point that 'market' can mean a 'perfect market': that is, atomic producers and consumers (all market players are price-takers) with perfect information and rationality, or 'real market', that is, any point of exchange of goods and services with varying gradations of market power possible (some market players are price-setters). Such market power in real markets is usually achieved by some combination of government and corporate cooperation in constructing barriers to entry (tariffs and so on), as well as by manipulating the information and/or rationality of other players (advertising is a manipulation of rationality, if you take rationality to include prudential [choice of ends] as well as instrumental [matching means to ends] forms). Perfect markets are said to reach an optimal 'equilibrium' (an economic term resonating with the thermodynamic sense) with the best possible distribution of goods and services, while real markets, notoriously, operate in far-from-equilibrium crises and often get trapped in 'sub-optimal' zones. Kauffman, who is so brilliant in developing the notion of sub-optimality in far-from-equilibrium biology, misses the obvious economic points. These points about

complex, far-from-equilibrium economics, while they do indicate the impossibility of successful central planning, do not by any means indicate that governments should not [cautiously] intervene to nudge economies out of sub-optimal zones. Only a blind libertarian ideological commitment equating all government action with totalitarian central planning could miss this point.

12. Kohler and Gummerman 2000.
13. Freeman 1995; Tschlacher and Scheier 2000; Ward 2002; Varela, Lachaux, Rodriguez, and Martinerie 2001.
14. Dyke 1990; Shermer 1995; Lindenfeld 1999.
15. Gharajedagh 1999; Olson and Eoyang 2001; Lomi and Larsen 2001.
16. Petitot, Varela, Pachoud, and Roy 1999.
17. Axelrod 1997; Cederman 1997.
18. Thrift 1999; Manson 2001.
19. Philips 1999a and 1999b.
20. Dyke 1988. At 1988: 359, Dyke cites Jacobs 1984 as being amenable to a nonlinear approach, a recommendation seconded by DeLanda 1997. See also Allen 1997.
21. Lansing 1991; Gimblett 2002.
22. We do not claim no geographers have shown an interest in Deleuze and Guattari prior to this work. Doel (1999) incorporates a wide range of postmodern thinkers in an attempt to refound geography as spatial science. In our opinion, however, Doel consistently conflates the Derridean and Deleuzoguattarian approaches and hence does not elaborate the historical-libidinal materialism we find so compelling in Deleuze and Guattari. At Doel 2000: 118–19, for instance, the 'Glunk' of Dr. Seuss as that which 'exemplifies the realist and materialist inalienability of existence pure and simple' will be opposed to a setting-into-motion by Deleuze's 'and' which 'enacts its unhinging and deconstruction'. For us, Deleuze and Guattari's realism and materialism cannot be reduced to a positing of 'existence', as this is only possible in a phenomenological arena Deleuze and Guattari circumvent, while 'deconstruction' is a Derridean term, about which Deleuze has said on the occasion of the 1972 Cerisy colloquium on Nietzsche: 'With regard to the method of deconstruction of texts, I see well what it is, I admire it greatly, but I don't see it having anything to do with my own' (Gandillac 1973: 186). On another occasion, Doel explicitly conflates the Deleuzean and Derridean projects: 'Accordingly, Gilles Deleuze and Félix Guattari, like Jacques Derrida and Jean-François Lyotard, are exemplary un-glunkers of pointillism, of the metaphysics of presence, and of the essentialist ontology of being' (2000: 120). We find this assimilation of Derrida and Deleuze problematic and restrictive, vitiating some but not all of the relevance of Doel's work to our project. The complexities of the Deleuze–Derrida relation are explored at length in Protevi 2001b and Patton and Protevi 2003.

Following the inclusion of Deleuze among the influences for the 'non-representational theory' proposed by Nigel Thrift, a few human geographers have turned to Deleuze in the last few years. None, however, see the connection with complexity theory we emphasize here. See Thrift 1996; Thrift and Dewsbury 2000; Dewsbury 2000; Harrison 2000.

Other geographical or geophilosophical treatments of Deleuze and Guattari have been briefer. The best sympathetic treatment of Deleuze and Guattari appears in Casey (1993). Casey's sensitive phenomenological treatment of the notion of 'smooth space' found in the section on nomads of *ATP* is exemplary in its rigor and nuance, and opens up rather than closes off avenues for interdisciplinary work. Casey's anthropological and phenomenological focus precludes, however, a grappling with the geological and ethological registers of *ATP* opened by the articulation with complexity theory.

Some contemporary geographers' engagements with Deleuze and Guattari have made the mistake of treating them under the rubric of 'postmodernism', following the lead of Fredric Jameson's 1984 essay 'Postmodernism, or, the cultural logic of late capitalism' (in Jameson 1991). For instance, under Jameson's tutelage, Harvey (1989) discusses only *AO*, and then only under the rubric of the 'psychological presuppositions' of 'postmodernism' (itself treated as a cultural efflorescence), its alleged 'conception of personality' (53). Similarly, Gregory (1994) conflates Deleuze and Guattari with Derrida in construing *ATP*'s cartography as 'pluralizing, disseminating, deterritorializing' (7n), thereby mixing Deleuze and Guattari's materialist notion of cartography with Derrida's concerns for signifier-produced meaning. Finally, Peet (1998) claims that Deleuze and Guattari 'argue' for 'fragmentation, multiplicity and indeterminacy' (195). This is at best a simplified reading of *AO* that completely ignores the cautious pragmatism of *ATP*, the last line of which is 'never believe a smooth space will save us' (a 'smooth space' being one of Deleuze and Guattari's names for a generator and multiplier of difference). Peet's final word is that *ATP* is a 'Nietzschean geography of forces and intensities' (212), which is not a bad description of it at all; unfortunately he never bothers to indicate in the slightest how *ATP* could be put to use by geographers. Peet explicitly confirms the regrettable tendency on the part of some geographers to try to dissuade readers from tackling *ATP*; we propose the present work as an attempt to open up rather than to close off paths for interdisciplinary work. Insofar as Harvey, Gregory, and Peet are strongly influenced by Marx, we will do our best to show the profound engagement with Marx that pervades all of Deleuze and Guattari's joint work.

23. For example, Cosgrove and Daniels 1988; Duncan 1990; Barnes and Duncan 1992; Benko and Strohmayer 1997. In the latter part of the

1990s, geographers, inspired in part by feminist thinking, turned increasingly to the body, the subject, and performativity; Butler 1993 is an example of a key text for them. See, for example, Pile and Thrift 1995; Jones, Nast, and Roberts 1997; Nast and Pile 1998. Many of these latter collections feature geographers who cross-fertilize phenomenological, structuralist, and post-structuralist approaches: for example, Lacan, Lefebvre, Merleau-Ponty, and Foucault.

24. Protevi 2001b highlights the breakdown of signification in the asignifying Derridean 'general text' as the interplay of 'force and signification', as well as juxtaposing it to the Deleuzoguattarian notion of 'body politic'.

25. For a critical commentary on *ATP*'s use of such sources, see Miller 1993 and 1998.

26. Derrida 1994 and 1997 are fascinating texts, with an extremely high level of philosophical sophistication and subtlety, but neither provides the opportunities for concrete analysis that a text like Hardt and Negri 2000 does, which counts Deleuze and Guattari among its primary influences.

27. They borrow the term 'plateau' from Gregory Bateson, a borrowing that shows not only Deleuze and Guattari's reach, but is especially appropriate to geophilosophy in that Bateson was himself a transdisciplinary and collaborative social scientist.

28. E. Holland (1999) provides an excellent account of this synthesis.

29. In *AO*, Deleuze and Guattari spend a lot of time on the question of the possible conflict between 'pre-conscious interests' and 'unconscious investments', or, more simply, between theory and practice in both their cognitive/rational (interests) and corporeal/emotional (investments) registers.

2. PHILOSOPHY AND SCIENCE

30. In one of his most interesting moves in *DR*, Deleuze turns to the 'Gothic' notions of pre-modern calculus (the infinitesimal, the approach to a limit, and so on) for help in constructing his ontology. See Smith (forthcoming) for details.

31. See 'Intellectuals and Power' in Foucault 1977.

32. Heidegger named his early project a 'fundamental ontology', but to his mind that was not included in what came to be called the 'metaphysics of presence'.

33. Deleuze 1995: 136.

34. Cited at Villani 1999: 130.

35. Harvey also has interesting remarks at the end of *Explanation* on functionalism and the General Systems Theory of Ludwig von Bertalanffy. Insofar as General Systems Theory, which came to attention in connection with cybernetics in the 1940s, is a forerunner of nonlinear dynamics, one could say that we want to update the last two chapters

of Harvey's *Explanation,* using Deleuze and Guattari as our philosophical resource.

36. Actually, complexity theory shows that the irreversibility of time is essential for many complex systems operating far-from-equilibrium in inorganic and organic registers well beyond the human and social.

37. Discipline tries to make social reality conform to rational choice models by normalizing humans, that is, by turning them into 'individuals' whose behaviors can be classified relative to the norm of a population of other such individuals. Classical and neo-classical economics make assumptions of these goals of disciplinary practice, thereby enabling them to model economies as 'equilibrium' systems. The result is an elegant model whose inability to predict reality is often blamed on some recalcitrant feature of reality: the model says markets should behave in such-and-such a fashion; real markets do not behave in this fashion; therefore there must be some government distortion of the real market preventing it from behaving in the way it should; therefore we must remove such distortion to 'allow' – that is, to make – the system behave the way the model says it should. The key point is that neoliberal economic prescriptions (in the Global South, under the pressure of the *IMF*, the development banks, and other institutions) try to bring such 'rational economic' behavior about by actively producing the social situations the model assumes: normalization of behavior by making people behave in individual self-interest (due to lack of social interaction/social security). The problem comes when people write about such economics as if they were only a matter of assumptions and models rather than prods for concerted efforts to produce a social reality conforming to the model's assumptions. See Dyke (1989) for an eloquent statement of this position of the relation of discipline and rationality.

This sort of production of predictable human behavior remains the basis for quantitative models of human development across the globe, particularly in those regions wearing the straightjacket of *IMF*-prescribed socioeconomic medicine ('structural readjustment'). The very uniformity of neoliberal prescriptions for diverse countries at first glance is counterintuitive, because extreme diversity, radically different geographies, and highly divergent histories would seem to demand different development strategies for each place. However, the monotony of a single and universalizing neoliberal model is based on the assumption that humans are essentially uniform and that their behavior, and the behavior of their localized aggregate, can be predicted based on the behavior of other humans and their aggregates in other societies at other times. As we point out at several places in this book, Deleuze's ontology, and the Deleuzoguattarian toolkit, present a multiverse of alternative approaches to 'mapping' the geographic and historic problems of human societies. Perhaps the greatest challenge for Deleuze-inspired social science in the twenty-first century, even beyond the challenges of complexity theory itself, is the overturning of positivism and its derivations across the physical/social science spectrum, and in particular anywhere the ideal of 'description and explanation' serves to hide the production of homogeneity in human and non-human registers. (DeLanda 1997: 174–9 provides a brief treatment of the spread of homogenizing and normalizing disciplinary practices in the organic realm by the production of genetically modified organisms [*GMOs*].)

38. DeLanda (2002: 70–81) provides a rigorous treatment of the 'philosophical transformation' of the mathematical concepts used in state space construction (see the section 'Complexity Theory', p. 16) and information theory to reach the philosophical concepts of multiplicities and the plane of consistency. The concept of multiplicities is purified by transforming state space construction to remove any traces of individuating processes in differentials (pure reciprocal determination rather than functions), singularities (whose existence and distribution are given in the vector field before the full construction of the phase portrait), and series (as infinite ordinal series). The concept of the meshing of the plane of consistency is purified by transforming information theory so that the linked change in probability of actual events that constitutes the emission of a 'quantum' of information becomes virtualized as the simple linkage of changes in the distribution of the singular and the ordinary within a series.

39. The three aspects of Deleuzean ontology explain the significance of the title of DeLanda's *Intensive Science and Virtual Philosophy*: complexity theory explores intensive processes ('intensive science'), while Deleuzean philosophy explicates the virtual realm ('virtual philosophy')

40. The following account relies on Allen 2001.

41. Technically speaking, a system never performs exactly as prescribed by such a point; in other words, attractors are never actualized, but systems always fluctuate in the vicinity of attractors.

42. Chapter I of *DR* (Deleuze 1994) contains a sustained critique of 'representation'.

43. The connection of the birth of classical mechanics and the military utility of calculating projectile trajectories is noted at DeLanda 1991: 39–40.

44. In his theorizing of singularities Deleuze relies upon Lautman 1946: 42: 'the field of vectors on the one hand, and the integral curves on the other, are two essentially distinct mathematical realities'. See Evens 2000; DeLanda 2002: 30–1; and Smith (forthcoming).

45. We have simplified Deleuze and Guattari's treatment of the relations of deterritorialization and reterritorialization here. In the Glossary we present a full treatment.

46. Allen 2001. For an alternative typology of eleven (!) forms of self-organization mentioned in the scientific literature, see Philips 1999a.

47. Allen 2001: 8. Allen classifies cellular automata as models of nonlinear

dynamic systems, claiming they don't allow for sub-level component learning because, by definition, they build in the behavior rules of the simplest level. Thus you can explore systems behavior, but not co-evolution of environment, system, and components. For this you need 'agent-based' modeling.

48. An excellent guide to complexity in biology is Solé and Goodwin 2000.

49. At Massumi 2002: 37 we find the unfortunate assertion that 'quantum indeterminacy is fed forward' through all strata. Even leaving aside the problem of aligning Heisenberg's anti-realist notion of 'indeterminacy' with Bohm's or Deleuze's realism, from our point of view, identifying all indeterminacy, undecidability, physical free play, political resistance, economic crisis, and so on, with somehow amplified quantum indeterminacy is speculative overkill. See Cohen and Stewart 1994: 425–7 for a critique of Penrose's analogous attempt to ground free will in quantum indeterminacy in *The Emperor's New Mind*. From an emergentist perspective, there are plenty of macro-level sources of unpredictability that retain their own specificity even as they have damped out quantum effects. Thus for the purposes of this book, we follow DeLanda in reading the plane of consistency in terms of the virtual realm for macro-systems (the patterns and thresholds of intensive processes, in other words) and leave open the question of the relation of quantum virtuality to the virtuality of attractors and bifurcators in complex systems. All this, however, is not to say there is no relation between Deleuze and Guattari's notion of the 'plane of consistency' and quantum mechanical notions, as is evident in the following passage: 'There is no doubt that mad physical particles crash through the strata as they accelerate, leaving minimal traces of their passage, escaping spatiotemporal and even existential coordinates as they tend toward a state of absolute deterritorialization, the state of unformed matter on the plane of consistency' (*ATP*: 55–6). For a bold attempt to relate Deleuze and the realist quantum mechanics of David Bohm, see Murphy 1998.

50. Lakoff and Nunez 2000: 110: '[T]he axiomatic method is the manifestation in Western mathematics of the folk theory of essences inherited from the Greeks.'

51. Once again, DeLanda 2002 is our guide here.

52. Deleuze will develop other names for 'Idea', including 'virtual multiplicity' in *ATP* and 'concept' in *WP*.

53. For a popular account of 'mutual bootstrapping', see Kauffman 1995.

54. Cohen and Stewart (1994) call this phenomenon 'complicity'.

55. Deleuze (1991: 269) points out a possible reading of Lucretius: the clinamen or 'swerve' is the least deviation from the laminar. In *ATP* (554n24) Deleuze and Guattari approvingly cite Serres 1977 which develops at length the thesis that ancient Greek atomistic physics was a fluid dynamics, not a solid one.

56. Deleuze once said in an interview that '*Anti-Oedipus* was about the univocity of the real, a sort of Spinozism of the unconscious. And I think '68 was this discovery itself. The people who hate '68, or say it was a mistake, see it as something symbolic or imaginary. But that's precisely what it wasn't, it was pure reality breaking through' (Deleuze 1995: 144–5).

57. Foucault's phrase in his Preface to the English translation of *Anti-Oedipus*, p. xii.

58. Here again an opportunity to articulate the work of Derrida, especially 'White Mythology' (in Derrida 1982), with that of Deleuze and Guattari. For Derrida, the signifying notion of metaphor must be placed in its 'economic' relation with Nietzsche's asignifying bodily notion laid out in the latter's 'On Truth and Lie'. The resultant economy of signifying and asignifying notions results in the articulation of a notion of 'metaphoricity', which can then be seen in terms of the general text and its interweaving of 'force and signification'.

3. TOWARD A GEOGRAPHY OF COMPLEX SPACES

59. For an overview of philosophical issues concerning emergence, see Silberstein and McGeever 1999; for emergence in a cognitive science perspective, see Thompson and Varela 2001; for an overview of agent-based computer modeling of emergent behavior, see J. Holland 1998.

60. Allen 1997: 1. 'Helpless slaves' indeed! Protevi 2001b examines analogous sorts of 'political physics' in Plato, Aristotle, and Kant.

61. The Introduction to Massumi 2002 contains an excellent critique of the tendency of cultural studies to stick with a social grid model of molar 'positions' rather than address the intensive molecular process that gives rise to such probability distributions, and that, once tapped into, provides the resources for 'molecular revolution', to use Guattari's term.

62. All of this, of course, assumes a neoliberal social framework. A more profound notion of human freedom is implicit in Deleuze and Guattari's notion of the 'Collectivity' that is the Body without Organs, formed on a plane of consistency that would destratify neoliberal social formations (*ATP*: 161). The inspiration here is Spinoza; see Negri 1991 (1981), Negri and Hardt 1994, and Hardt and Negri 2000.

63. 'And unfortunate in many others', they add immediately thereafter.

64. Juarrero (1999) investigates this rehabilitation of the Aristotelian notion of 'final cause' in terms of 'action theory'.

65. See also the denial of emergence at the level of social structure in the Rom Harré school of critical realism, as in López and Potter 2001.

66. In his last interviews, Varela insists autopoiesis is only valid on the biological level and should not be extended to social systems because of the problem of 'fascism' (what Deleuze and Guattari in *ATP* call 'totalitarianism').

67. Such transformations are what Foucault called the domain of

'incorporeal materialism' (see 'The Discourse on Language' at Foucault 1972: 231).

68. Henri Lefebvre notwithstanding.

APPENDIX: CASE STUDY – ENTANGLED SPACES AND SEMIOTICS IN OLANCHO

75. See also Bonta 2003 for published details on the region, and Bonta (forthcoming) for an *ATP*-inspired case study.

76. We use 'land' in its *ATP* sense (see Glossary) as ground that has been striated by capital; this does not fully capture what 'land users' are doing, but does point up Olanchanos' primary (though not only) view of the earth as far as their livelihoods are concerned.

77. See the second sense of 'Landscape' in the Glossary – *not* landscape as face correlate.

78. For the case of an extreme clarifying a norm, we cite a certain hillside coffee farm that rode a small landslide downslope during Hurricane Mitch and was deposited on top of another coffee farm belonging to a different owner. For the time that the plants on top survived, the bewilderment of the owners over their new land tenure can be imagined.

79. Useful published secondary sources for Contact-period historical geography include Chamberlain 1966; MacLeod 1973; Newson 1986.

80. Possible proof of this is the relatively small number of disappearances achieved by the paranoid 1980s Cold War State in Honduras (less than two hundred) that stand in strong contrast to the thousands achieved in neighboring countries.

81. Small farmers do own cattle, but only as elements in diversified land-use regimes; smallholder landscapes are heavily fenced in part because the few cattle that are present still cause a lot of damage. The difference between smallholder and rancher is one of degree and of definition, but there is a clear boundary between one who calls himself a 'rancher' (*ganadero*) and one who calls himself a *campesino*.

82. The classic critique of development remains Sachs 1992. The contributors, for example Arturo Escobar and Gustavo Esteva, are major voices in the academic-activist assault on 'development': see Escobar 1995 and Esteva 1998.

83. Sundberg 1998 and 1999 document a parallel process among conservationist NGOs in the Guatemalan Petén.

84. Bonta came to Olancho in 1991 as a Peace Corps volunteer assigned to this park, charged with achieving its conservation.

85. In other words, we don't wish to enter into the discussion of whether the State is the best guarantor of peace and stability because people are inherently violent and unfair to each other. The State, in 2003, has hardly proven itself yet to be a guarantor of any type of non-violence and fairness, not in Honduras and probably not anywhere.

86. Bankrolled in this case by private investors, the Honduran State, and the Central American Bank for Economic Integration.
87. See 'Molar' and 'Molecular' in the Glossary for the clarification of their relationship to global and local, general and particular.
88. Title of a classic 1885 [1996] essay by Peter Kropotkin.

Bibliography

Allen, Peter M. (1997) *Cities and Regions as Self-Organizing Systems*, Amsterdam: Gordon and Breach.

Allen, Peter M. (2001) 'The dynamics of knowledge and ignorance: learning the new systems science', in M. Matthies, H. Malchow, and J. Kriz (eds), *Integrative Systems Approaches to Natural and Social Dynamics: Systems Science 2000*, New York: Springer-Verlag, pp. 3–29.

Anguiano, Ramón de (1997 [1801]) 'Censo levantado en 1801, por el gobernador Intendente y Comandante General, Don Ramón de Anguiano', in Antionio Vallejo (1997 [1893]), *Primer anuario estadístico correspondiente al año de 1889*, Tegucigalpa: Editorial Universitaria, pp. 119–35.

Ansell Pearson, Keith (1997) *Viroid Life: Perspectives on Nietzsche and the Transhuman Condition*, London: Routledge.

Ansell Pearson, Keith (1999) *Germinal Life: The Difference and Repetition of Deleuze*, London: Routledge.

Axelrod, Robert (1997) *The Complexity of Cooperation: Agent-Based Models of Competition and Collaboration*, Princeton: Princeton University Press.

Barnes, T., and J. Duncan (eds) (1992) *Writing Worlds: Discourse, Text and Metaphor in the Representation of Landscape*, London: Routledge.

Bataille, Georges (1988) *The Accursed Share: An Essay on General Economy*, trans. Robert Hurley, New York: Zone Books.

Bateson, Gregory (1999) *Steps to an Ecology of Mind: Collected Essays in Anthropology, Psychiatry, Evolution, and Epistemology*, Chicago: University of Chicago Press.

Benko, G., and U. Strohmayer (eds) (1997) *Space and Social Theory: Interpreting Modernity and Postmodernity*, Oxford: Blackwell.

Blackburn, Robin (1997) *The Making of New World Slavery*, London: Verso.

Bonta, Mark A. (2001) 'Mapping *enredos* of complex spaces: a regional geography of Olancho, Honduras', unpublished doctoral dissertation, Baton Rouge: Louisiana State University.

Bonta, Mark A. (2003) *Seven Names for the Bellbird: Conservation Geography in Honduras*, College Station, TX: Texas A&M University Press.

Bonta, Mark A. (Forthcoming 2004) 'Becoming-forest, becoming-local: transformations of a protected area in Honduras', *Geoforum*.

Boundas, Constantin (1996) 'Deleuze-Bergson: an ontology of the virtual', in Paul Patton (ed.), *Deleuze: A Critical Reader*, Oxford: Blackwell.

Braidotti, Rosi (2002) *Metamorphoses: Towards a Materialist Theory of Becoming*, Cambridge: Polity.

Braudel, Ferdnand (1985) *Civilization and Capitalism 15th–18th Century*, London: HarperCollins, 3 vols.

Buchanan, Ian, and Claire Colebrook (eds) (2000) *Deleuze and Feminist Theory*, Edinburgh: Edinburgh University Press.

Butler, Judith (1993) *Bodies That Matter: On the Discursive Limits of 'Sex'*, London: Routledge.

Butzer, Karl (1976) *Early Hydraulic Civilization in Egypt: A Study in Cultural Ecology*, Chicago: University of Chicago Press.

Butzer, Karl (1996) 'Irrigation, raised fields and state management: Wittfogel redux?', *Antiquity*, 70, pp. 200–4.

Campbell, Edward (2000) 'Boulez and Expression: A Deleuzoguattarian Approach', dissertation, University of Edinburgh.

Canetti, Elias (1963) *Crowds and Power*, trans. Carol Stewart, New York: Viking Press.

Casey, Edward (1993) *Getting Back into Place*, Bloomington: Indiana University Press.

Cederman, Lars-Erik (1997) *Emergent Actors in World Politics: How States and Nations Develop and Dissolve*, Princeton: Princeton University Press.

Chamberlain, Robert S. (1966 [1953]) 'The conquest and colonization of Honduras 1502–1550', *Carnegie Institute of Washington Publication*, 598; reprinted New York: Octagon Books.

Clark, Andy (1997) *Being There: Putting Brain, Body, and World Back Together Again*, Cambridge, MA: MIT Press.

Clastres, Pierre (1987) *Society against the State: Essays in Political Anthropology*, trans. R. Hurley, New York: Zone Books.

Cohen, Jack, and Ian Stewart (1994) *The Collapse of Chaos*, New York: Penguin.

Cosgrove, D., and S. Daniels (eds) (1988) *The Iconography of Landscape: Essays on the Symbolic Representation, Design, and Use of Past Environments*, Cambridge: Cambridge University Press.

De Certeau, Michel (1984) *The Practice of Everyday Life*, trans. S. Rendall, Berkeley: University of California Press.

DeLanda, Manuel (1991) *War in the Age of Intelligent Machines*, New York: Zone Books.

DeLanda, Manuel (1992) 'Nonorganic Life', in Jonathan Crary and Sanford Kwinter (eds), *Incorporations: Zone 6*, New York: Zone Books, pp. 129–67.

DeLanda, Manuel (1997) *A Thousand Years of Nonlinear History*, New York: Zone Books.

DeLanda, Manuel (2001) 'An ontology for the social sciences', http://www.uiuc.edu/unit/STIM/delanda1.pdf.

DeLanda, Manuel (2002) *Intensive Science and Virtual Philosophy*, London: Continuum.

DeLanda, Manuel (2003) 'Interview with C-Theory', www.ctheory.net.

Deleuze, Gilles (1978) 'Second lesson on Kant: 21st March, 1978', www.webdeleuze.com.

Deleuze, Gilles (1988a [1986]) *Foucault*, trans. Seán Hand, Minneapolis: University of Minnesota Press.

Deleuze, Gilles (1988b [1970]) *Spinoza: Practical Philosophy*, trans. Robert Hurley, San Francisco: City Lights.

Deleuze, Gilles (1989 [1985]) *Cinema 2: The Time Image*, trans. Hugh Tomlinson and Robert Galeta, London: Athlone.

Deleuze, Gilles (1991 [1969]) *The Logic of Sense*, trans. Mark Lester with Charles Stivale, New York: Columbia University Press.

Deleuze, Gilles (1992 [1968]) *Expressionism in Philosophy: Spinoza*, trans. Martin Joughin, New York: Zone Books.

Deleuze, Gilles (1994 [1968]) *Difference and Repetition*, trans. Paul Patton, New York: Columbia University Press.

Deleuze, Gilles (1995 [1990]) *Negotiations 1972–1990*, trans. Martin Joughin, New York: Columbia University Press

Deleuze, Gilles, and Félix Guattari (1984 [1972]) *Anti-Oedipus*, trans. Robert Hurley, Mark Seem, and Helen R. Lane, London: Athlone Press.

Deleuze, Gilles, and Félix Guattari (1986 [1975]) *Kafka: Toward a Minor Literature*, trans. Dana Polan, Minneapolis: University of Minnesota Press.

Deleuze, Gilles, and Félix Guattari (1987 [1980]) *A Thousand Plateaus*, trans. Brian Massumi, London: Athlone Press.

Deleuze, Gilles, and Félix Guattari (1994 [1991]) *What Is Philosophy?*, trans. Hugh Tomlinson and Graham Burchell, New York: Columbia University Press.

Denevan, William (1961) 'The upland pine forests of Nicaragua: A study in cultural plant geography', *University of California Publications in Geography*, 12.4, pp. 251–320.

Dennett, Daniel (1991) *Consciousness Explained*, Boston: Little, Brown.

Derrida, Jacques (1982 [1972]) *Margins: Of Philosophy*, trans. Alan Bass, Chicago: University of Chicago Press.

Derrida, Jacques (1994 [1993]) *Specters of Marx*, trans. Peggy Kamuf, London: Routledge.

Derrida, Jacques (1997 [1994]) *Politics of Friendship*, trans. George Collins, London: Verso.

Dewsbury, John-David (2000) 'Performativity and the event: enacting a philosophy of difference', *Environment and Planning D: Society and Space*, 18, pp. 473–96.

Doel, Marcus (1999) *Poststructuralist Geographies: The Diabolical Art of Spatial Science*, Lanham, MD: Rowman and Littlefield.

Doel, Marcus (2000) 'Un-glunking geography: spatial science after Dr. Seuss and Gilles Deleuze', in Mike Crang and Nigel Thrift (eds), *Thinking Space*, London: Routledge.

Duncan, J. S. (1990) *The City as Text: The Politics of Landscape Interpretation in the Kandyan Kingdom*, Cambridge: Cambridge University Press.

Dyke, Chuck (1988) 'Cities as dissipative systems', in Bruce H. Weber, David J. Depew, and James D. Smith (eds), *Entropy, Information and Evolution*, Cambridge, MA: MIT Press, pp. 355–67.

Dyke, Chuck (1989) *The Evolutionary Dynamics of Complex Systems: A Study in Biosocial Complexity*, New York: Oxford University Press.

Dyke, Chuck (1990) 'Strange attraction, curious liaison: Clio meets chaos', *The Philosophical Forum*, 21.4, pp. 369–92.

Eliade, Mircea (1996 [1958]) *Patterns of Comparative Religions*, trans. Rosemary Sheed, Lincoln: University of Nebraska Press.

Escobar, Arturo (1995) *Encountering Development: The Making and Unmaking of the Third World*, Princeton: Princeton University Press.

Esteva, Gustavo (1998) 'Beyond development, what?', with M. S. Prakash, *Development in Practice*, 8.3, pp. 280–96.

Evens, Aden (2000) 'Math anxiety', *Angelaki*, 5.3, pp. 105–15.

Foucault, Michel (1972 [1971]) *The Archaeology of Knowledge,* trans. A. M. Sheridan Smith, New York: Pantheon.

Foucault, Michel (1977) *Language, Counter-Memory, Practice,* trans. Donald Bouchard and Sherry Simon, Ithaca, New York: Cornell University Press.

Foucault, Michel (1979) *Discipline and Punish,* trans. Alan Sheridan, New York: Vintage.

Freeman, Walter (1995) *Societies of Brains: A Study in the Neuroscience of Love and Hate,* Hillsdale, NJ: Lawrence Erlbaum.

Gandillac, Maurice de (ed.) (1973) *Nietzsche aujourd'hui? Tome 1: Intensités,* Paris: Union générale d'éditions.

Gharajedagh, Jamshid (1999) *Systems Thinking: Managing Chaos and Complexity: A Platform for Designing Business Architecture,* Boston: Butterworth-Heinemann.

Giddens, Anthony (1984) *The Constitution of Society: Outline of the Theory of Structuration,* Berkeley: University of California Press.

Gimblett, H. Randy (ed.) (2002) *Integrating Geographic Information Systems and Agent-Based Modeling Techniques for Simulating Social and Ecological Processes,* New York: Oxford University Press.

Gleick, James (1987) *Chaos: Making a New Science,* New York: Penguin.

Graham, Daniel (2002) 'Paper arrows: peasant resistance and territoriality in Honduras', M.A. thesis, University of California-Berkeley.

Gregory, Derek (1994) *Geographical Imaginations,* Oxford: Blackwell.

Hardt, Michael, and Antonio Negri (2000) *Empire,* Cambridge, MA: Harvard University Press.

Harrison, Paul (2000) 'Making sense: embodiment and the sensibilities of the everyday', *Environment and Planning D: Society and Space,* 18, pp. 497–517.

Harrison, Robert P. (1992) *Forests: The Shadow of Civilization,* Chicago: University of Chicago Press.

Harvey, David (1969) *Explanation in Geography,* London: Edward Arnold.

Harvey, David (1984) 'On the history and present conditions of geography: an historical materialist approach', *Professional Geographer,* 3, pp. 1–11.

Harvey, David (1989) *The Condition of Postmodernity,* Oxford: Blackwell.

Holland, Eugene (1999) *Deleuze and Guattari's* Anti-Oedipus: *Introduction to Schizoanalysis,* New York: Routledge.

209

Holland, John (1998) *Emergence: From Chaos to Order*, Reading, MA: Addison-Wesley.

Jacobs, Jane (1984) *Cities and the Wealth of Nations*, New York: Random House.

Jameson, Fredric (1991) *Postmodernism, or, The Cultural Logic of Late Capitalism*, Durham: Duke University Press.

Johannessen, Carl (1963) 'Savannas of interior Honduras', *Ibero-Americana*, 46.

Jones, J. P. III, H. J. Nast, and S. M. Roberts (eds) (1997) *Thresholds in Feminist Geography: Difference, Methodology, Representation*, Lanham, MD: Rowman and Littlefield.

Juarrero, Alicia (1999) *Dynamics in Action*, Cambridge, MA: MIT Press.

Kauffman, Stuart (1995) *At Home in the Universe*, Oxford: Oxford University Press.

Kauffman, Stuart (2000) *Investigations*, Oxford: Oxford University Press.

Kellert, Stephen (1993) *In the Wake of Chaos*, Chicago: University of Chicago Press.

Kniffen, Fred (1936) 'Louisiana house types', *Annals, Association of American Geographers*, 26, pp. 179–93.

Kohler, Timothy, and George Gummerman (eds) (2000) *Dynamics in Human and Primate Societies: Agent Based Modeling of Social and Spatial Processes*, New York: Oxford.

Kropotkin, Peter (1989 [1902]) *Mutual Aid: A Factor of Evolution*, Montreal: Black Rose Books.

Kropotkin, Peter (1996 [1885]) 'What geography ought to be', in John Agnew, David N. Livingstone, and Alisdair Rogers (eds), *Human Geography: An Essential Anthropology*, Oxford, UK: Blackwell, pp. 139–54.

Lakoff, George and Mark Johnson (1999) *Philosophy in the Flesh: The Embodied Mind and Its Challenge to Western Thought*, New York: Basic Books.

Lakoff, George, and Rafael Núñez (2000). *Where Mathematics Comes From: How the Embodied Mind Brings Mathematics into Being*, New York: Basic Books.

Lansing, John Stephen (1991) *Priests and Programmers*, Princeton: Princeton University Press.

Lautman, Albert (1946) *Le problème du temps* and *Symétrie et dissymétrie en mathématiques et en physique*, Paris: Hermann.

Lindenfeld, David (1999) Causality, chaos theory, and the end of the Weimar Republic: a commentary on Henry Turner's Hitler's Thirty Days to Power', *History and Theory*, 38, pp. 281–99.

Lomi, Alesandro, and Erik Larsen (eds) (2001) *Dynamics of Organizations: Computational Modeling and Organization Theories*, Cambridge, MA: MIT Press.

López, José, and Garry Potter (2001) *After Postmodernism: An Introduction to Critical Realism*, London: Athlone.

Lorraine, Tamsin (1999) *Irigaray and Deleuze: Experiments in Visceral Philosophy*, Ithaca: Cornell University Press.

MacLeod, Murdo (1973) *Spanish Central America: A Socio-economic History, 1520–1720*, Berkeley: University of California Press.

Mahan, Alfred T. (1987 [1890]) *The Influence of Sea-Power upon History, 1660–1783*, New York: Dover Publications.

Manson, Steven M. (2001) 'Simplifying complexity: a review of complexity theory', *Geoforum*, 32.3, pp. 405–14.

Margulis, Lynn (1998) *Symbiotic Planet: A New Look at Evolution*, New York: Basic Books.

Massumi, Brian (1992) *A User's Guide to Capitalism and Schizophrenia: Deviations from Deleuze and Guattari*, Cambridge, MA: MIT Press.

Massumi, Brian (2002) *Parables for the Virtual*, Durham: Duke University Press.

Mathewson, Kent (1985) 'Carl Sauer special session II: south by southwest – an antimodernist apotheosis', *Geographers on Film* 1982 G. 2.

Miller, Christopher (1993) 'The postidentitarian predicament in the footnotes of *A Thousand Plateaus*', *Diacritics*, 23.3, pp. 6–35.

Miller, Christopher (1998) *Nationalists and Nomads: Essays on Francophone African Literature and Culture*, Chicago: University of Chicago Press.

Mumford, Lewis (1970) *The Pentagon of Power*, New York: Harcourt Brace Jovanovich.

Murphy, Tim (1998) 'Quantum ontology: a virtual mechanics of becoming', in Eleanor Kaufman and Kevin Jon Keller (eds), *Deleuze and Guattari: New Mappings in Politics, Philosophy and Culture*, Minneapolis: University of Minnesota Press, pp. 211–29.

Nast, H., and S. Pile (eds) (1998) *Places through the Body*, London: Routledge.

Negri, Antonio (1991 [1981]) *The Savage Anomaly: The Power of Spinoza's Metaphysics and Politics*, trans. Michael Hardt, Minneapolis: University of Minnesota Press.

Negri, Antonio, and Michael Hardt (1994) *Labor of Dionysus: A Critique of the State Form*, Minneapolis: University of Minnesota Press.

Newson, Linda (1986) *The Cost of Conquest: Indian Decline in Honduras under Spanish Rule*, Boulder, CO: Westview.

Olkowski, Dorothea (1999) *Gilles Deleuze and the Ruin of Representation*, Berkeley: University of California Press.

Olson, Edwin, and Eoyang, Glenda (2001) *Facilitating Organization Change: Lessons from Complexity Science*, San Francisco: Jossey-Bass/Pfeiffer.

Pacotte, Julienne (1936) *Le réseau arborescent, scheme primordial de la pensée*, Paris: Hermann.

Patton, Paul, and John Protevi (eds) (2003) *Between Deleuze and Derrida*, London: Continuum.

Peet, R. (1998) *Modern Geographical Thought*, Oxford: Blackwell.

Penrose, Roger (1989) *The Emperor's New Mind: Concerning Computers, Minds and the Laws of Physics*, London: Penguin.

Petitot, Jean, Francisco Varela, Bernard Pachoud, and Jean-Michel Roy (eds) (1999) *Naturalizing Phenomenology: Issues in Contemporary Phenomenology and the Cognitive Sciences*, Stanford: Stanford University Press.

Philips, Jonathan (1999a) 'Divergence, convergence, and self-organization in landscapes', *Annals of the Association of American Geographers*, 89, pp. 466–88.

Philips, Jonathan (1999b) *Earth Surface Systems: Complexity, Order, and Scale*, Oxford: Blackwell.

Pile, S., and N. Thrift (eds) (1995) *Mapping the Subject: Geographies of Cultural Transformation*, London: Routledge.

Prigogine, Ilya, and Isabelle Stengers (1984) *Order out of Chaos: Man's New Dialogue with Nature*, New York: Bantam.

Protevi, John (1994) *Time and Exteriority: Aristotle, Heidegger, Derrida*, Lewisburg: Bucknell University Press.

Protevi, John (1998) 'The "sense" of "sight": Heidegger and Merleau-Ponty on the meaning of bodily and existential sight', *Research in Phenomenology*, 28, pp. 211–23.

Protevi, John (2001a) 'The organism as judgment of God', in *Deleuze and Religion*, Mary Bryden (ed.), London: Routledge, pp. 30–42.

Protevi, John (2001b) *Political Physics: Deleuze, Derrida and the Body Politic*, London: Athlone.

Reclus, Elisée (1897) *The Earth and its Inhabitants*, New York: D. Appleton and Company.

Ronai, Maurice (1976) 'Paysages', *Hérodote*, 1, pp. 125–59.

Sachs, Wolfgang (ed.) (1992) *The Development Dictionary: A Guide to Knowledge as Power*, Atlantic Heights, NJ: Zed Books.

Sauer, Carl O., and John B. Leighly (1963) *Land and Life: A Selection from the Writings of Carl Ortwin Sauer*, Berkeley: University of California Press.

Serres, Michel (1977). *La naissance de la physique dans le texte de Lucrèce*, Paris: Minuit.

Shermer, Michael (1995) 'Exorcising LaPlace's demon: chaos and antichaos, history and metahistory', *History and Theory*, 34.1, pp. 59–83.

Silberstein, Michael, and John McGeever (1999) 'The search for ontological emergence', *The Philosophical Quarterly*, 49, pp. 182–200.

Simondon, Gilbert (1995 [1964]) *L'individu et sa genèse physico-biologique*, Grenoble: Millon.

Smith, Daniel (1997) 'A life of pure immanence: Deleuze's *Critique et Clinique* Project', in Gilles Deleuze, *Essays Clinical and Critical*, trans. Daniel Smith and Michael Greco, Minneapolis: University of Minnesota Press.

Smith, Daniel (forthcoming) 'Mathematics and the theory of multiplicities: Badiou and Deleuze revisited', *Southern Journal of Philosophy*.

Sokal, Alan, and Jean Bricmont (1998) *Fashionable Nonsense: Postmodern Intellectuals and the Abuse of Science*, New York: Picador.

Solé, Richard, and Brian Goodwin (2000) *Signs of Life: How Complexity Pervades Biology*, New York: Basic Books.

Steinberg, Philip (2001) *The Social Construction of the Ocean*, Cambridge: Cambridge University Press.

Sundberg, Juanita (1998) 'Strategies for authenticity, space, and place in the Maya Biosphere Reserve, Petén, Guatemala', *Yearbook, Conference of Latin Americanist Geographers*, 24, pp. 85–96.

Sundberg, Juanita (1999) 'Conservation encounters: NGOs, local people, and changing cultural landscapes', PhD dissertation, University of Texas-Austin.

Thanem, Torkild, Manuel DeLanda, and John Protevi (forthcoming) 'Deleuzean interrogations: a conversation with Manuel DeLanda, John Protevi, and Torkild Thanem', *Tamara: A Journal of Radical Organization Theory*.

Thesiger, Wilfred (1959) *Arabian Sands*, London: Longmans, Green.

Theweleit, Klaus (1987 and 1989) *Male Fantasies*, 2 vols, Minneapolis: University of Minnesota Press.

Thompson, Evan, and Francisco Varela (2001) 'Radical embodiment: neuronal dynamics and consciousness', *Trends in Cognitive Science*, 5, pp. 418–25.

Thrift, Nigel (1996) *Spatial Formations*, London: Sage.

Thrift, Nigel (1999) 'The place of complexity', *Theory, Culture and Society*, 16.3, pp. 31–69.

Thrift, Nigel, and John-David Dewsbury (2000) 'Dead geographies – and how to make them live', *Environment and Planning D: Society and Space*, 18, pp. 411–32.

Tschlacher, Wolfgang, and Christian Scheier (2000) 'Embodied cognitive science: concepts, methods and implications for psychology', in M. Matties, H. Malchow, and J. Kriz (eds), *Integrative Systems Approaches to Natural and Social Dynamics*, New York: Springer Verlag, pp. 551–67.

Uexküll, Jakob Johann von (1965) *Mondes animaux et monde humaine*, Paris: Gonthier.

Varela, Francisco, Evan Thompson, and Elizabeth Rosch (1991) *The Embodied Mind*, Cambridge, MA: MIT Press.

Varela, Francisco (1992) 'The re-enchantment of the concrete', in Jonathan Crary and Sanford Kwinter (eds), *Incorporations: Zone 6*, New York: Zone Books, pp. 320–38.

Varela, Francisco (1999) 'The specious present: a neurophenomenology of time consciousness', in Petitot, Varela, Pachoud, and Roy, pp. 266–314.

Varela, Francisco, Jean-Phillipe Lachaux, Eugenio Rodriguez, and Jacques Martinerie (2001) 'The brainweb: phase synchronization and large-scale integration', *Nature Reviews: Neuroscience*, 2, pp. 229–39.

Villani, Arnaud (1999). *La guêpe et l'orchidée: Essai sur Gilles Deleuze*, Paris: Belin.

Ward, Lawrence (2002) *Dynamical Cognitive Science*, Cambridge, MA: MIT Press.

West, Robert Cooper (1998 [1958]) 'Sociopolitical aspects of mining in the Pacific lowlands of Colombia', *Latin American Geography: Historical-Geographical Essays, 1941–1998*, Geoscience and Man, vol. 35, Baton Rouge, LA: Geoscience Publications, pp. 103–12.

Wickens, J. S. (1986) 'Evolutionary self-organization and entropic dissipation in biological and socioeconomic systems', *Journal of Social and Biological Structures*, 9, pp. 261–73.

Wittfogel, Karl August (1957) *Oriental Despotism: A Comparative Study of Total Power*, New Haven, CT: Yale University Press.